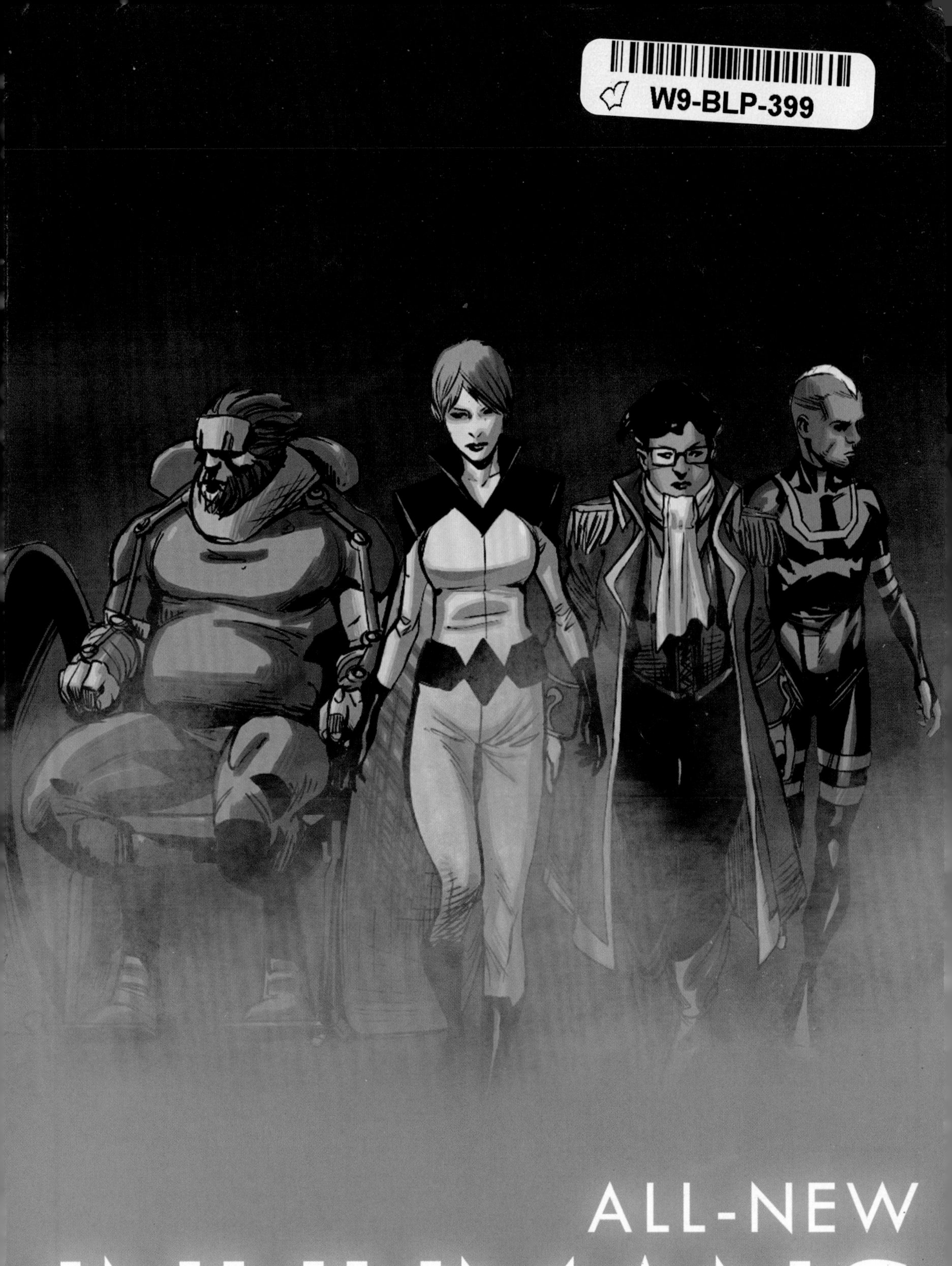

ALL-NEW INHUMANS

JENNIFER GRÜNWALD
COLLECTION EDITOR

SARAH BRUNSTAD
ASSOCIATE EDITOR

ALEX STARBUCK
ASSOCIATE MANAGING EDITOR

MARK D. BEAZLEY
EDITOR, SPECIAL PROJECTS

JEFF YOUNGQUIST
VP, PRODUCTION & SPECIAL PROJECTS

DAVID GABRIEL
SVP PRINT, SALES & MARKETING

ADAM DEL RE
BOOK DESIGNER

AXEL ALONSO
EDITOR IN CHIEF

JOE QUESADA
CHIEF CREATIVE OFFICER

DAN BUCKLEY
PUBLISHER

ALAN FINE
EXECUTIVE PRODUCER

ALL-NEW INHUMANS VOL. 1: GLOBAL OUTREACH. Contains material originally published in magazine form as ALL-NEW INHUMANS #1-4 and ALL-NEW, ALL-DIFFERENT POINT ONE #1. First printing 2016. ISBN# 978-0-7851-9638-9. Published by MARVEL WORLDWIDE, INC., a subsidiary of MARVEL ENTERTAINMENT, LLC. OFFICE OF PUBLICATION: 135 West 50th Street, New York, NY 10020. Copyright © 2016 MARVEL No similarity between any of the names, characters, persons, and/or institutions in this magazine with those of any living or dead person or institution is intended, and any such similarity which may exist is purely coincidental. **Printed in Canada.** ALAN FINE, President, Marvel Entertainment; DAN BUCKLEY, President, TV, Publishing & Brand Management; JOE QUESADA, Chief Creative Officer; TOM BREVOORT, SVP of Publishing; DAVID BOGART, SVP of Business Affairs & Operations, Publishing & Partnership; C.B. CEBULSKI, VP of Brand Management & Development, Asia; DAVID GABRIEL, SVP of Sales & Marketing, Publishing; JEFF YOUNGQUIST, VP of Production & Special Projects; DAN CARR, Executive Director of Publishing Technology; ALEX MORALES, Director of Publishing Operations; SUSAN CRESPI, Production Manager; STAN LEE, Chairman Emeritus. For information regarding advertising in Marvel Comics or on Marvel.com, please contact Vit DeBellis, Integrated Sales Manager, at vdebellis@marvel.com. For Marvel subscription inquiries, please call 888-511-5480. **Manufactured between 3/25/2016 and 5/2/2016 by SOLISCO PRINTERS, SCOTT, QC, CANADA.**

10 9 8 7 6 5 4 3 2 1

ALL-NEW INHUMANS
GLOBAL OUTREACH

"SUBLIMATION"
(FROM *ALL-NEW, ALL-DIFFERENT POINT ONE #1*)

CHARLES SOULE
WRITER

STEFANO CASELLI
ARTIST

ANDRES MOSSA
COLOR ARTIST

ALL-NEW INHUMANS #1
BACKUP STORY

JAMES ASMUS & CHARLES SOULE
WRITERS

STEFANO CASELLI
ARTIST

ANDRES MOSSA
COLOR ARTIST

ALL-NEW INHUMANS #1-4

JAMES ASMUS & CHARLES SOULE
WRITERS

STEFANO CASELLI
ARTIST

ANDRES MOSSA
COLOR ARTIST

VC'S CLAYTON COWLES
(#1, #3-4 & ALL-NEW, ALL-DIFFERENT POINT ONE #1)
& JOE SABINO (#2)
LETTERERS

STEFANO CASELLI (#1),
JAMAL CAMPBELL (#2) AND
STEFANO CASELLI & ANDRES MOSSA (#3-4)
COVER ART

CHARLES BEACHAM
ASSISTANT EDITOR

NICK LOWE
EDITOR

INHUMANS CREATED BY
STAN LEE & JACK KIRBY

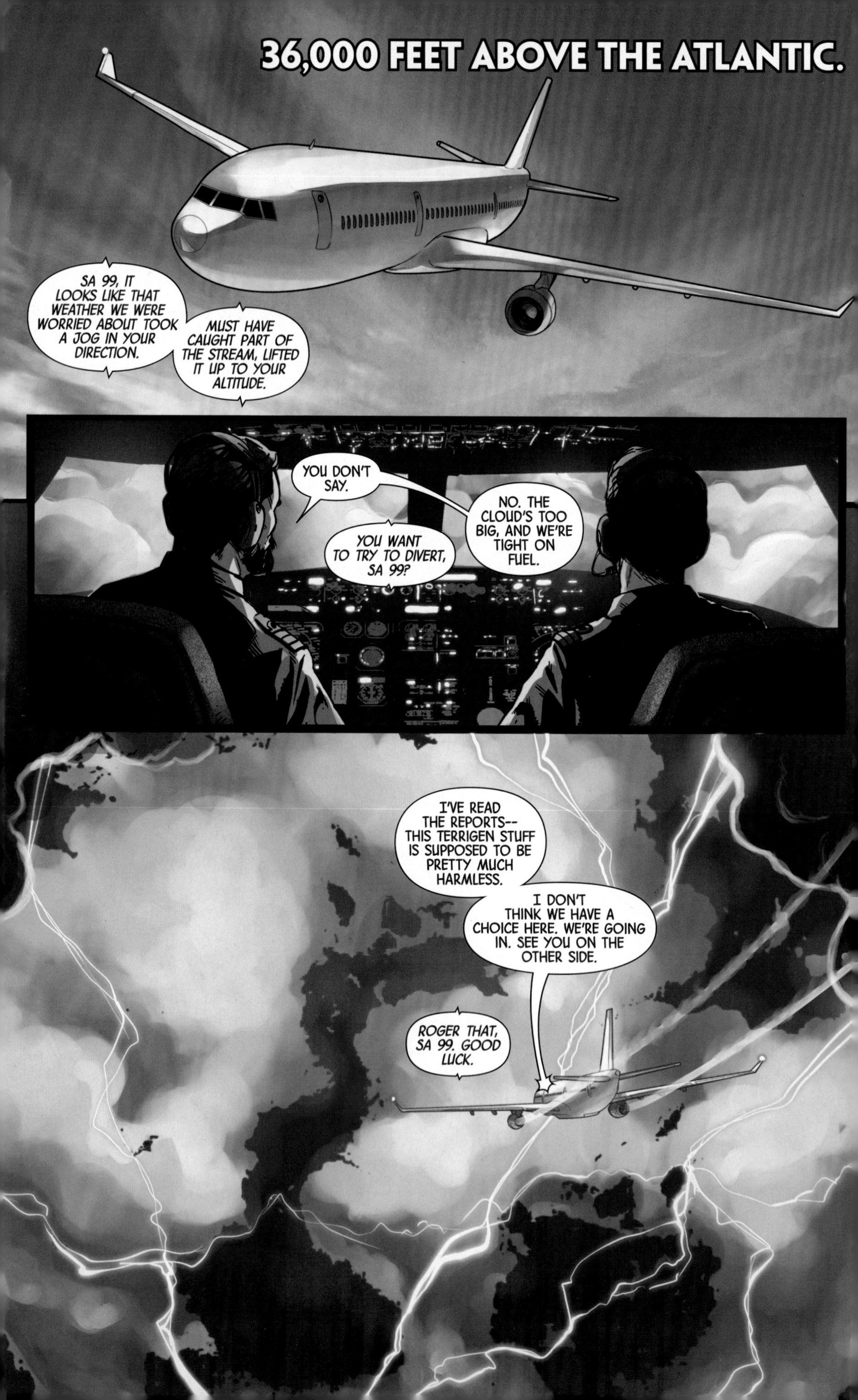
36,000 FEET ABOVE THE ATLANTIC.
SA 99, IT LOOKS LIKE THAT WEATHER WE WERE WORRIED ABOUT TOOK A JOG IN YOUR DIRECTION.
MUST HAVE CAUGHT PART OF THE STREAM, LIFTED IT UP TO YOUR ALTITUDE.
YOU DON'T SAY.
YOU WANT TO TRY TO DIVERT, SA 99?
NO. THE CLOUD'S TOO BIG, AND WE'RE TIGHT ON FUEL.
I'VE READ THE REPORTS-- THIS TERRIGEN STUFF IS SUPPOSED TO BE PRETTY MUCH HARMLESS.
I DON'T THINK WE HAVE A CHOICE HERE. WE'RE GOING IN. SEE YOU ON THE OTHER SIDE.
ROGER THAT, SA 99. GOOD LUCK.

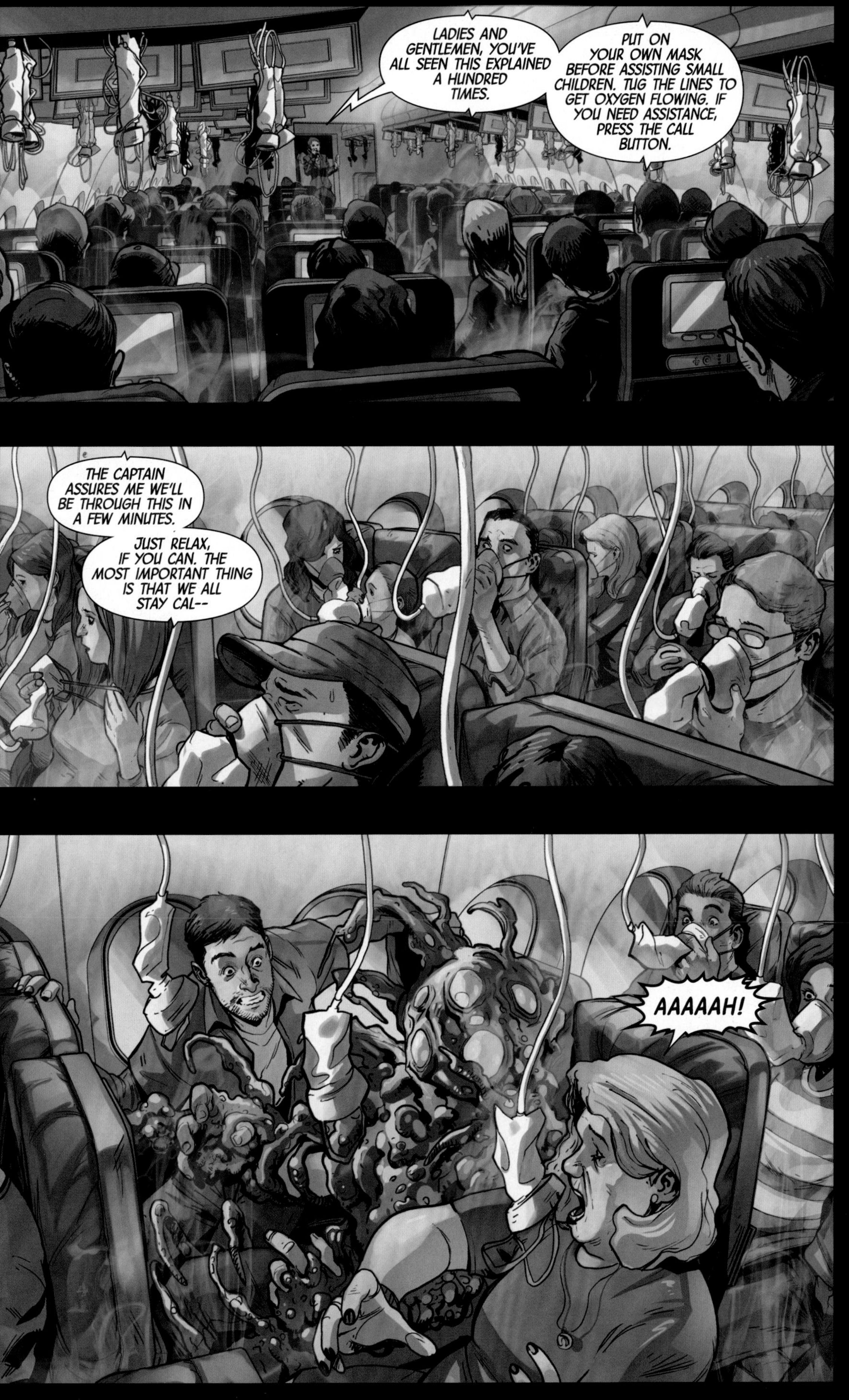
LADIES AND GENTLEMEN, YOU'VE ALL SEEN THIS EXPLAINED A HUNDRED TIMES.
PUT ON YOUR OWN MASK BEFORE ASSISTING SMALL CHILDREN. TUG THE LINES TO GET OXYGEN FLOWING. IF YOU NEED ASSISTANCE, PRESS THE CALL BUTTON.
THE CAPTAIN ASSURES ME WE'LL BE THROUGH THIS IN A FEW MINUTES.
JUST RELAX, IF YOU CAN. THE MOST IMPORTANT THING IS THAT WE ALL STAY CAL--
AAAAAH!

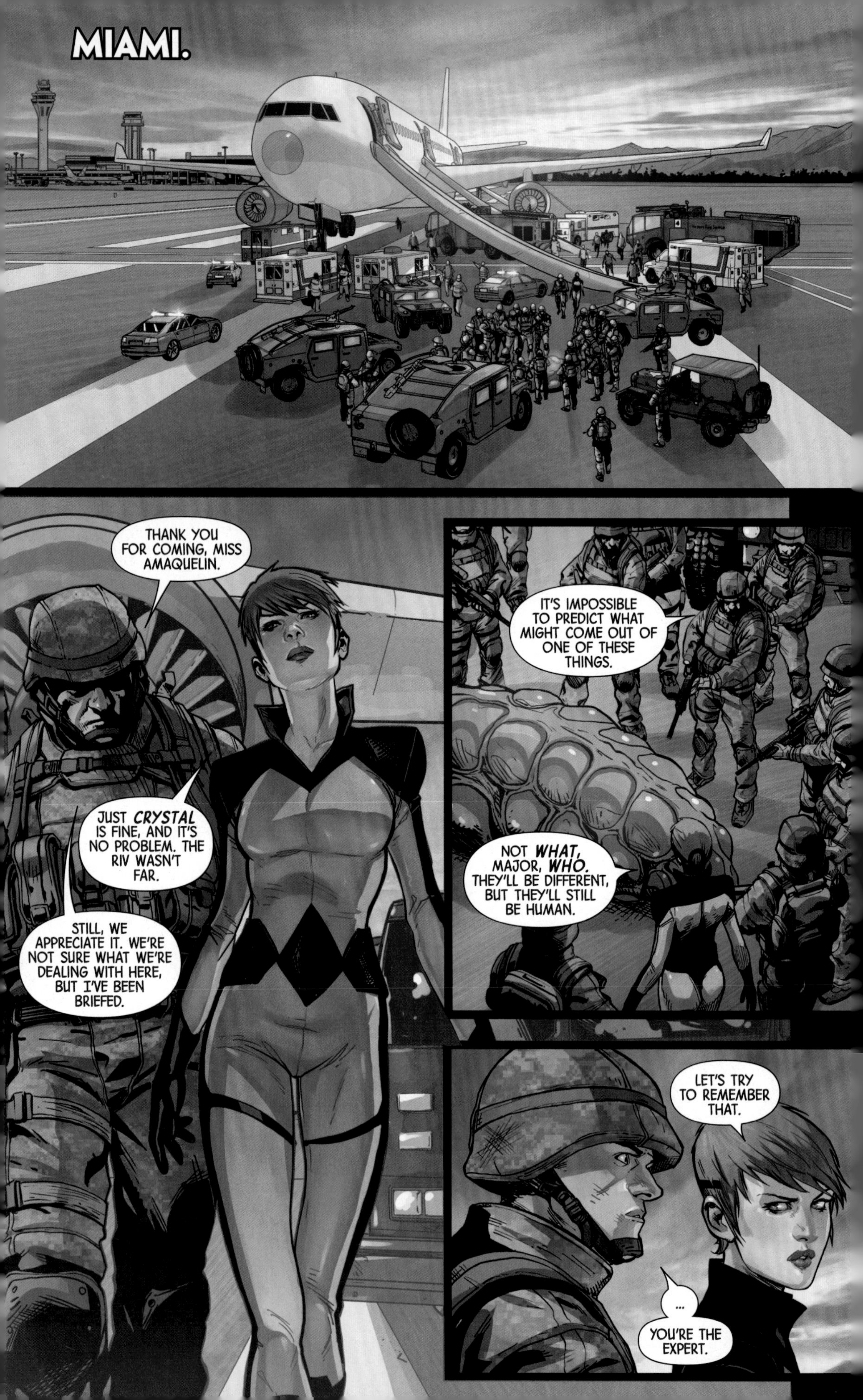
MIAMI.
THANK YOU FOR COMING, MISS AMAQUELIN.
JUST CRYSTAL IS FINE, AND IT'S NO PROBLEM. THE RIV WASN'T FAR.
STILL, WE APPRECIATE IT. WE'RE NOT SURE WHAT WE'RE DEALING WITH HERE, BUT I'VE BEEN BRIEFED.
IT'S IMPOSSIBLE TO PREDICT WHAT MIGHT COME OUT OF ONE OF THESE THINGS.
NOT WHAT, MAJOR, WHO. THEY'LL BE DIFFERENT, BUT THEY'LL STILL BE HUMAN.
LET'S TRY TO REMEMBER THAT.
...
YOU'RE THE EXPERT.

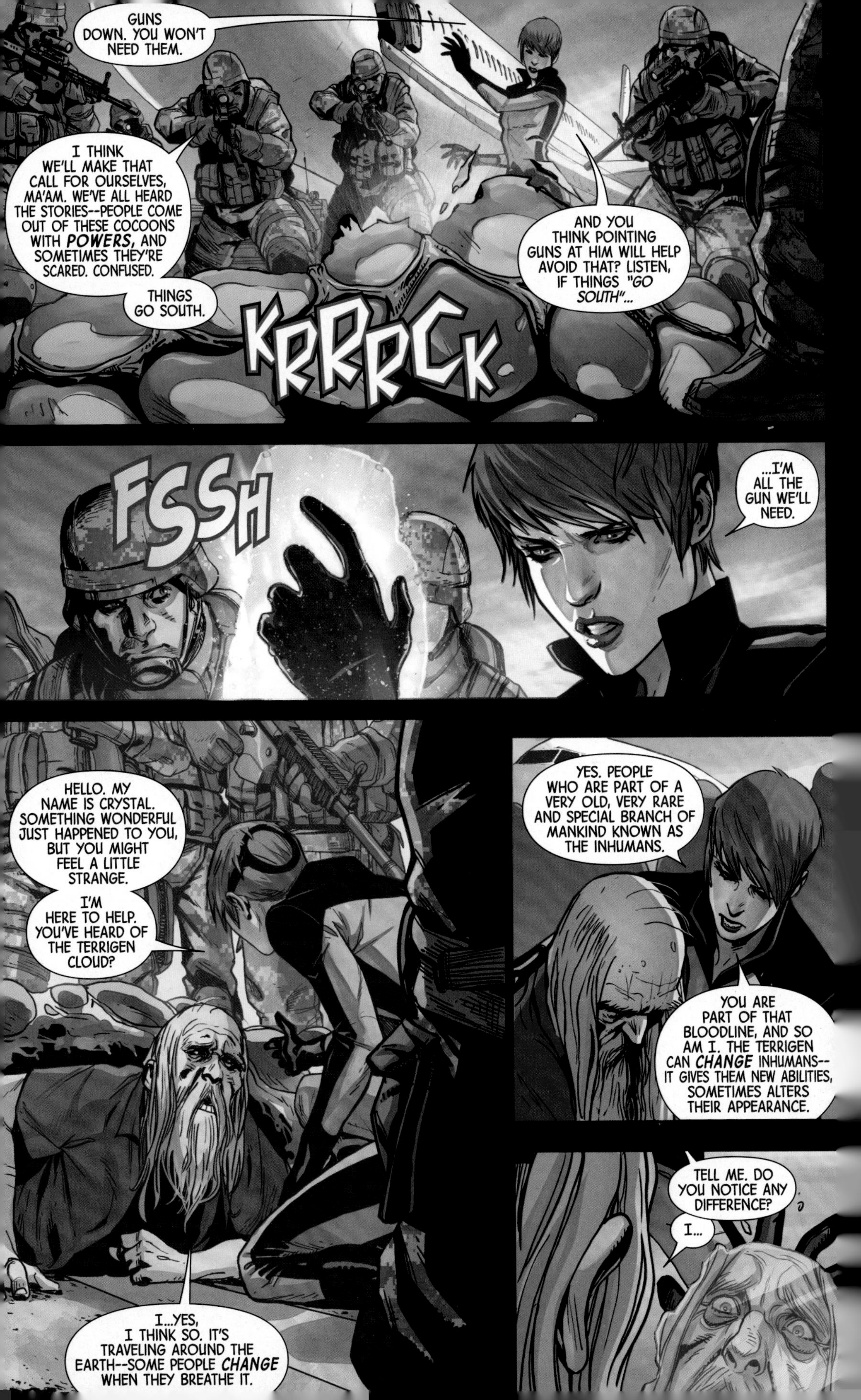
GUNS DOWN. YOU WON'T NEED THEM.
I THINK WE'LL MAKE THAT CALL FOR OURSELVES, MA'AM. WE'VE ALL HEARD THE STORIES--PEOPLE COME OUT OF THESE COCOONS WITH POWERS, AND SOMETIMES THEY'RE SCARED. CONFUSED.
THINGS GO SOUTH.
AND YOU THINK POINTING GUNS AT HIM WILL HELP AVOID THAT? LISTEN, IF THINGS "GO SOUTH"...
KRRRCK
FSSH
...I'M ALL THE GUN WE'LL NEED.
HELLO. MY NAME IS CRYSTAL. SOMETHING WONDERFUL JUST HAPPENED TO YOU, BUT YOU MIGHT FEEL A LITTLE STRANGE.
I'M HERE TO HELP. YOU'VE HEARD OF THE TERRIGEN CLOUD?
I...YES, I THINK SO. IT'S TRAVELING AROUND THE EARTH--SOME PEOPLE CHANGE WHEN THEY BREATHE IT.
YES. PEOPLE WHO ARE PART OF A VERY OLD, VERY RARE AND SPECIAL BRANCH OF MANKIND KNOWN AS THE INHUMANS.
YOU ARE PART OF THAT BLOODLINE, AND SO AM I. THE TERRIGEN CAN CHANGE INHUMANS--IT GIVES THEM NEW ABILITIES, SOMETIMES ALTERS THEIR APPEARANCE.
TELL ME. DO YOU NOTICE ANY DIFFERENCE?
I...

...I'M TWENTY-THREE YEARS OLD.

NNNNGH!

I NEED HELP HERE! A MEDIC!

I... CAN'T...I...I'M NOT...

JUST LIE STILL, SIR. YOU'RE GOING TO BE FINE.

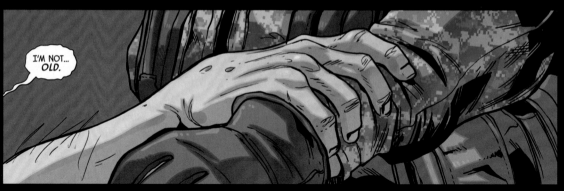

I'M NOT... OLD.

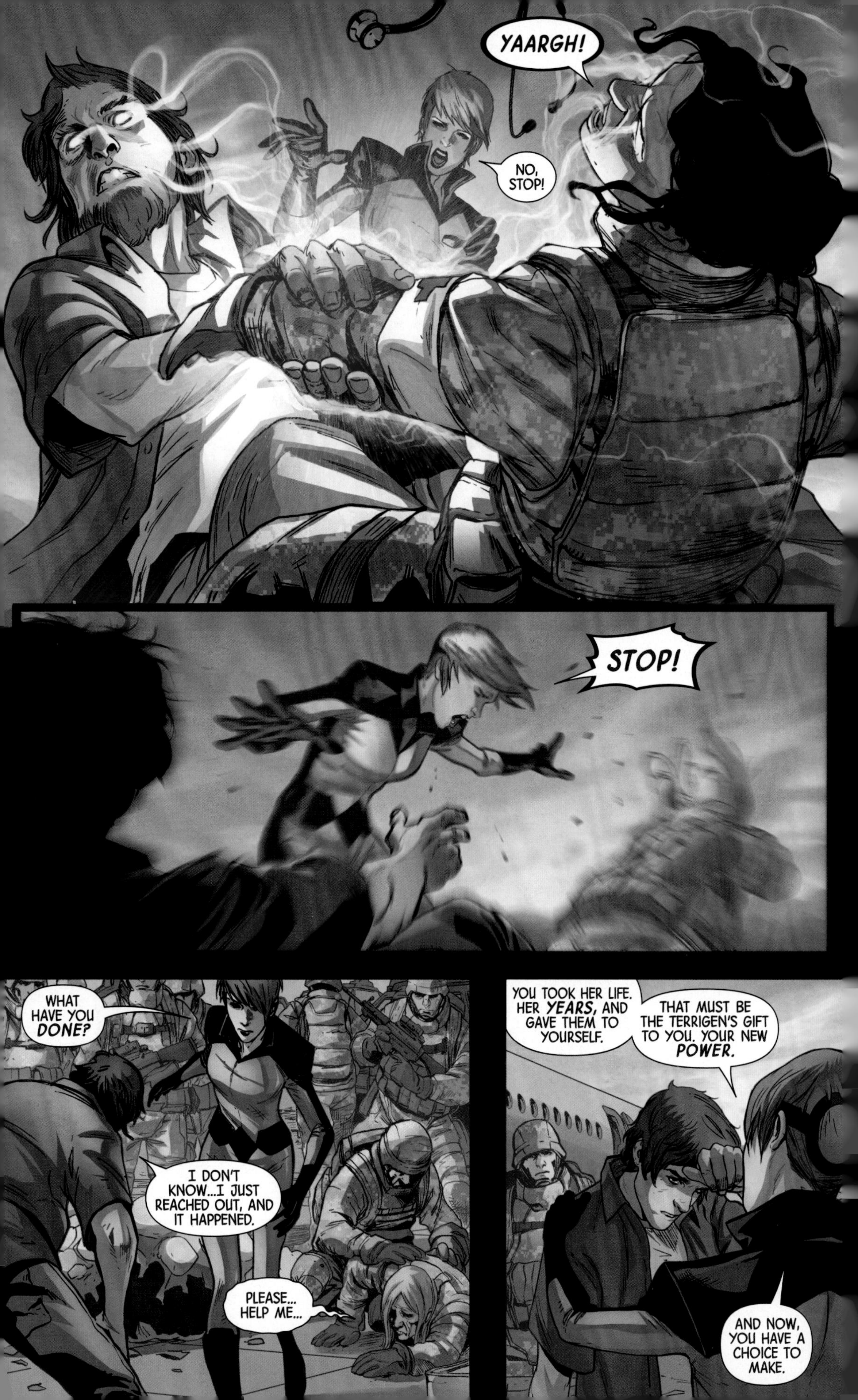
YAARGH!
NO, STOP!
STOP!
WHAT HAVE YOU DONE?
I DON'T KNOW...I JUST REACHED OUT, AND IT HAPPENED.
PLEASE... HELP ME...
YOU TOOK HER LIFE. HER YEARS, AND GAVE THEM TO YOURSELF.
THAT MUST BE THE TERRIGEN'S GIFT TO YOU. YOUR NEW POWER.
AND NOW, YOU HAVE A CHOICE TO MAKE.

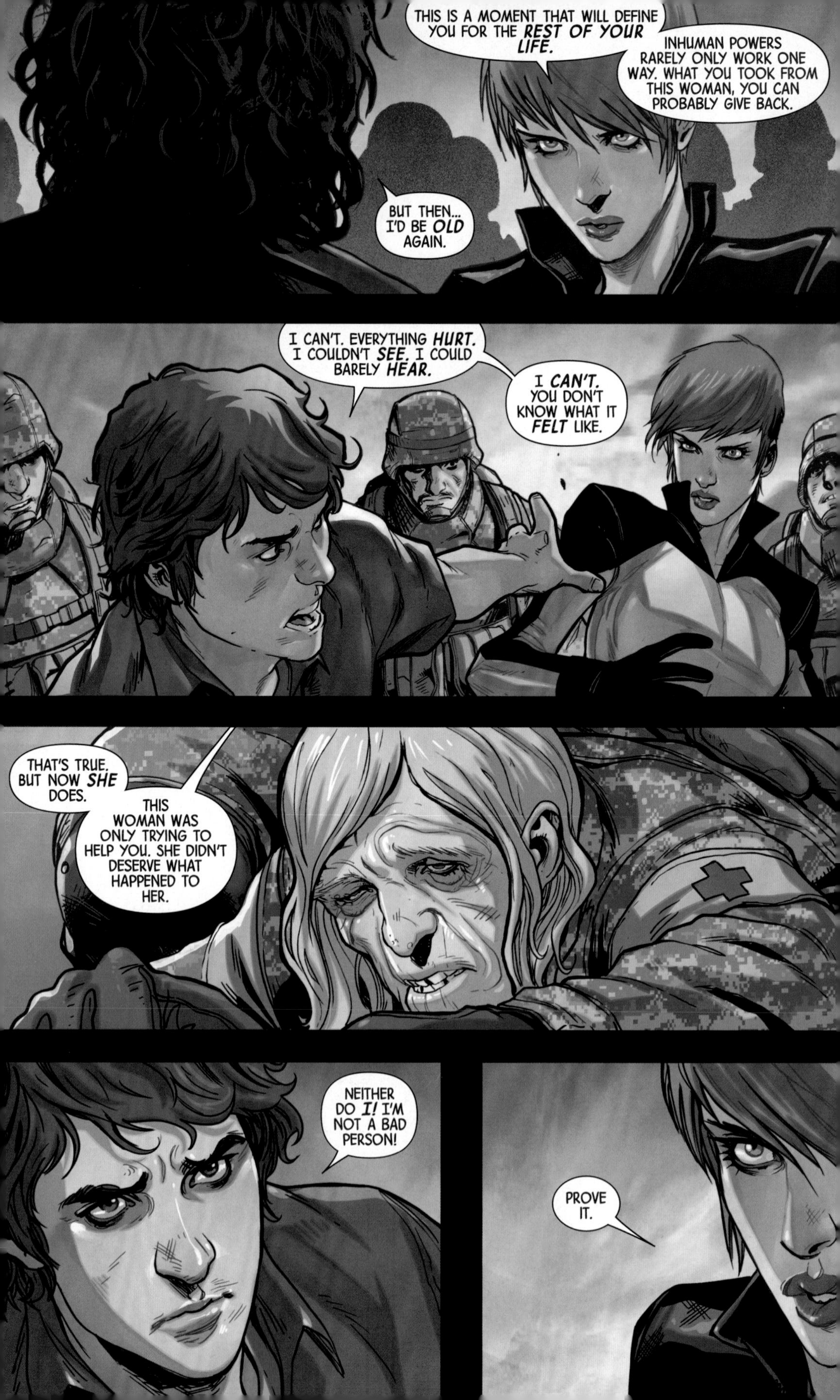
THIS IS A MOMENT THAT WILL DEFINE YOU FOR THE REST OF YOUR LIFE.
INHUMAN POWERS RARELY ONLY WORK ONE WAY. WHAT YOU TOOK FROM THIS WOMAN, YOU CAN PROBABLY GIVE BACK.
BUT THEN... I'D BE OLD AGAIN.
I CAN'T. EVERYTHING HURT. I COULDN'T SEE. I COULD BARELY HEAR.
I CAN'T. YOU DON'T KNOW WHAT IT FELT LIKE.
THAT'S TRUE. BUT NOW SHE DOES.
THIS WOMAN WAS ONLY TRYING TO HELP YOU. SHE DIDN'T DESERVE WHAT HAPPENED TO HER.
NEITHER DO I! I'M NOT A BAD PERSON!
PROVE IT.

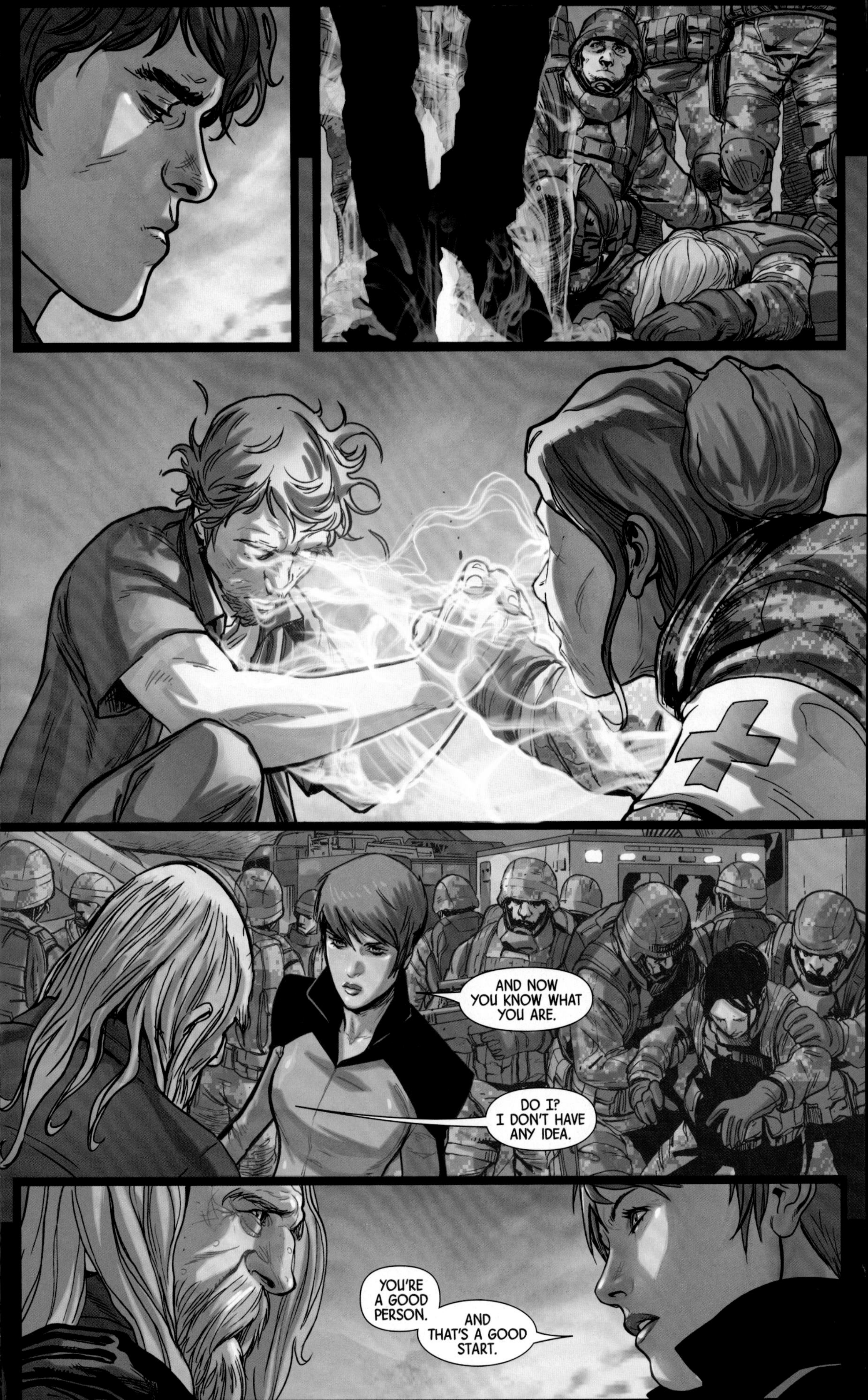
AND NOW YOU KNOW WHAT YOU ARE.
DO I? I DON'T HAVE ANY IDEA.
YOU'RE A GOOD PERSON.
AND THAT'S A GOOD START.

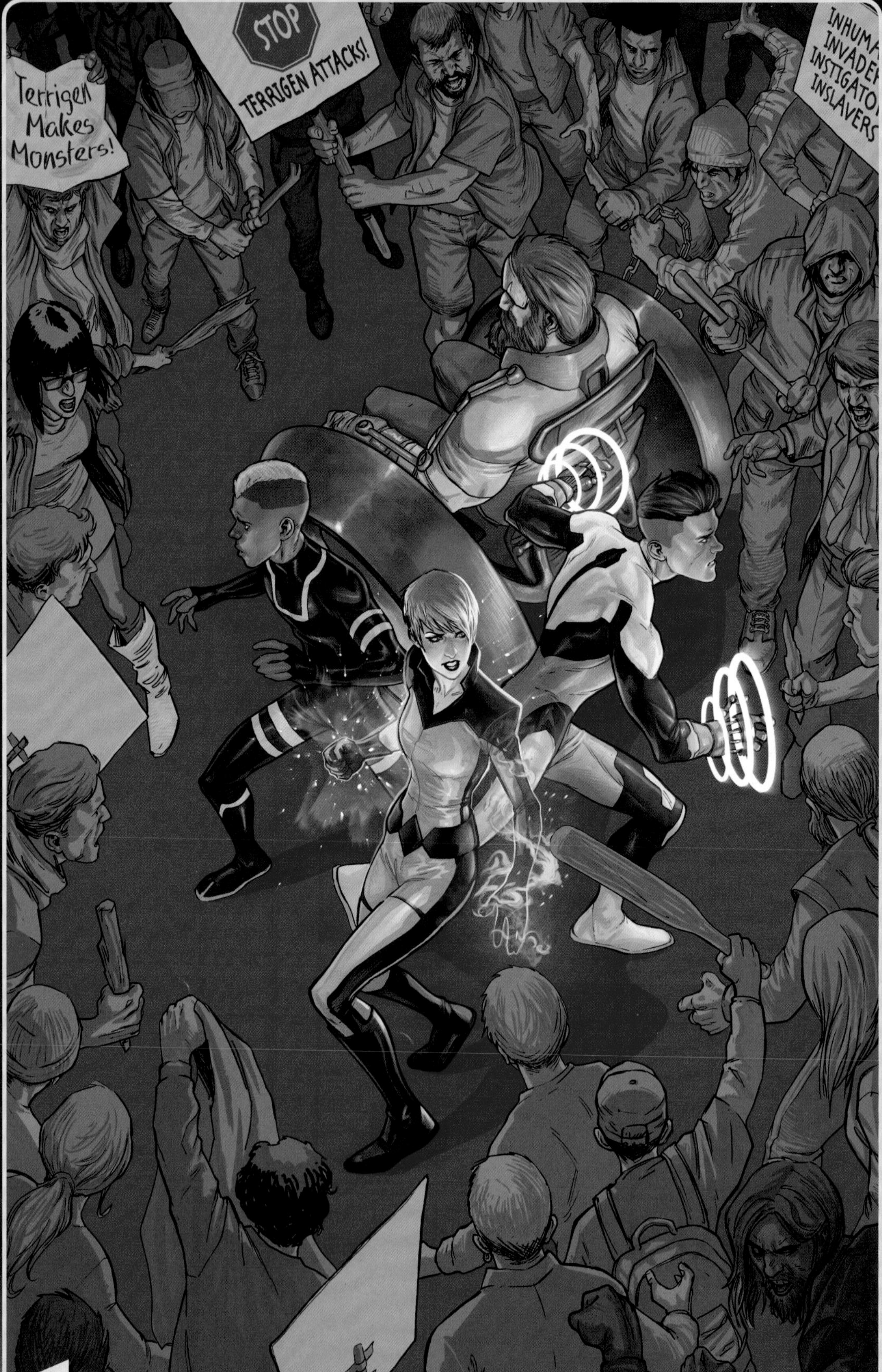
Terrigen Makes Monsters!
STOP
TERRIGEN ATTACKS!
INSLAVERS

1

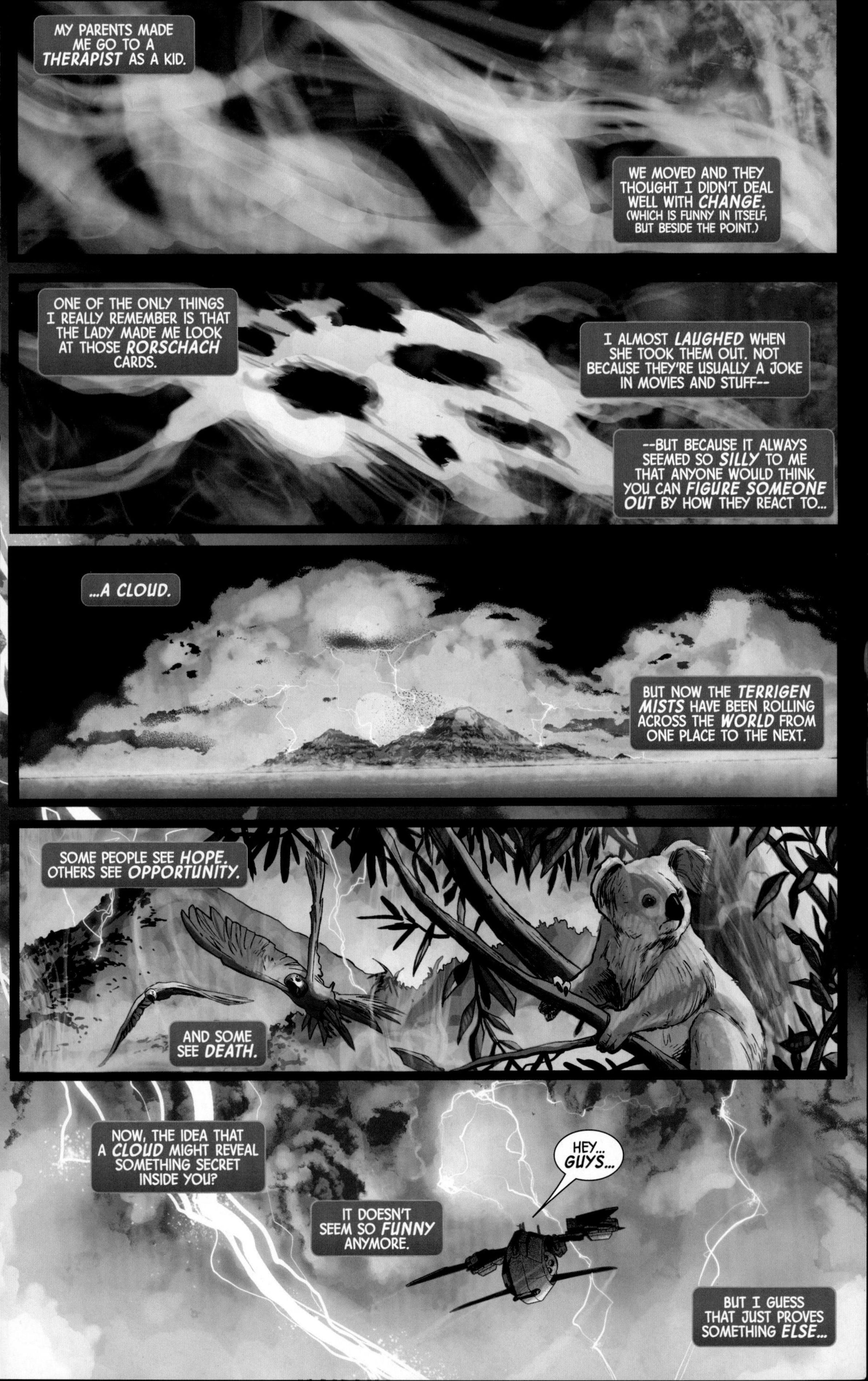
MY PARENTS MADE ME GO TO A *THERAPIST* AS A KID.
WE MOVED AND THEY THOUGHT I DIDN'T DEAL WELL WITH *CHANGE.* (WHICH IS FUNNY IN ITSELF, BUT BESIDE THE POINT.)
ONE OF THE ONLY THINGS I REALLY REMEMBER IS THAT THE LADY MADE ME LOOK AT THOSE *RORSCHACH* CARDS.
I ALMOST *LAUGHED* WHEN SHE TOOK THEM OUT. NOT BECAUSE THEY'RE USUALLY A JOKE IN MOVIES AND STUFF--
--BUT BECAUSE IT ALWAYS SEEMED SO *SILLY* TO ME THAT ANYONE WOULD THINK YOU CAN *FIGURE SOMEONE OUT* BY HOW THEY REACT TO...
...A CLOUD.
BUT NOW THE *TERRIGEN MISTS* HAVE BEEN ROLLING ACROSS THE *WORLD* FROM ONE PLACE TO THE NEXT.
SOME PEOPLE SEE *HOPE.* OTHERS SEE *OPPORTUNITY.*
AND SOME SEE *DEATH.*
NOW, THE IDEA THAT A *CLOUD* MIGHT REVEAL SOMETHING SECRET INSIDE YOU?
HEY... *GUYS...*
IT DOESN'T SEEM SO *FUNNY* ANYMORE.
BUT I GUESS THAT JUST PROVES SOMETHING *ELSE...*

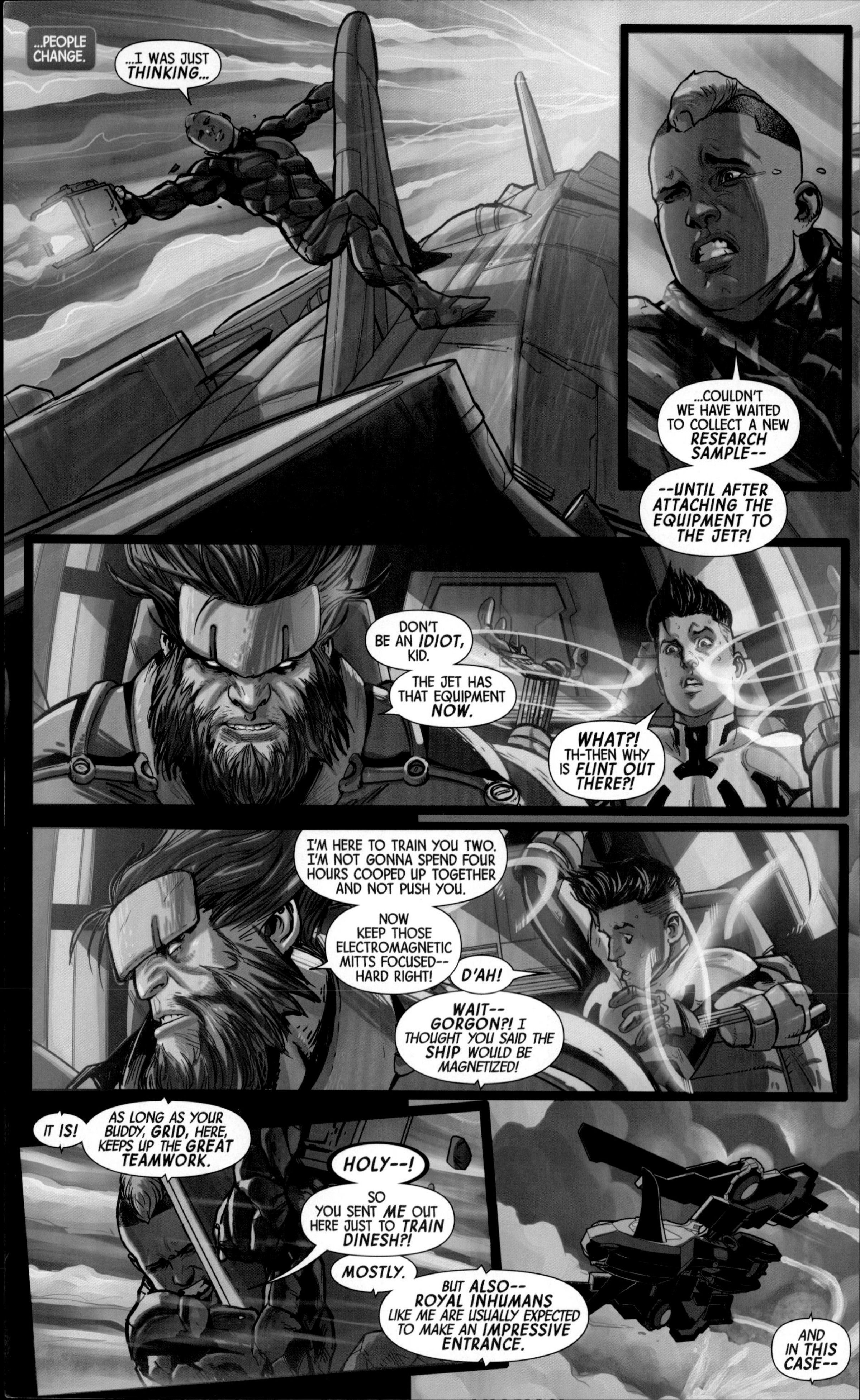
...PEOPLE CHANGE.
...I WAS JUST THINKING...
...COULDN'T WE HAVE WAITED TO COLLECT A NEW RESEARCH SAMPLE--
--UNTIL AFTER ATTACHING THE EQUIPMENT TO THE JET?!
DON'T BE AN IDIOT, KID.
THE JET HAS THAT EQUIPMENT NOW.
WHAT?! TH-THEN WHY IS FLINT OUT THERE?!
I'M HERE TO TRAIN YOU TWO. I'M NOT GONNA SPEND FOUR HOURS COOPED UP TOGETHER AND NOT PUSH YOU.
NOW KEEP THOSE ELECTROMAGNETIC MITTS FOCUSED-- HARD RIGHT!
D'AH!
WAIT-- GORGON?! I THOUGHT YOU SAID THE SHIP WOULD BE MAGNETIZED!
IT IS!
AS LONG AS YOUR BUDDY, GRID, HERE, KEEPS UP THE GREAT TEAMWORK.
HOLY--!
SO YOU SENT ME OUT HERE JUST TO TRAIN DINESH?!
MOSTLY.
BUT ALSO-- ROYAL INHUMANS LIKE ME ARE USUALLY EXPECTED TO MAKE AN IMPRESSIVE ENTRANCE.
AND IN THIS CASE--

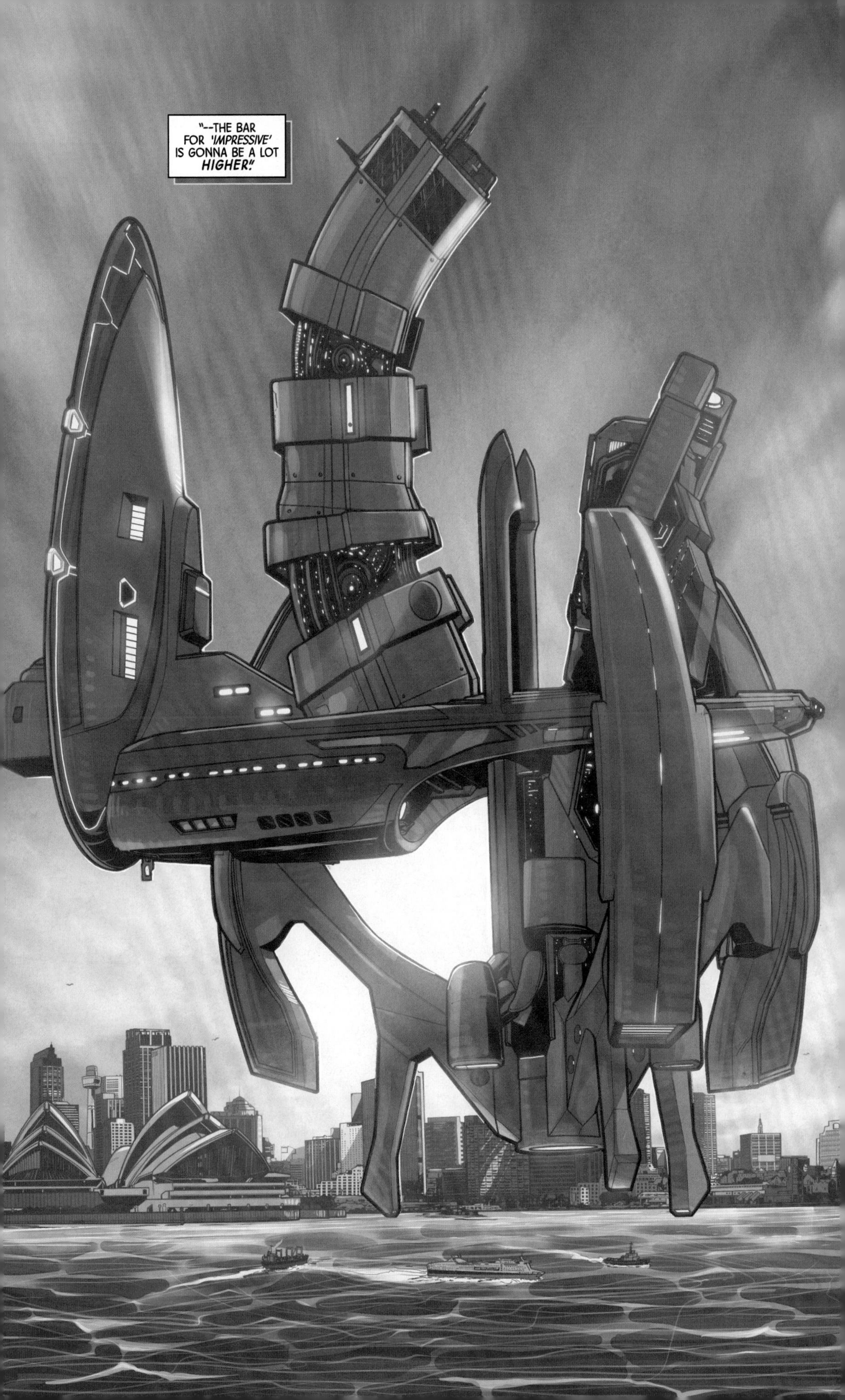
"--THE BAR FOR 'IMPRESSIVE' IS GONNA BE A LOT HIGHER!"

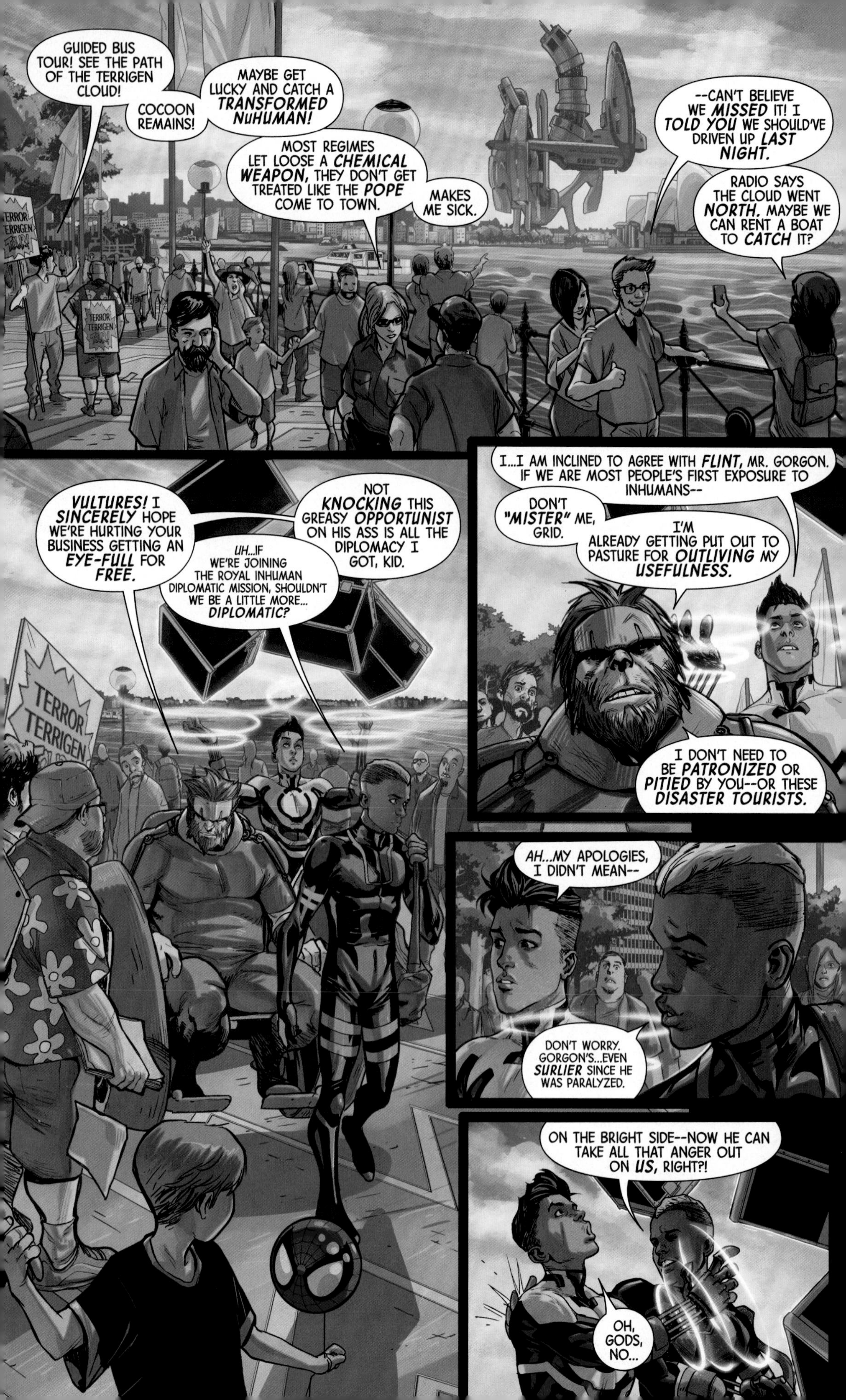
GUIDED BUS TOUR! SEE THE PATH OF THE TERRIGEN CLOUD!
COCOON REMAINS!
MAYBE GET LUCKY AND CATCH A TRANSFORMED NuHUMAN!
MOST REGIMES LET LOOSE A CHEMICAL WEAPON, THEY DON'T GET TREATED LIKE THE POPE COME TO TOWN.
MAKES ME SICK.
--CAN'T BELIEVE WE MISSED IT! I TOLD YOU WE SHOULD'VE DRIVEN UP LAST NIGHT.
RADIO SAYS THE CLOUD WENT NORTH. MAYBE WE CAN RENT A BOAT TO CATCH IT?
TERROR TERRIGEN TOUR!
TERROR TERRIGEN TOUR!
VULTURES! I SINCERELY HOPE WE'RE HURTING YOUR BUSINESS GETTING AN EYE-FULL FOR FREE.
NOT KNOCKING THIS GREASY OPPORTUNIST ON HIS ASS IS ALL THE DIPLOMACY I GOT, KID.
UH...IF WE'RE JOINING THE ROYAL INHUMAN DIPLOMATIC MISSION, SHOULDN'T WE BE A LITTLE MORE... DIPLOMATIC?
TERROR TERRIGEN
I...I AM INCLINED TO AGREE WITH FLINT, MR. GORGON. IF WE ARE MOST PEOPLE'S FIRST EXPOSURE TO INHUMANS--
DON'T "MISTER" ME, GRID.
I'M ALREADY GETTING PUT OUT TO PASTURE FOR OUTLIVING MY USEFULNESS.
I DON'T NEED TO BE PATRONIZED OR PITIED BY YOU--OR THESE DISASTER TOURISTS.
AH...MY APOLOGIES, I DIDN'T MEAN--
DON'T WORRY. GORGON'S...EVEN SURLIER SINCE HE WAS PARALYZED.
ON THE BRIGHT SIDE--NOW HE CAN TAKE ALL THAT ANGER OUT ON US, RIGHT?!
OH, GODS, NO...

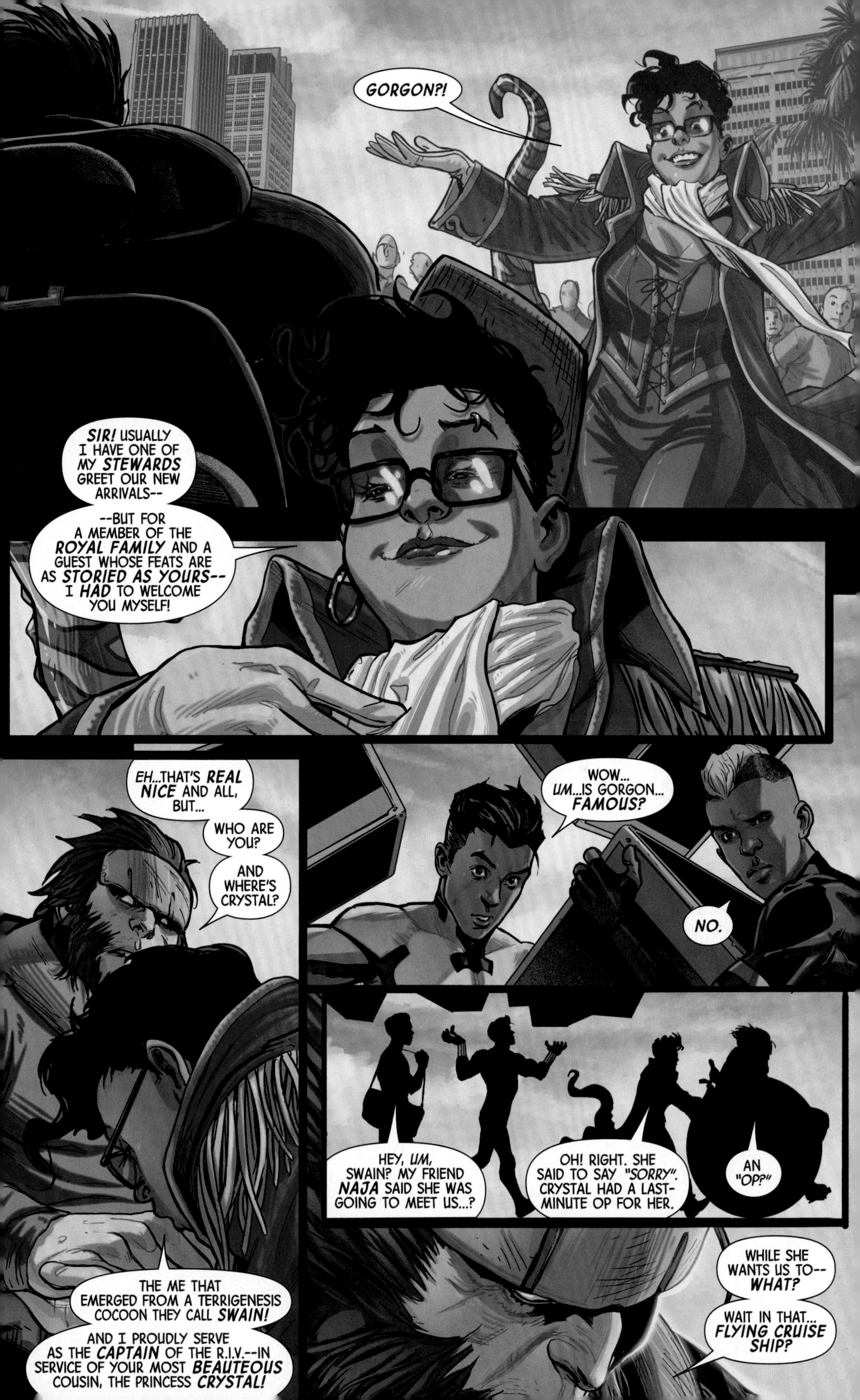
GORGON?!
SIR! USUALLY I HAVE ONE OF MY STEWARDS GREET OUR NEW ARRIVALS--
--BUT FOR A MEMBER OF THE ROYAL FAMILY AND A GUEST WHOSE FEATS ARE AS STORIED AS YOURS-- I HAD TO WELCOME YOU MYSELF!
EH...THAT'S REAL NICE AND ALL, BUT...
WHO ARE YOU?
AND WHERE'S CRYSTAL?
THE ME THAT EMERGED FROM A TERRIGENESIS COCOON THEY CALL SWAIN!
AND I PROUDLY SERVE AS THE CAPTAIN OF THE R.I.V.--IN SERVICE OF YOUR MOST BEAUTEOUS COUSIN, THE PRINCESS CRYSTAL!
WOW... UM...IS GORGON... FAMOUS?
NO.
HEY, UM, SWAIN? MY FRIEND NAJA SAID SHE WAS GOING TO MEET US...?
OH! RIGHT. SHE SAID TO SAY "SORRY". CRYSTAL HAD A LAST-MINUTE OP FOR HER.
AN "OP?"
WHILE SHE WANTS US TO-- WHAT?
WAIT IN THAT... FLYING CRUISE SHIP?

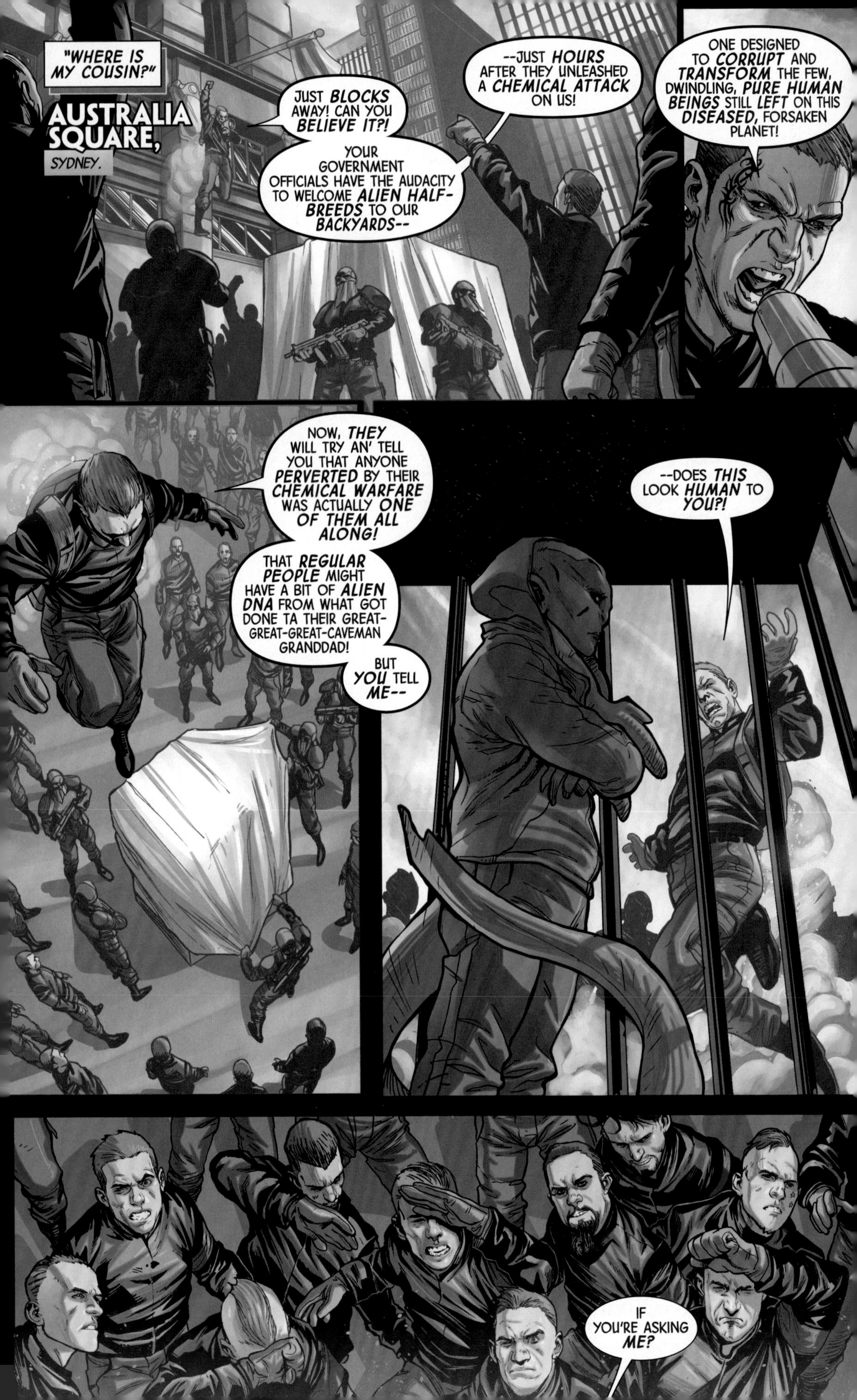
"WHERE IS MY COUSIN?"
AUSTRALIA SQUARE,
SYDNEY.
JUST BLOCKS AWAY! CAN YOU BELIEVE IT?!
YOUR GOVERNMENT OFFICIALS HAVE THE AUDACITY TO WELCOME ALIEN HALF-BREEDS TO OUR BACKYARDS--
--JUST HOURS AFTER THEY UNLEASHED A CHEMICAL ATTACK ON US!
ONE DESIGNED TO CORRUPT AND TRANSFORM THE FEW, DWINDLING, PURE HUMAN BEINGS STILL LEFT ON THIS DISEASED, FORSAKEN PLANET!
NOW, THEY WILL TRY AN' TELL YOU THAT ANYONE PERVERTED BY THEIR CHEMICAL WARFARE WAS ACTUALLY ONE OF THEM ALL ALONG!
THAT REGULAR PEOPLE MIGHT HAVE A BIT OF ALIEN DNA FROM WHAT GOT DONE TA THEIR GREAT-GREAT-GREAT-CAVEMAN GRANDDAD!
BUT YOU TELL ME--
--DOES THIS LOOK HUMAN TO YOU?!
IF YOU'RE ASKING ME?

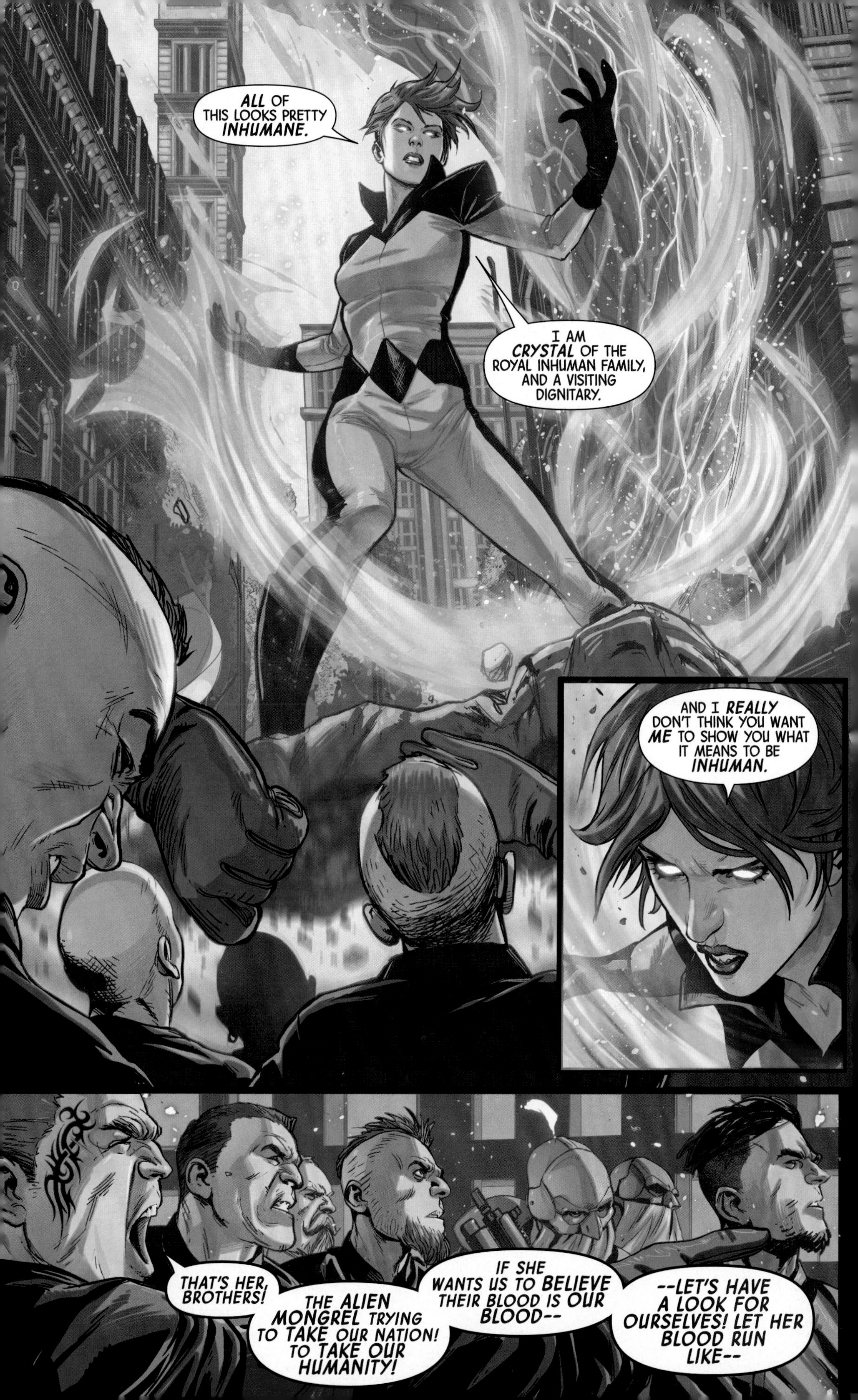
ALL OF THIS LOOKS PRETTY INHUMANE.
I AM CRYSTAL OF THE ROYAL INHUMAN FAMILY, AND A VISITING DIGNITARY.
AND I REALLY DON'T THINK YOU WANT ME TO SHOW YOU WHAT IT MEANS TO BE INHUMAN.
THAT'S HER, BROTHERS!
THE ALIEN MONGREL TRYING TO TAKE OUR NATION! TO TAKE OUR HUMANITY!
IF SHE WANTS US TO BELIEVE THEIR BLOOD IS OUR BLOOD--
--LET'S HAVE A LOOK FOR OURSELVES! LET HER BLOOD RUN LIKE--

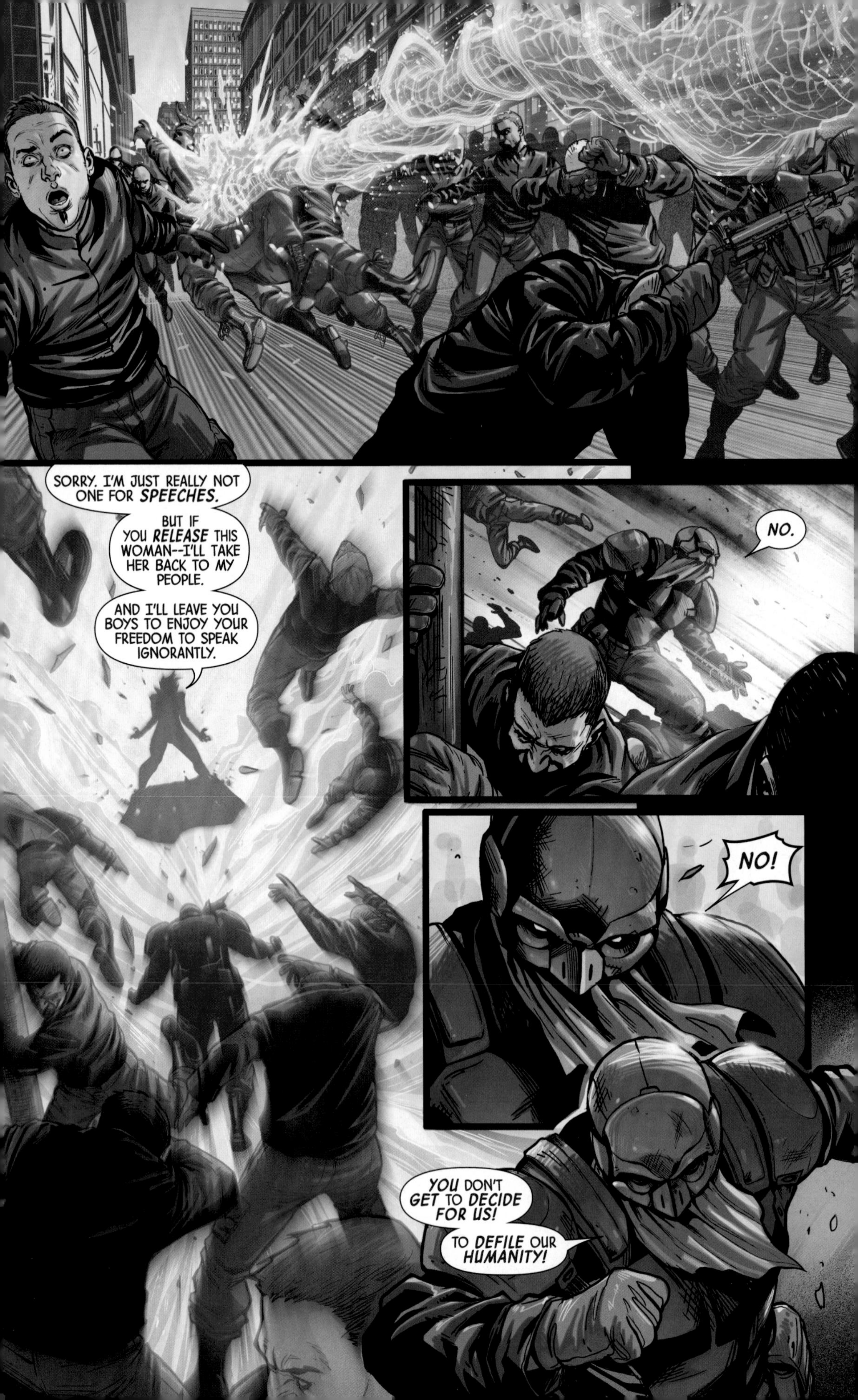
SORRY. I'M JUST REALLY NOT ONE FOR SPEECHES.
BUT IF YOU RELEASE THIS WOMAN--I'LL TAKE HER BACK TO MY PEOPLE.
AND I'LL LEAVE YOU BOYS TO ENJOY YOUR FREEDOM TO SPEAK IGNORANTLY.
NO.
NO!
YOU DON'T GET TO DECIDE FOR US!
TO DEFILE OUR HUMANITY!

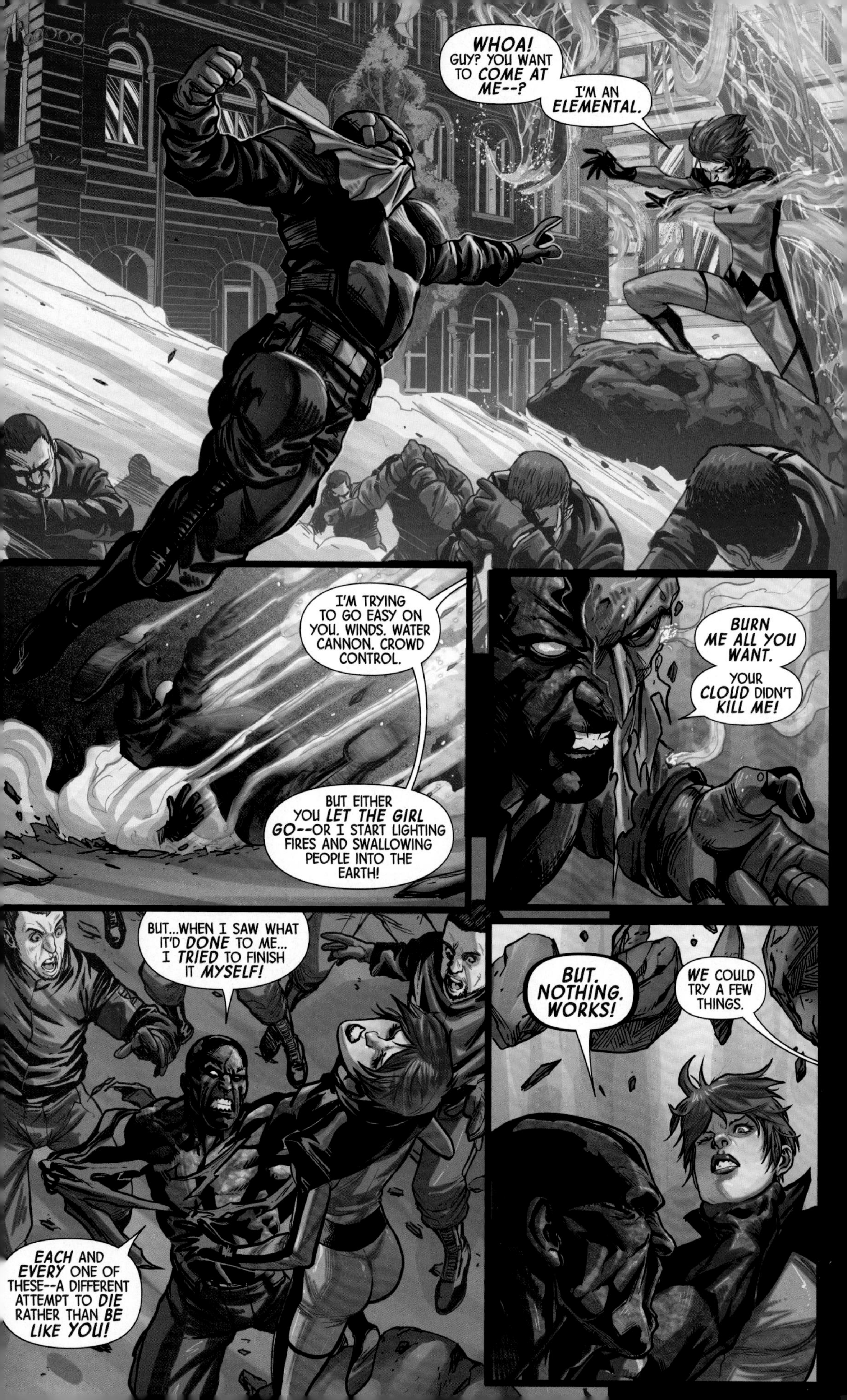
WHOA! GUY? YOU WANT TO COME AT ME--?
I'M AN ELEMENTAL.
I'M TRYING TO GO EASY ON YOU. WINDS. WATER CANNON. CROWD CONTROL.
BUT EITHER YOU LET THE GIRL GO--OR I START LIGHTING FIRES AND SWALLOWING PEOPLE INTO THE EARTH!
BURN ME ALL YOU WANT.
YOUR CLOUD DIDN'T KILL ME!
BUT...WHEN I SAW WHAT IT'D DONE TO ME... I TRIED TO FINISH IT MYSELF!
EACH AND EVERY ONE OF THESE--A DIFFERENT ATTEMPT TO DIE RATHER THAN BE LIKE YOU!
BUT. NOTHING. WORKS!
WE COULD TRY A FEW THINGS.

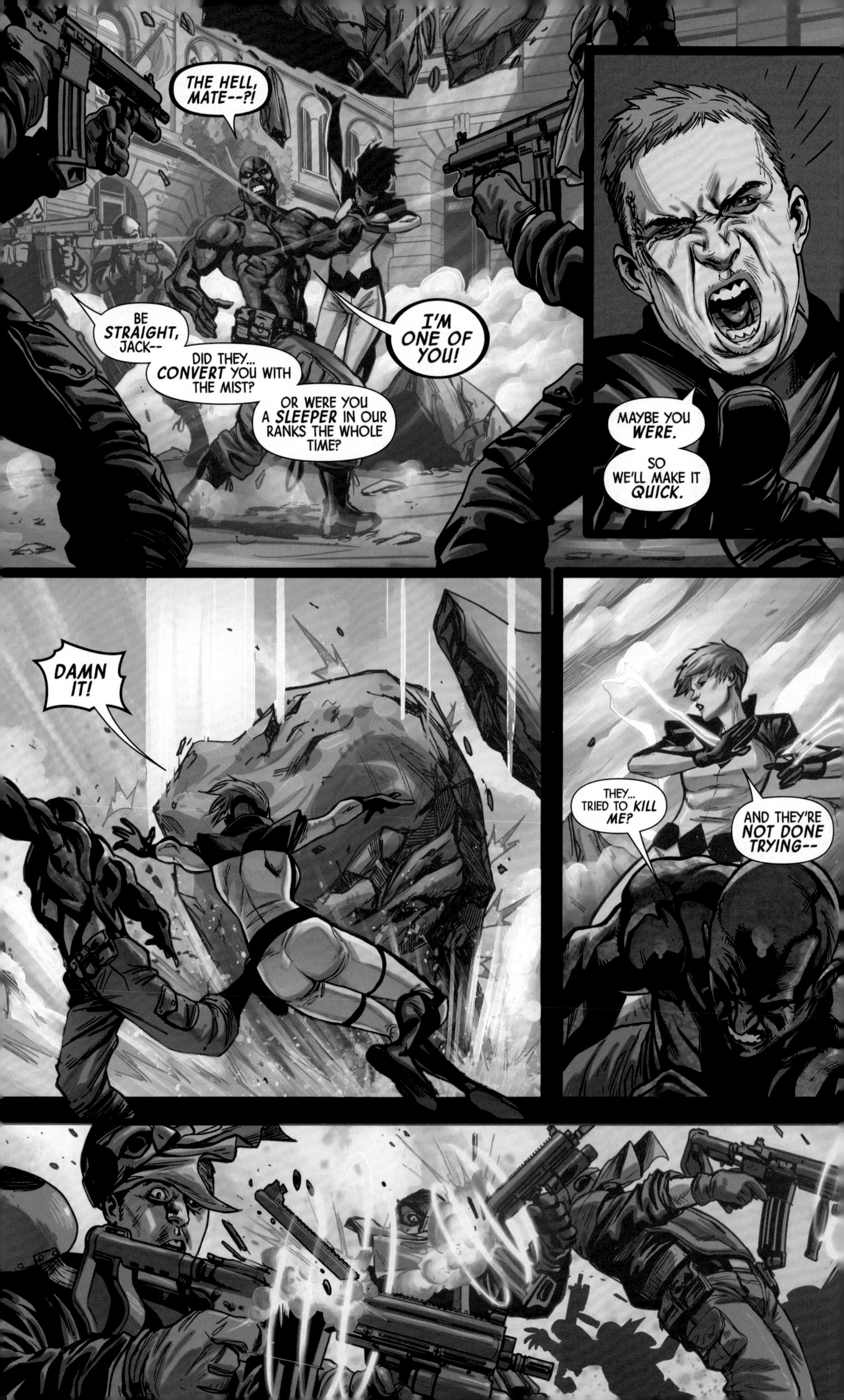
THE HELL, MATE--?!
BE STRAIGHT, JACK--
DID THEY... CONVERT YOU WITH THE MIST?
OR WERE YOU A SLEEPER IN OUR RANKS THE WHOLE TIME?
I'M ONE OF YOU!
MAYBE YOU WERE.
SO WE'LL MAKE IT QUICK.
DAMN IT!
THEY... TRIED TO KILL ME?
AND THEY'RE NOT DONE TRYING--

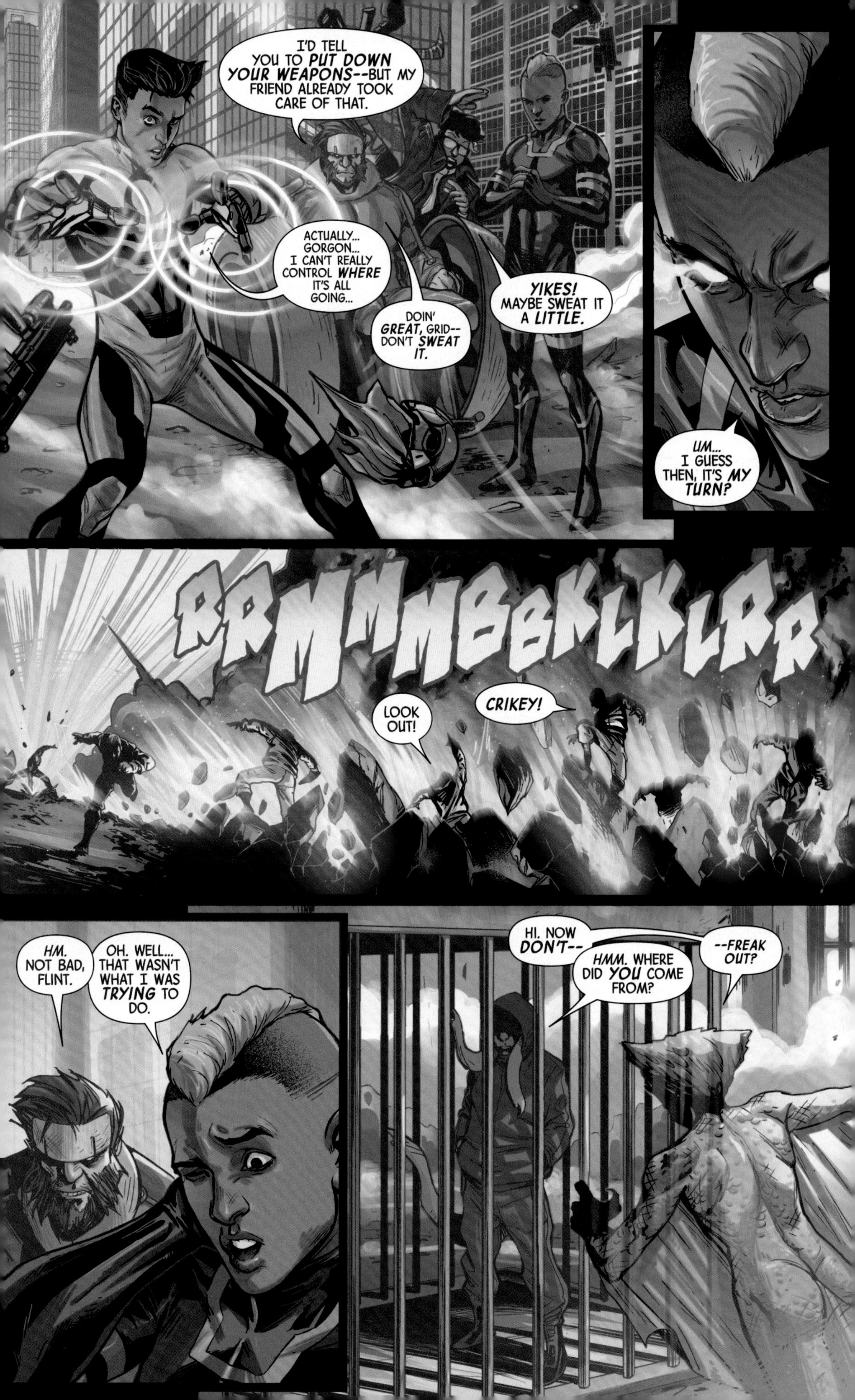
I'D TELL YOU TO PUT DOWN YOUR WEAPONS--BUT MY FRIEND ALREADY TOOK CARE OF THAT.
ACTUALLY... GORGON... I CAN'T REALLY CONTROL WHERE IT'S ALL GOING...
DOIN' GREAT, GRID--DON'T SWEAT IT.
YIKES! MAYBE SWEAT IT A LITTLE.
UM... I GUESS THEN, IT'S MY TURN?
RRMMMBBKLKLRR
LOOK OUT!
CRIKEY!
HM. NOT BAD, FLINT.
OH. WELL... THAT WASN'T WHAT I WAS TRYING TO DO.
HI. NOW DON'T--
--FREAK OUT?
HMM. WHERE DID YOU COME FROM?

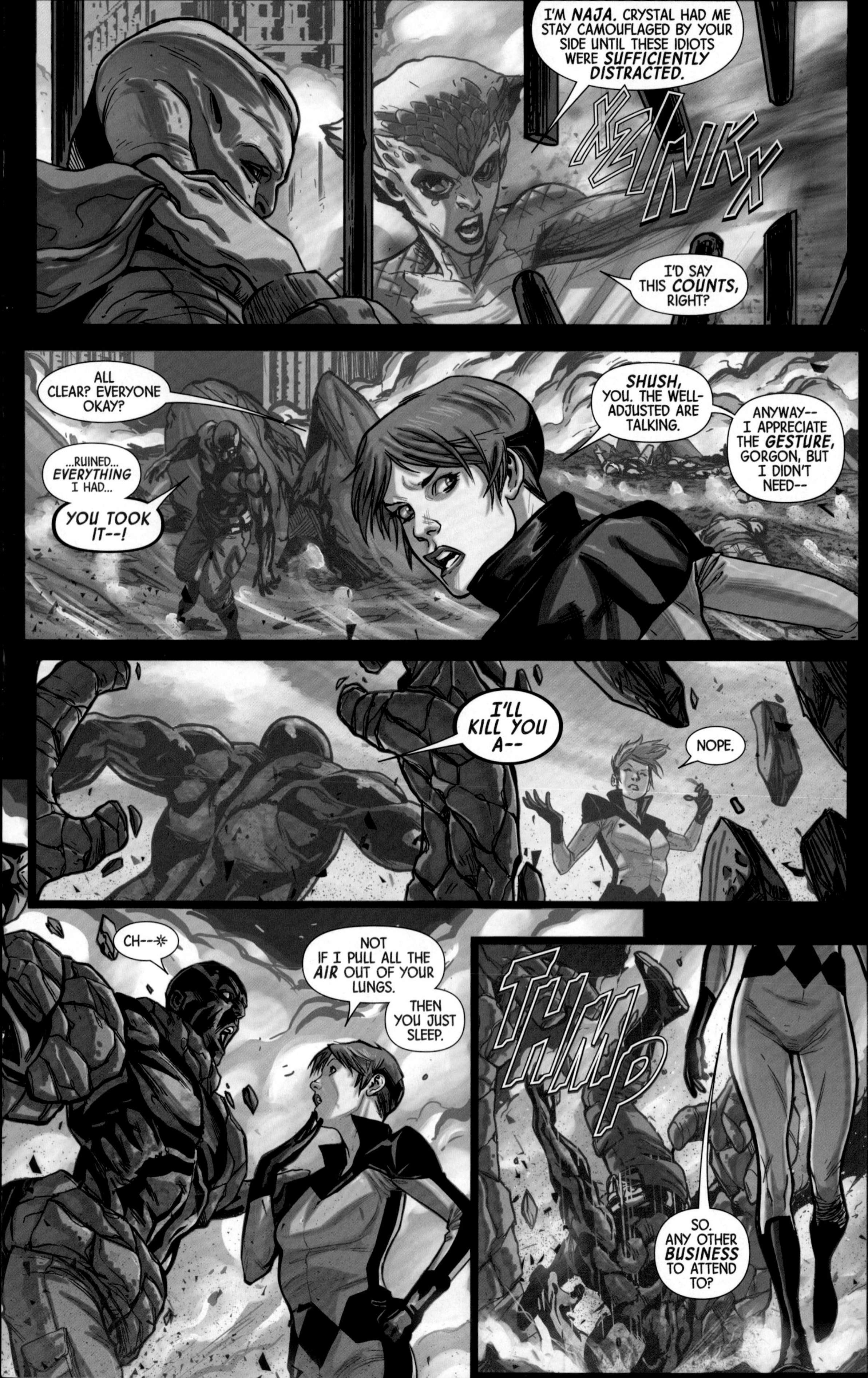
I'M NAJA. CRYSTAL HAD ME STAY CAMOUFLAGED BY YOUR SIDE UNTIL THESE IDIOTS WERE SUFFICIENTLY DISTRACTED.
XZINKX
I'D SAY THIS COUNTS, RIGHT?
ALL CLEAR? EVERYONE OKAY?
...RUINED... EVERYTHING I HAD...
YOU TOOK IT--!
SHUSH, YOU. THE WELL-ADJUSTED ARE TALKING.
ANYWAY-- I APPRECIATE THE GESTURE, GORGON, BUT I DIDN'T NEED--
I'LL KILL YOU A--
NOPE.
CH--
NOT IF I PULL ALL THE AIR OUT OF YOUR LUNGS.
THEN YOU JUST SLEEP.
THUMP
SO. ANY OTHER BUSINESS TO ATTEND TO?

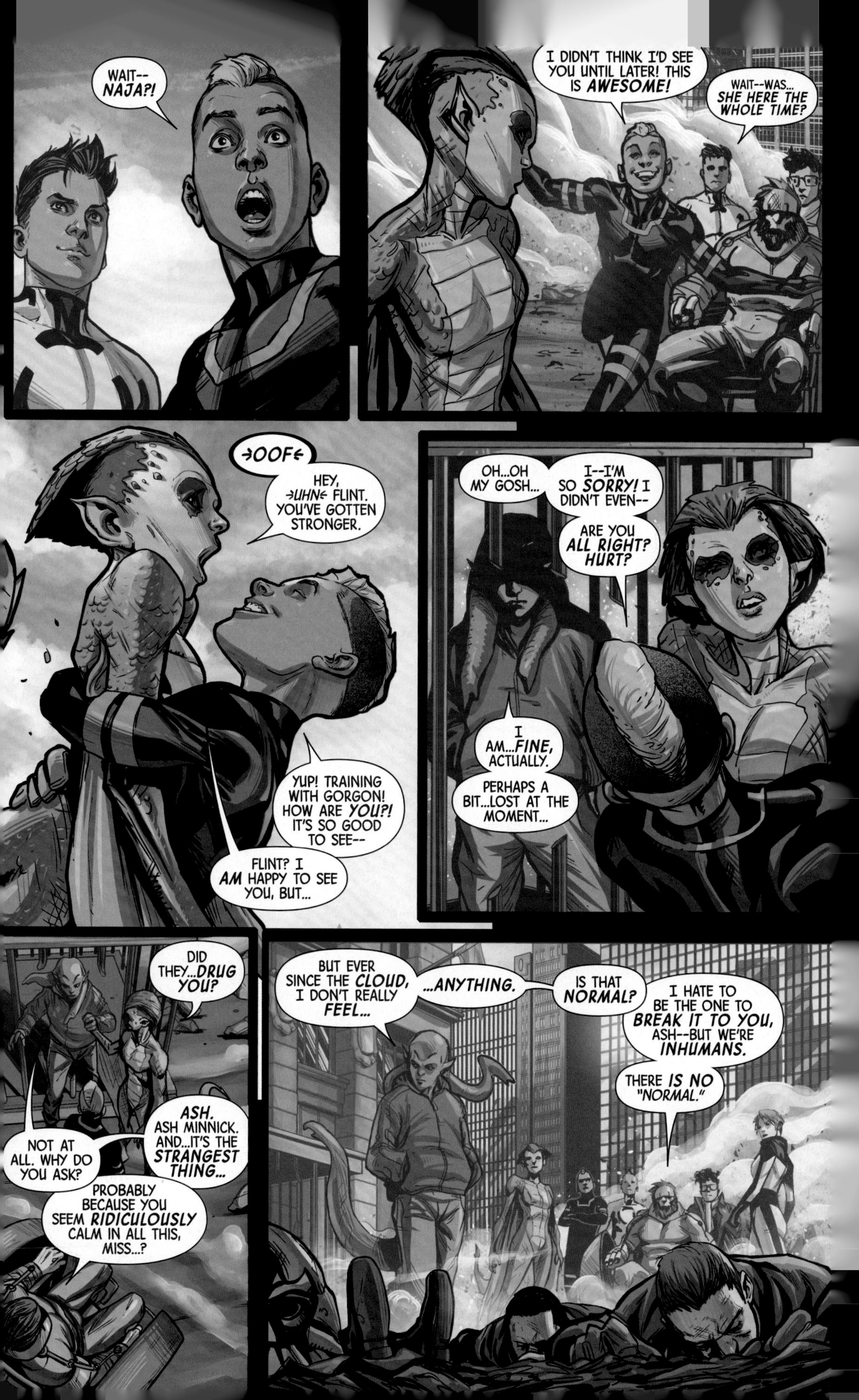
WAIT--
NAJA?!
I DIDN'T THINK I'D SEE YOU UNTIL LATER! THIS IS AWESOME!
WAIT--WAS... SHE HERE THE WHOLE TIME?
→OOF←
HEY, →UHN← FLINT. YOU'VE GOTTEN STRONGER.
YUP! TRAINING WITH GORGON! HOW ARE YOU?! IT'S SO GOOD TO SEE--
FLINT? I AM HAPPY TO SEE YOU, BUT...
OH...OH MY GOSH...
I--I'M SO SORRY! I DIDN'T EVEN--
ARE YOU ALL RIGHT? HURT?
I AM...FINE, ACTUALLY.
PERHAPS A BIT...LOST AT THE MOMENT...
DID THEY...DRUG YOU?
NOT AT ALL. WHY DO YOU ASK?
PROBABLY BECAUSE YOU SEEM RIDICULOUSLY CALM IN ALL THIS, MISS...?
ASH. ASH MINNICK. AND...IT'S THE STRANGEST THING...
BUT EVER SINCE THE CLOUD, I DON'T REALLY FEEL...
...ANYTHING.
IS THAT NORMAL?
I HATE TO BE THE ONE TO BREAK IT TO YOU, ASH--BUT WE'RE INHUMANS.
THERE IS NO "NORMAL."

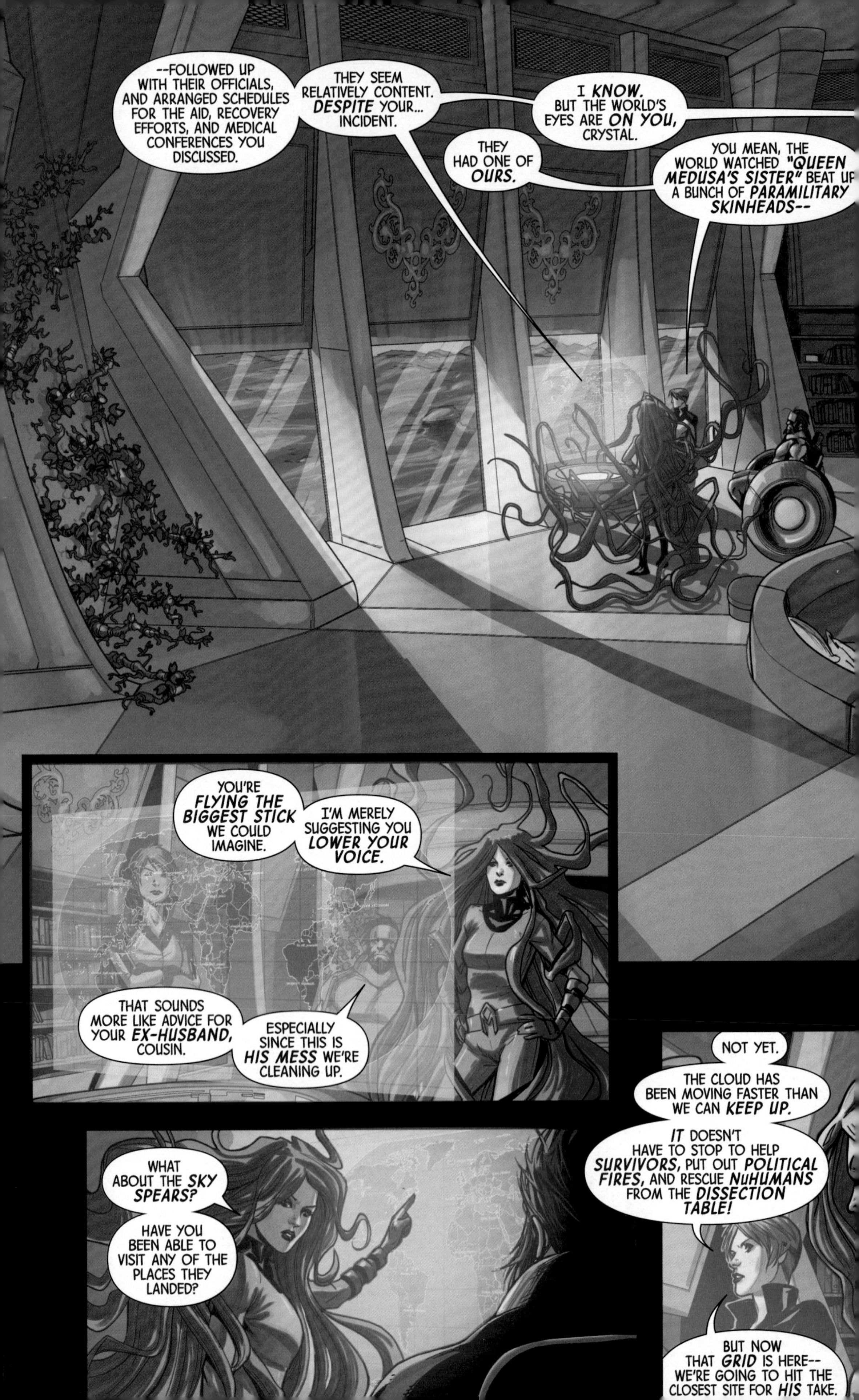
--FOLLOWED UP WITH THEIR OFFICIALS, AND ARRANGED SCHEDULES FOR THE AID, RECOVERY EFFORTS, AND MEDICAL CONFERENCES YOU DISCUSSED.
THEY SEEM RELATIVELY CONTENT. DESPITE YOUR... INCIDENT.
THEY HAD ONE OF OURS.
I KNOW. BUT THE WORLD'S EYES ARE ON YOU, CRYSTAL.
YOU MEAN, THE WORLD WATCHED "QUEEN MEDUSA'S SISTER" BEAT UP A BUNCH OF PARAMILITARY SKINHEADS--
YOU'RE FLYING THE BIGGEST STICK WE COULD IMAGINE.
I'M MERELY SUGGESTING YOU LOWER YOUR VOICE.
THAT SOUNDS MORE LIKE ADVICE FOR YOUR EX-HUSBAND, COUSIN.
ESPECIALLY SINCE THIS IS HIS MESS WE'RE CLEANING UP.
WHAT ABOUT THE SKY SPEARS?
HAVE YOU BEEN ABLE TO VISIT ANY OF THE PLACES THEY LANDED?
NOT YET.
THE CLOUD HAS BEEN MOVING FASTER THAN WE CAN KEEP UP.
IT DOESN'T HAVE TO STOP TO HELP SURVIVORS, PUT OUT POLITICAL FIRES, AND RESCUE NuHUMANS FROM THE DISSECTION TABLE!
BUT NOW THAT GRID IS HERE-- WE'RE GOING TO HIT THE CLOSEST SITE FOR HIS TAKE.

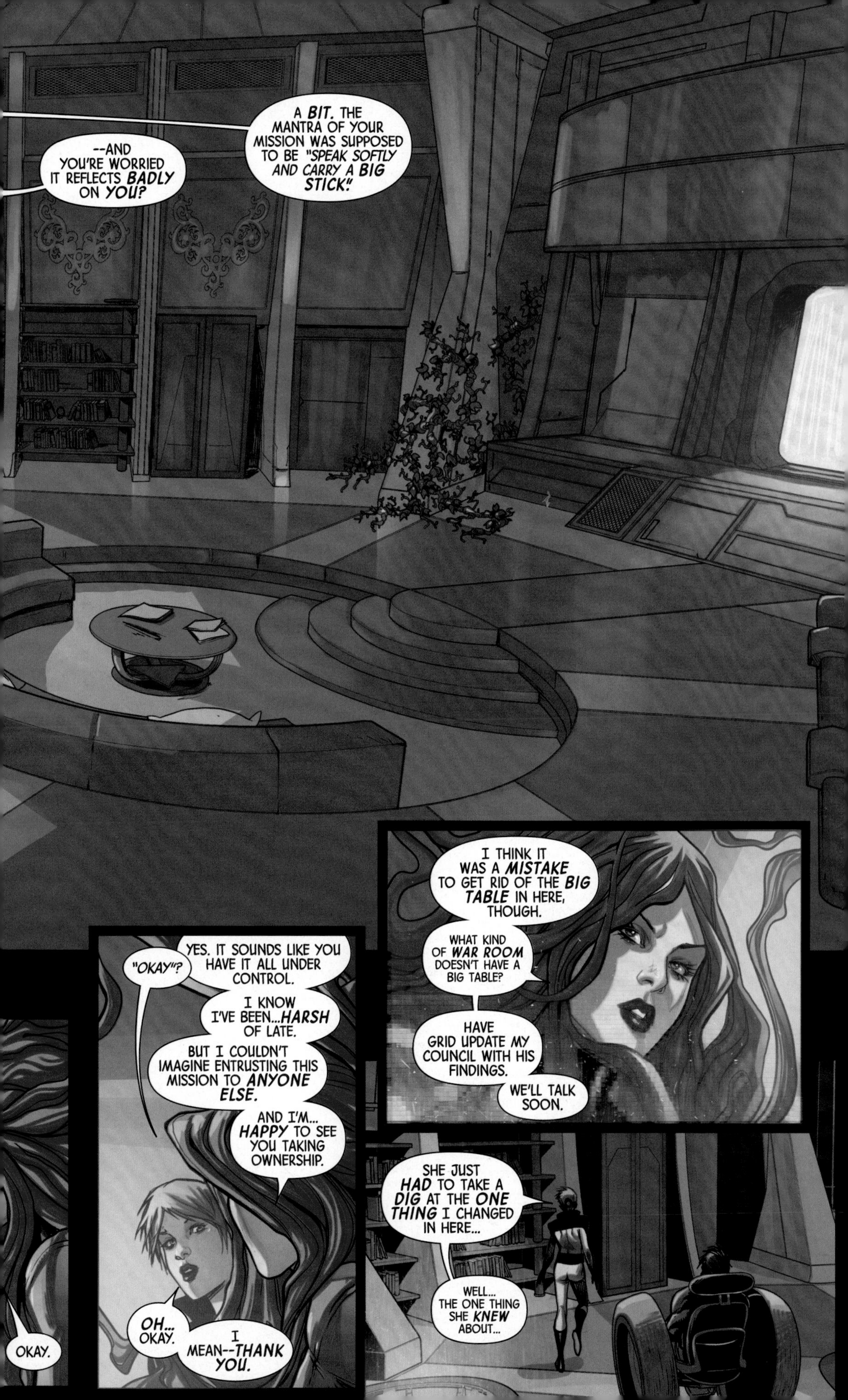
--AND YOU'RE WORRIED IT REFLECTS BADLY ON YOU?
A BIT. THE MANTRA OF YOUR MISSION WAS SUPPOSED TO BE "SPEAK SOFTLY AND CARRY A BIG STICK."
YES. IT SOUNDS LIKE YOU HAVE IT ALL UNDER CONTROL.
I KNOW I'VE BEEN...HARSH OF LATE.
BUT I COULDN'T IMAGINE ENTRUSTING THIS MISSION TO ANYONE ELSE.
AND I'M... HAPPY TO SEE YOU TAKING OWNERSHIP.
"OKAY"?
OKAY.
OH... OKAY.
I MEAN--THANK YOU.
I THINK IT WAS A MISTAKE TO GET RID OF THE BIG TABLE IN HERE, THOUGH.
WHAT KIND OF WAR ROOM DOESN'T HAVE A BIG TABLE?
HAVE GRID UPDATE MY COUNCIL WITH HIS FINDINGS.
WE'LL TALK SOON.
SHE JUST HAD TO TAKE A DIG AT THE ONE THING I CHANGED IN HERE...
WELL... THE ONE THING SHE KNEW ABOUT...

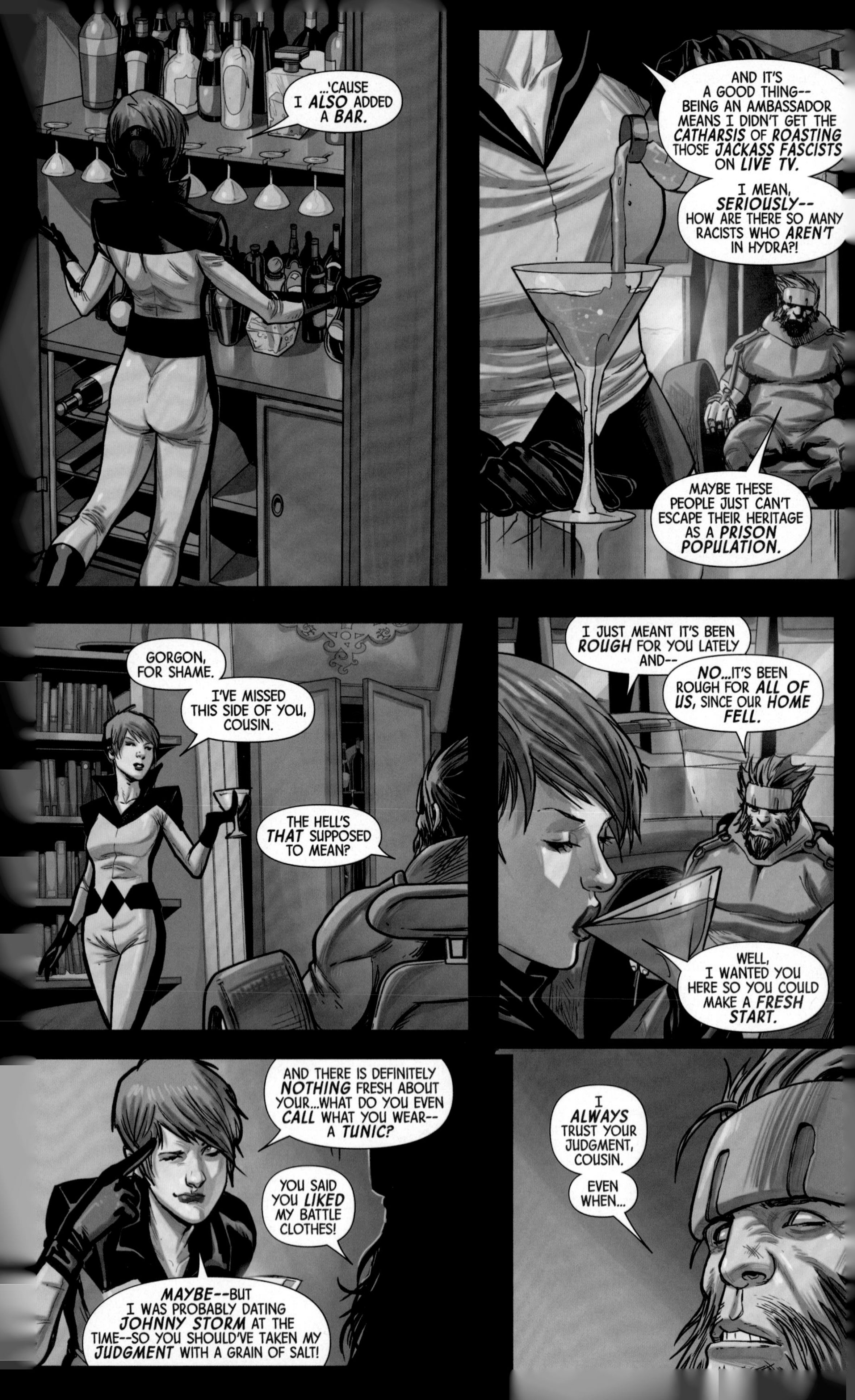
...'CAUSE I ALSO ADDED A BAR.
AND IT'S A GOOD THING-- BEING AN AMBASSADOR MEANS I DIDN'T GET THE CATHARSIS OF ROASTING THOSE JACKASS FASCISTS ON LIVE TV.
I MEAN, SERIOUSLY-- HOW ARE THERE SO MANY RACISTS WHO AREN'T IN HYDRA?!
MAYBE THESE PEOPLE JUST CAN'T ESCAPE THEIR HERITAGE AS A PRISON POPULATION.
GORGON, FOR SHAME.
I'VE MISSED THIS SIDE OF YOU, COUSIN.
THE HELL'S THAT SUPPOSED TO MEAN?
I JUST MEANT IT'S BEEN ROUGH FOR YOU LATELY AND--
NO...IT'S BEEN ROUGH FOR ALL OF US, SINCE OUR HOME FELL.
WELL, I WANTED YOU HERE SO YOU COULD MAKE A FRESH START.
AND THERE IS DEFINITELY NOTHING FRESH ABOUT YOUR...WHAT DO YOU EVEN CALL WHAT YOU WEAR-- A TUNIC?
YOU SAID YOU LIKED MY BATTLE CLOTHES!
MAYBE--BUT I WAS PROBABLY DATING JOHNNY STORM AT THE TIME--SO YOU SHOULD'VE TAKEN MY JUDGMENT WITH A GRAIN OF SALT!
I ALWAYS TRUST YOUR JUDGMENT, COUSIN.
EVEN WHEN...

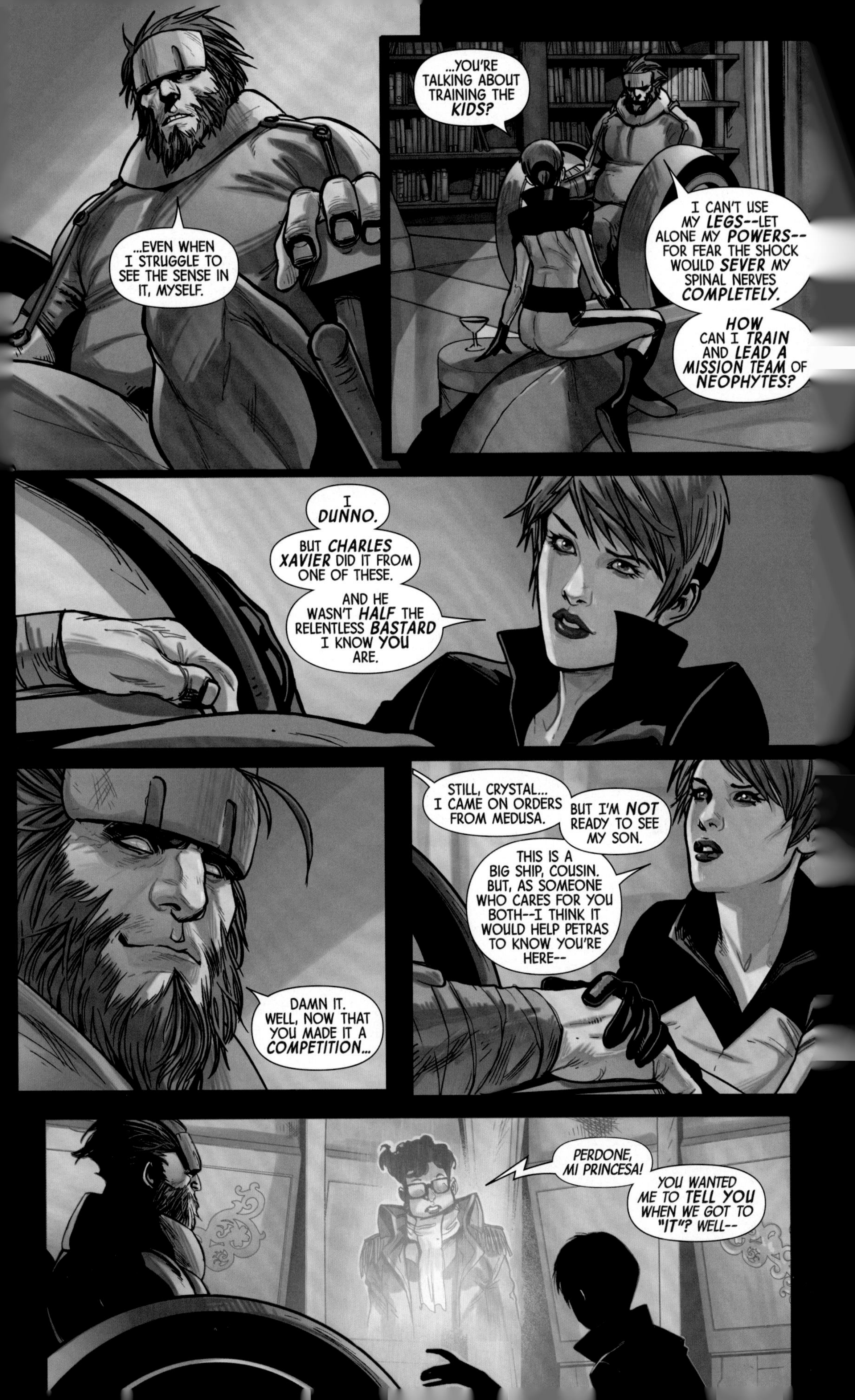
...EVEN WHEN I STRUGGLE TO SEE THE SENSE IN IT, MYSELF.
...YOU'RE TALKING ABOUT TRAINING THE KIDS?
I CAN'T USE MY LEGS--LET ALONE MY POWERS--FOR FEAR THE SHOCK WOULD SEVER MY SPINAL NERVES COMPLETELY.
HOW CAN I TRAIN AND LEAD A MISSION TEAM OF NEOPHYTES?
I DUNNO.
BUT CHARLES XAVIER DID IT FROM ONE OF THESE.
AND HE WASN'T HALF THE RELENTLESS BASTARD I KNOW YOU ARE.
DAMN IT. WELL, NOW THAT YOU MADE IT A COMPETITION...
STILL, CRYSTAL... I CAME ON ORDERS FROM MEDUSA.
BUT I'M NOT READY TO SEE MY SON.
THIS IS A BIG SHIP, COUSIN. BUT, AS SOMEONE WHO CARES FOR YOU BOTH--I THINK IT WOULD HELP PETRAS TO KNOW YOU'RE HERE--
PERDONE, MI PRINCESA!
YOU WANTED ME TO TELL YOU WHEN WE GOT TO "IT"? WELL--

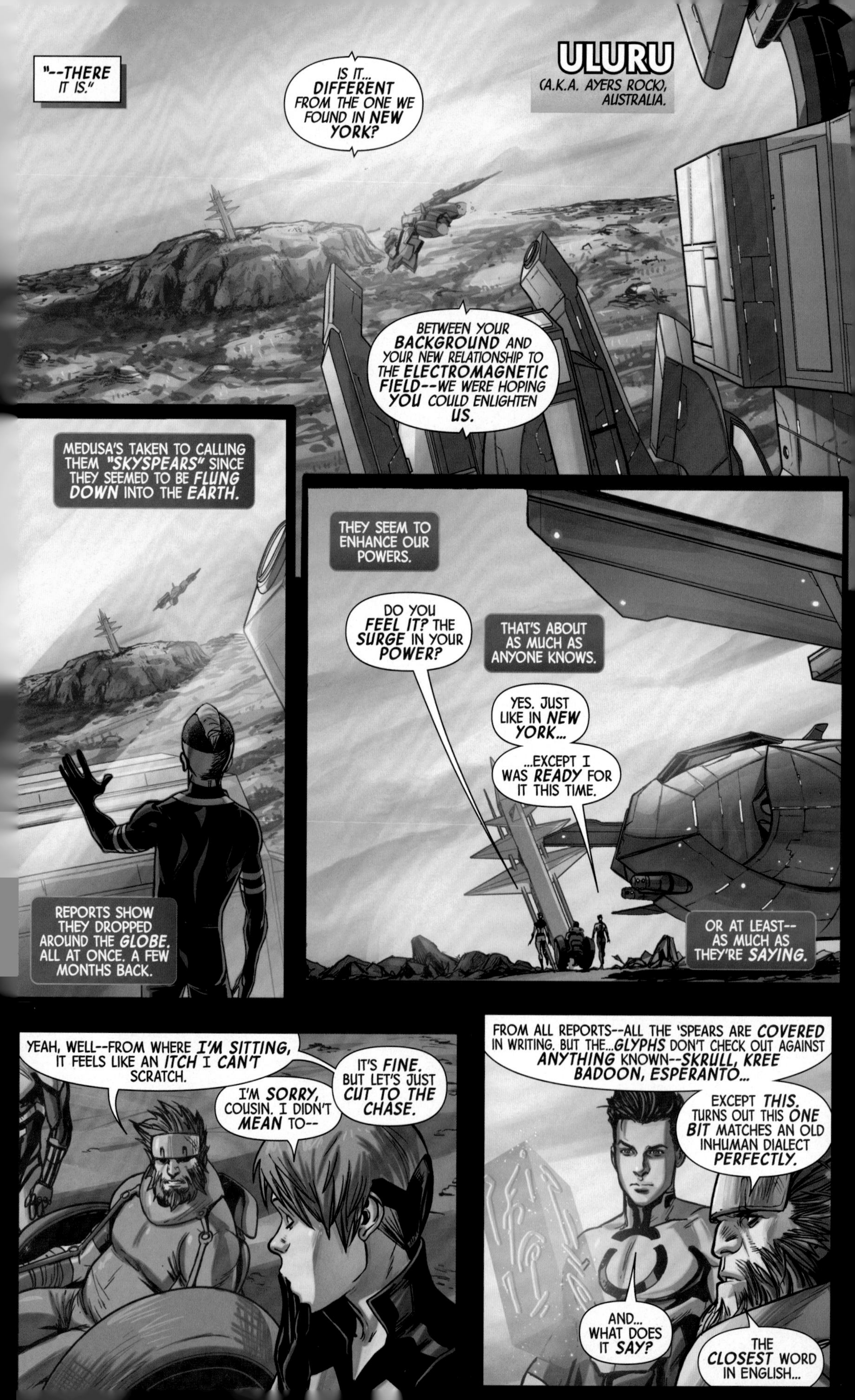
"--THERE IT IS."
IS IT... DIFFERENT FROM THE ONE WE FOUND IN NEW YORK?
ULURU
(A.K.A. AYERS ROCK), AUSTRALIA.
BETWEEN YOUR BACKGROUND AND YOUR NEW RELATIONSHIP TO THE ELECTROMAGNETIC FIELD--WE WERE HOPING YOU COULD ENLIGHTEN US.
MEDUSA'S TAKEN TO CALLING THEM "SKYSPEARS" SINCE THEY SEEMED TO BE FLUNG DOWN INTO THE EARTH.
REPORTS SHOW THEY DROPPED AROUND THE GLOBE, ALL AT ONCE, A FEW MONTHS BACK.
THEY SEEM TO ENHANCE OUR POWERS.
DO YOU FEEL IT? THE SURGE IN YOUR POWER?
THAT'S ABOUT AS MUCH AS ANYONE KNOWS.
YES. JUST LIKE IN NEW YORK...
...EXCEPT I WAS READY FOR IT THIS TIME.
OR AT LEAST-- AS MUCH AS THEY'RE SAYING.
YEAH, WELL--FROM WHERE I'M SITTING, IT FEELS LIKE AN ITCH I CAN'T SCRATCH.
I'M SORRY, COUSIN. I DIDN'T MEAN TO--
IT'S FINE. BUT LET'S JUST CUT TO THE CHASE.
FROM ALL REPORTS--ALL THE 'SPEARS ARE COVERED IN WRITING. BUT THE...GLYPHS DON'T CHECK OUT AGAINST ANYTHING KNOWN--SKRULL, KREE BADOON, ESPERANTO...
EXCEPT THIS. TURNS OUT THIS ONE BIT MATCHES AN OLD INHUMAN DIALECT PERFECTLY.
AND... WHAT DOES IT SAY?
THE CLOSEST WORD IN ENGLISH...

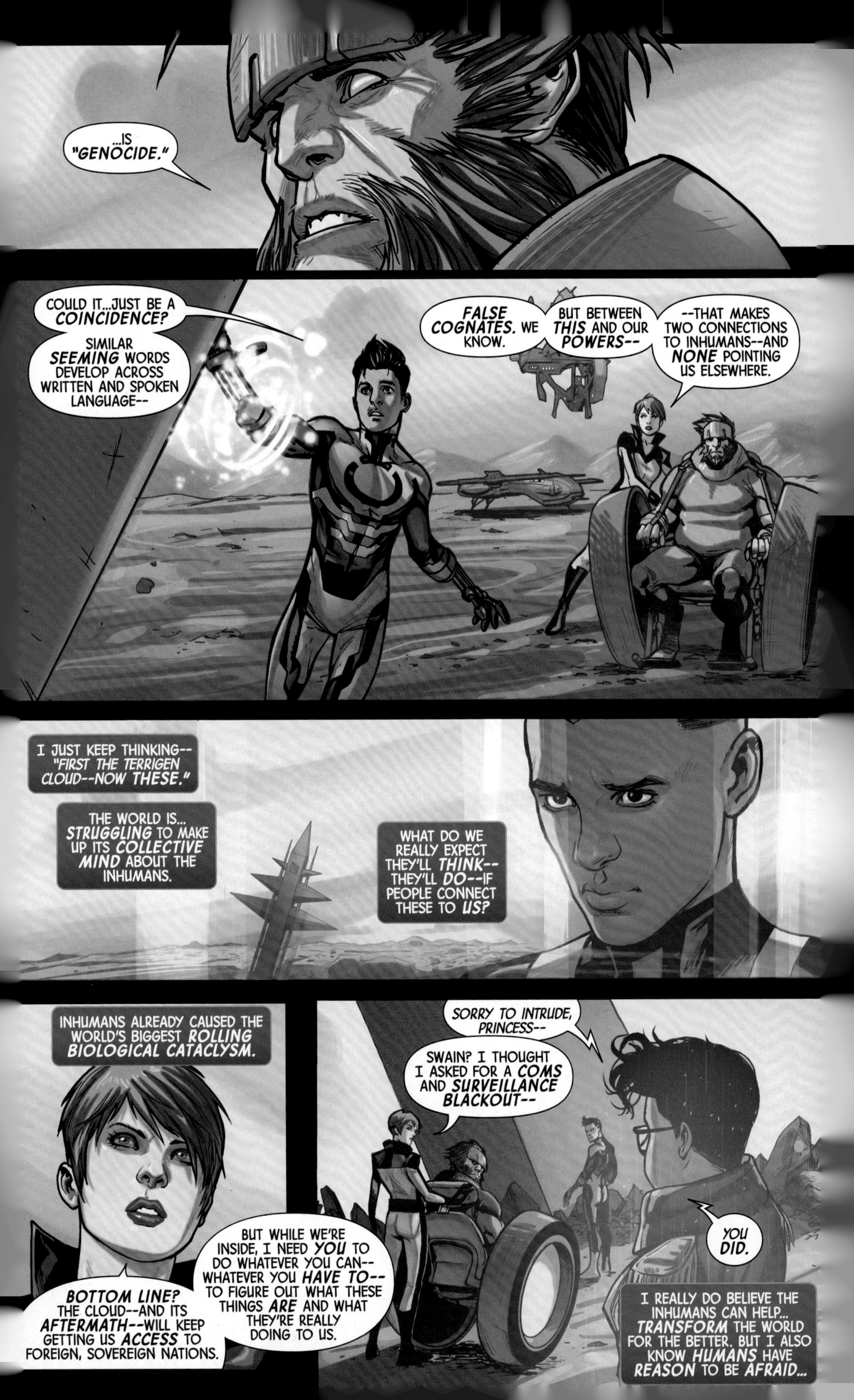

...IS "GENOCIDE."
COULD IT...JUST BE A COINCIDENCE?
SIMILAR SEEMING WORDS DEVELOP ACROSS WRITTEN AND SPOKEN LANGUAGE--
FALSE COGNATES. WE KNOW.
BUT BETWEEN THIS AND OUR POWERS--
--THAT MAKES TWO CONNECTIONS TO INHUMANS--AND NONE POINTING US ELSEWHERE.
I JUST KEEP THINKING-- "FIRST THE TERRIGEN CLOUD--NOW THESE."
THE WORLD IS... STRUGGLING TO MAKE UP ITS COLLECTIVE MIND ABOUT THE INHUMANS.
WHAT DO WE REALLY EXPECT THEY'LL THINK-- THEY'LL DO--IF PEOPLE CONNECT THESE TO US?
INHUMANS ALREADY CAUSED THE WORLD'S BIGGEST ROLLING BIOLOGICAL CATACLYSM.
BOTTOM LINE? THE CLOUD--AND ITS AFTERMATH--WILL KEEP GETTING US ACCESS TO FOREIGN, SOVEREIGN NATIONS.
BUT WHILE WE'RE INSIDE, I NEED YOU TO DO WHATEVER YOU CAN--WHATEVER YOU HAVE TO--TO FIGURE OUT WHAT THESE THINGS ARE AND WHAT THEY'RE REALLY DOING TO US.
SORRY TO INTRUDE, PRINCESS--
SWAIN? I THOUGHT I ASKED FOR A COMS AND SURVEILLANCE BLACKOUT--
YOU DID.
I REALLY DO BELIEVE THE INHUMANS CAN HELP... TRANSFORM THE WORLD FOR THE BETTER. BUT I ALSO KNOW HUMANS HAVE REASON TO BE AFRAID...

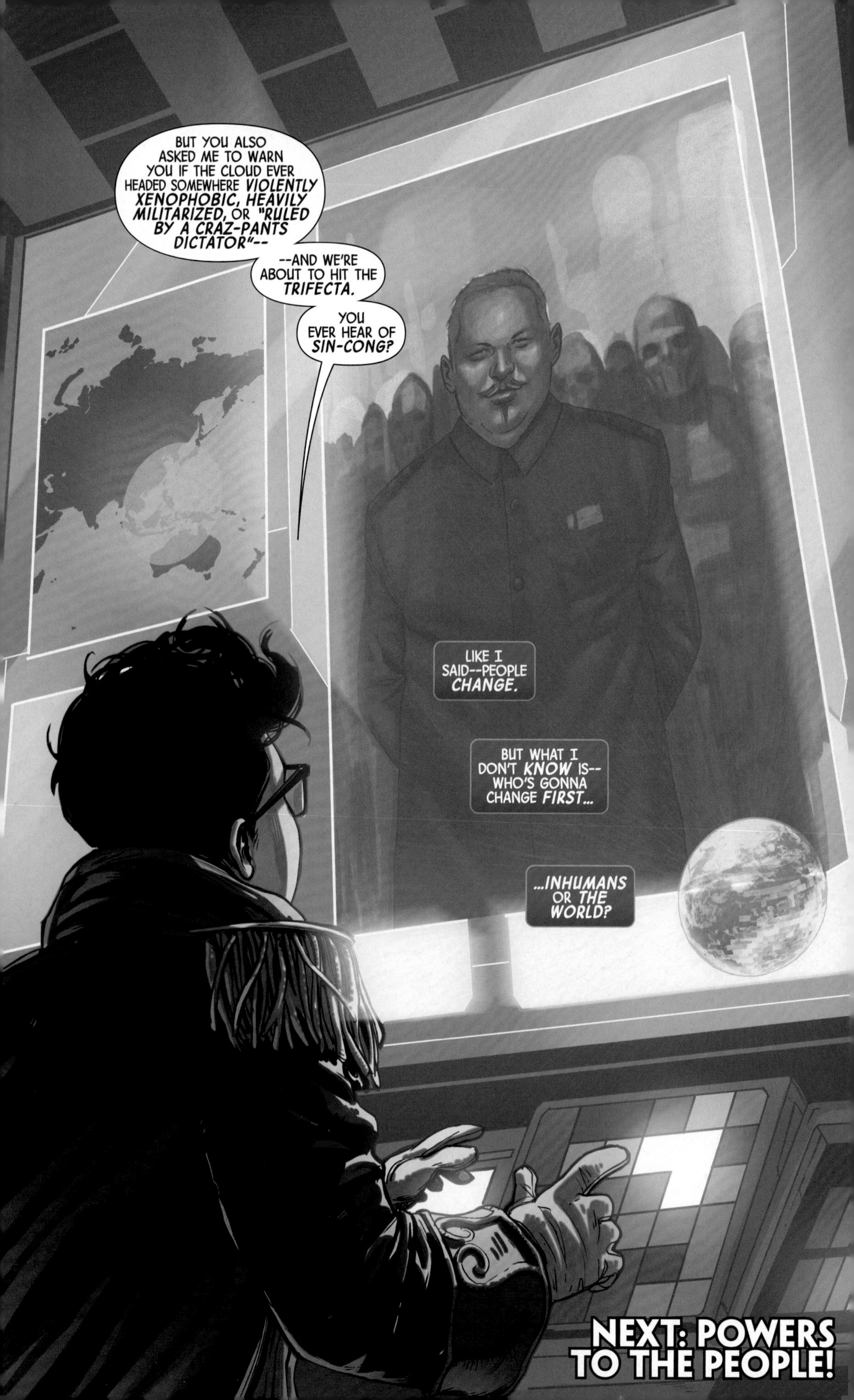
BUT YOU ALSO ASKED ME TO WARN YOU IF THE CLOUD EVER HEADED SOMEWHERE VIOLENTLY XENOPHOBIC, HEAVILY MILITARIZED, OR "RULED BY A CRAZ-PANTS DICTATOR"--
--AND WE'RE ABOUT TO HIT THE TRIFECTA.
YOU EVER HEAR OF SIN-CONG?
LIKE I SAID--PEOPLE CHANGE.
BUT WHAT I DON'T KNOW IS--WHO'S GONNA CHANGE FIRST...
...INHUMANS OR THE WORLD?
NEXT: POWERS TO THE PEOPLE!

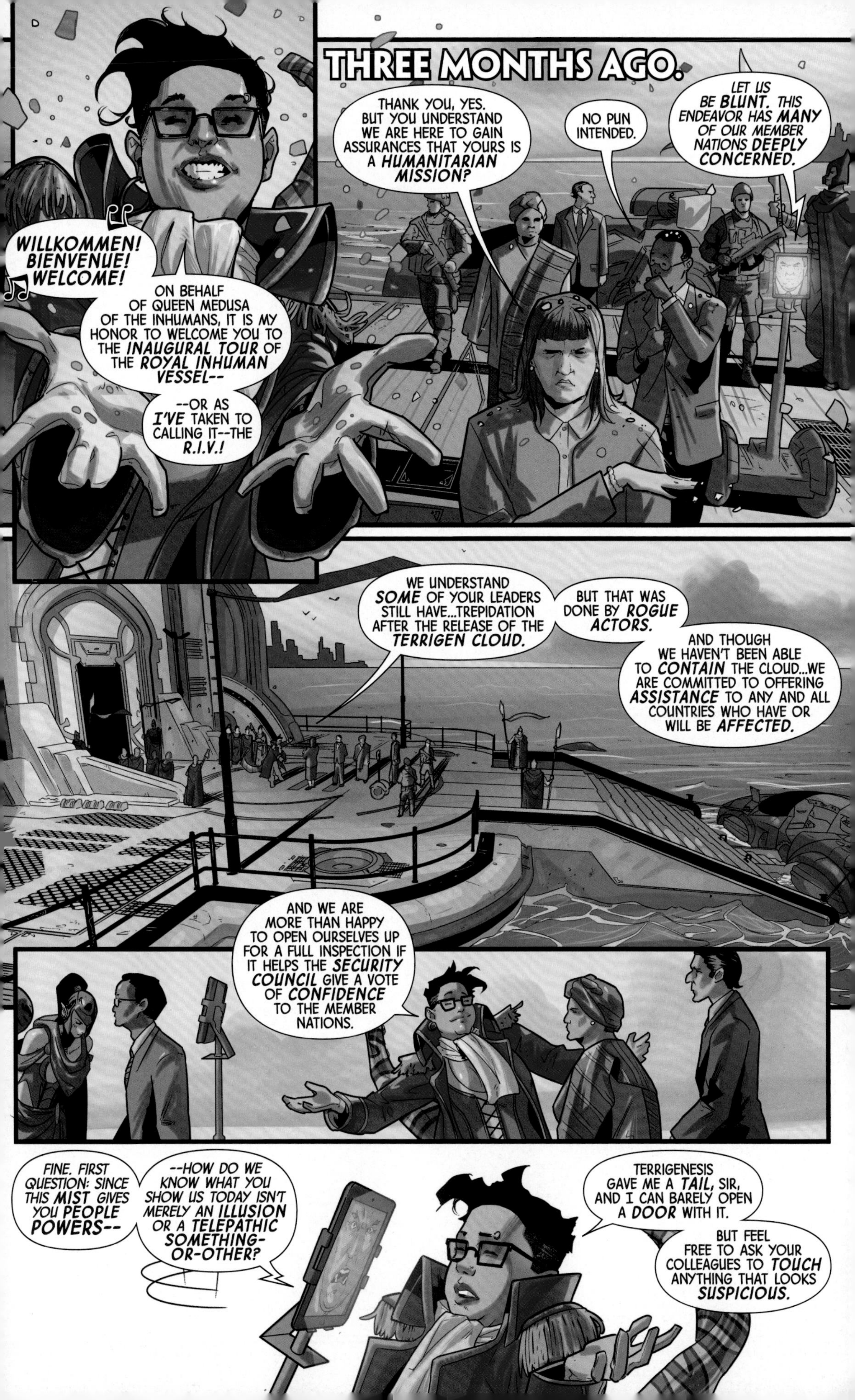
THREE MONTHS AGO.
WILLKOMMEN! BIENVENUE! WELCOME!
ON BEHALF OF QUEEN MEDUSA OF THE INHUMANS, IT IS MY HONOR TO WELCOME YOU TO THE INAUGURAL TOUR OF THE ROYAL INHUMAN VESSEL--
--OR AS I'VE TAKEN TO CALLING IT--THE R.I.V.!
THANK YOU, YES. BUT YOU UNDERSTAND WE ARE HERE TO GAIN ASSURANCES THAT YOURS IS A HUMANITARIAN MISSION?
NO PUN INTENDED.
LET US BE BLUNT. THIS ENDEAVOR HAS MANY OF OUR MEMBER NATIONS DEEPLY CONCERNED.
WE UNDERSTAND SOME OF YOUR LEADERS STILL HAVE...TREPIDATION AFTER THE RELEASE OF THE TERRIGEN CLOUD.
BUT THAT WAS DONE BY ROGUE ACTORS.
AND THOUGH WE HAVEN'T BEEN ABLE TO CONTAIN THE CLOUD...WE ARE COMMITTED TO OFFERING ASSISTANCE TO ANY AND ALL COUNTRIES WHO HAVE OR WILL BE AFFECTED.
AND WE ARE MORE THAN HAPPY TO OPEN OURSELVES UP FOR A FULL INSPECTION IF IT HELPS THE SECURITY COUNCIL GIVE A VOTE OF CONFIDENCE TO THE MEMBER NATIONS.
FINE. FIRST QUESTION: SINCE THIS MIST GIVES YOU PEOPLE POWERS--
--HOW DO WE KNOW WHAT YOU SHOW US TODAY ISN'T MERELY AN ILLUSION OR A TELEPATHIC SOMETHING-OR-OTHER?
TERRIGENESIS GAVE ME A TAIL, SIR, AND I CAN BARELY OPEN A DOOR WITH IT.
BUT FEEL FREE TO ASK YOUR COLLEAGUES TO TOUCH ANYTHING THAT LOOKS SUSPICIOUS.

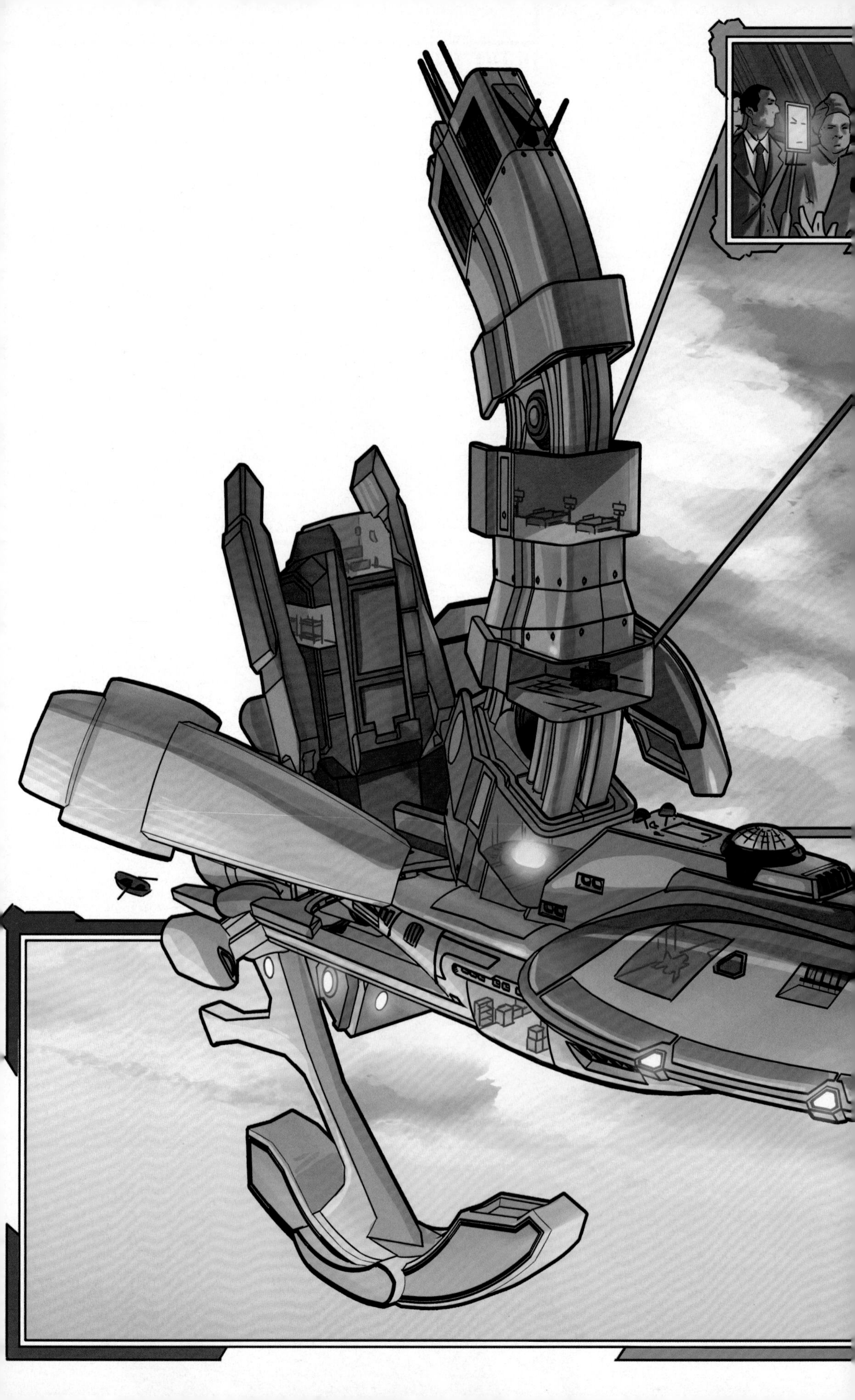

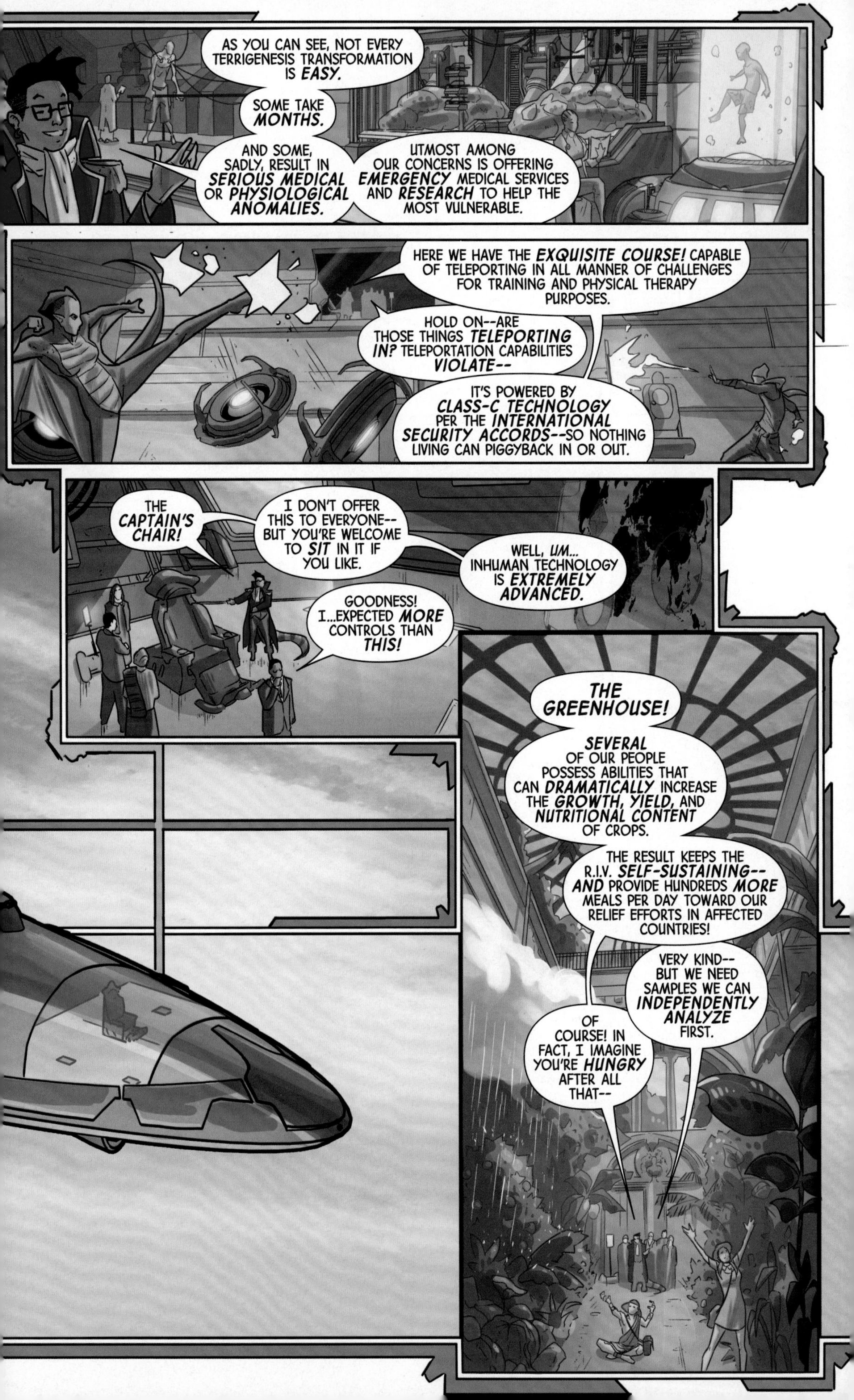
AS YOU CAN SEE, NOT EVERY TERRIGENESIS TRANSFORMATION IS EASY.
SOME TAKE MONTHS.
AND SOME, SADLY, RESULT IN SERIOUS MEDICAL OR PHYSIOLOGICAL ANOMALIES.
UTMOST AMONG OUR CONCERNS IS OFFERING EMERGENCY MEDICAL SERVICES AND RESEARCH TO HELP THE MOST VULNERABLE.
HERE WE HAVE THE EXQUISITE COURSE! CAPABLE OF TELEPORTING IN ALL MANNER OF CHALLENGES FOR TRAINING AND PHYSICAL THERAPY PURPOSES.
HOLD ON--ARE THOSE THINGS TELEPORTING IN? TELEPORTATION CAPABILITIES VIOLATE--
IT'S POWERED BY CLASS-C TECHNOLOGY PER THE INTERNATIONAL SECURITY ACCORDS--SO NOTHING LIVING CAN PIGGYBACK IN OR OUT.
THE CAPTAIN'S CHAIR!
I DON'T OFFER THIS TO EVERYONE--BUT YOU'RE WELCOME TO SIT IN IT IF YOU LIKE.
WELL, UM... INHUMAN TECHNOLOGY IS EXTREMELY ADVANCED.
GOODNESS! I...EXPECTED MORE CONTROLS THAN THIS!
THE GREENHOUSE!
SEVERAL OF OUR PEOPLE POSSESS ABILITIES THAT CAN DRAMATICALLY INCREASE THE GROWTH, YIELD, AND NUTRITIONAL CONTENT OF CROPS.
THE RESULT KEEPS THE R.I.V. SELF-SUSTAINING--AND PROVIDE HUNDREDS MORE MEALS PER DAY TOWARD OUR RELIEF EFFORTS IN AFFECTED COUNTRIES!
VERY KIND--BUT WE NEED SAMPLES WE CAN INDEPENDENTLY ANALYZE FIRST.
OF COURSE! IN FACT, I IMAGINE YOU'RE HUNGRY AFTER ALL THAT--

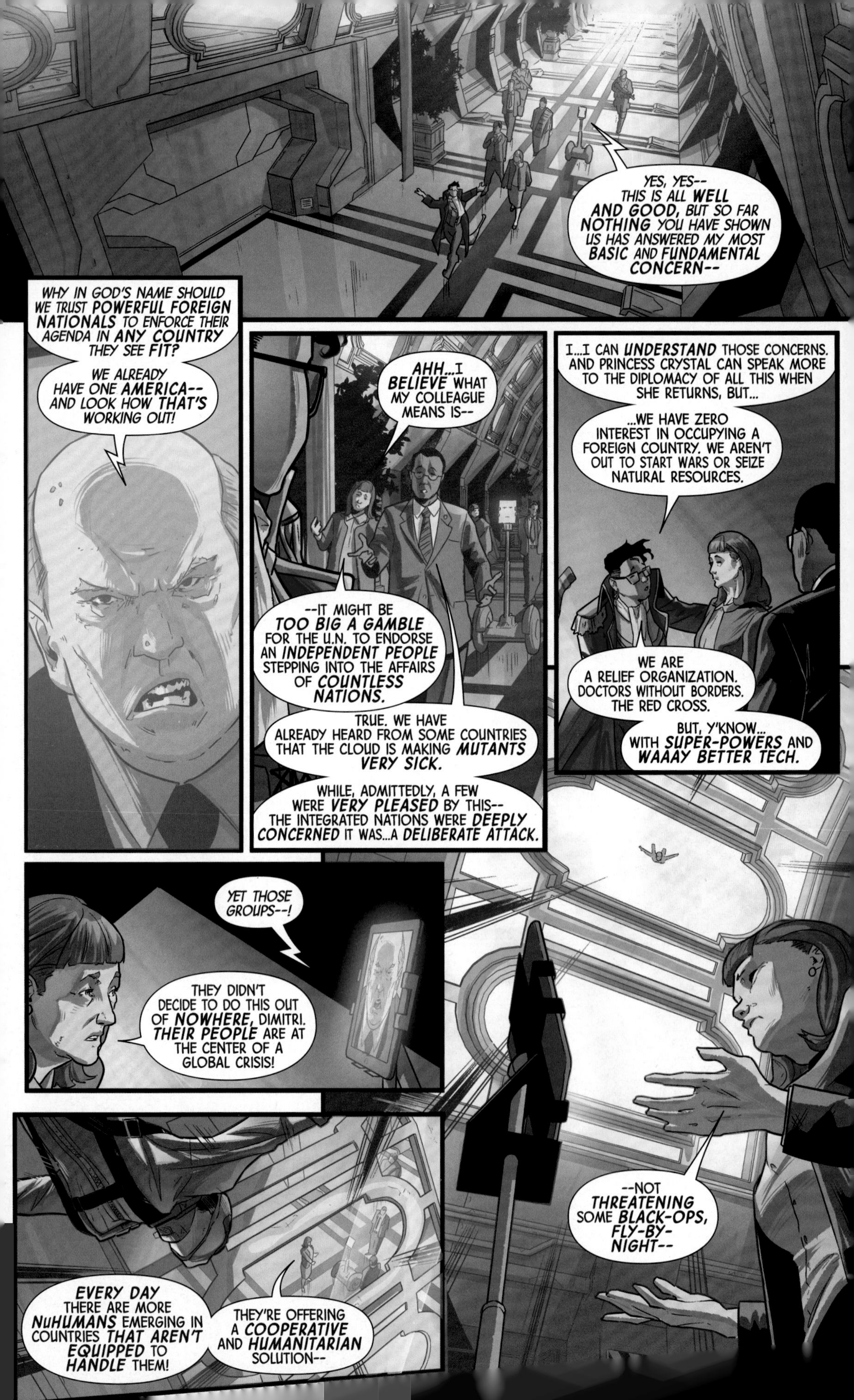
YES, YES-- THIS IS ALL WELL AND GOOD, BUT SO FAR NOTHING YOU HAVE SHOWN US HAS ANSWERED MY MOST BASIC AND FUNDAMENTAL CONCERN--
WHY IN GOD'S NAME SHOULD WE TRUST POWERFUL FOREIGN NATIONALS TO ENFORCE THEIR AGENDA IN ANY COUNTRY THEY SEE FIT?
WE ALREADY HAVE ONE AMERICA-- AND LOOK HOW THAT'S WORKING OUT!
AHH...I BELIEVE WHAT MY COLLEAGUE MEANS IS--
--IT MIGHT BE TOO BIG A GAMBLE FOR THE U.N. TO ENDORSE AN INDEPENDENT PEOPLE STEPPING INTO THE AFFAIRS OF COUNTLESS NATIONS.
TRUE. WE HAVE ALREADY HEARD FROM SOME COUNTRIES THAT THE CLOUD IS MAKING MUTANTS VERY SICK.
WHILE, ADMITTEDLY, A FEW WERE VERY PLEASED BY THIS-- THE INTEGRATED NATIONS WERE DEEPLY CONCERNED IT WAS...A DELIBERATE ATTACK.
I...I CAN UNDERSTAND THOSE CONCERNS. AND PRINCESS CRYSTAL CAN SPEAK MORE TO THE DIPLOMACY OF ALL THIS WHEN SHE RETURNS, BUT...
...WE HAVE ZERO INTEREST IN OCCUPYING A FOREIGN COUNTRY. WE AREN'T OUT TO START WARS OR SEIZE NATURAL RESOURCES.
WE ARE A RELIEF ORGANIZATION. DOCTORS WITHOUT BORDERS. THE RED CROSS.
BUT, Y'KNOW... WITH SUPER-POWERS AND WAAAY BETTER TECH.
YET THOSE GROUPS--!
THEY DIDN'T DECIDE TO DO THIS OUT OF NOWHERE, DIMITRI. THEIR PEOPLE ARE AT THE CENTER OF A GLOBAL CRISIS!
EVERY DAY THERE ARE MORE NUHUMANS EMERGING IN COUNTRIES THAT AREN'T EQUIPPED TO HANDLE THEM!
THEY'RE OFFERING A COOPERATIVE AND HUMANITARIAN SOLUTION--
--NOT THREATENING SOME BLACK-OPS, FLY-BY-NIGHT--

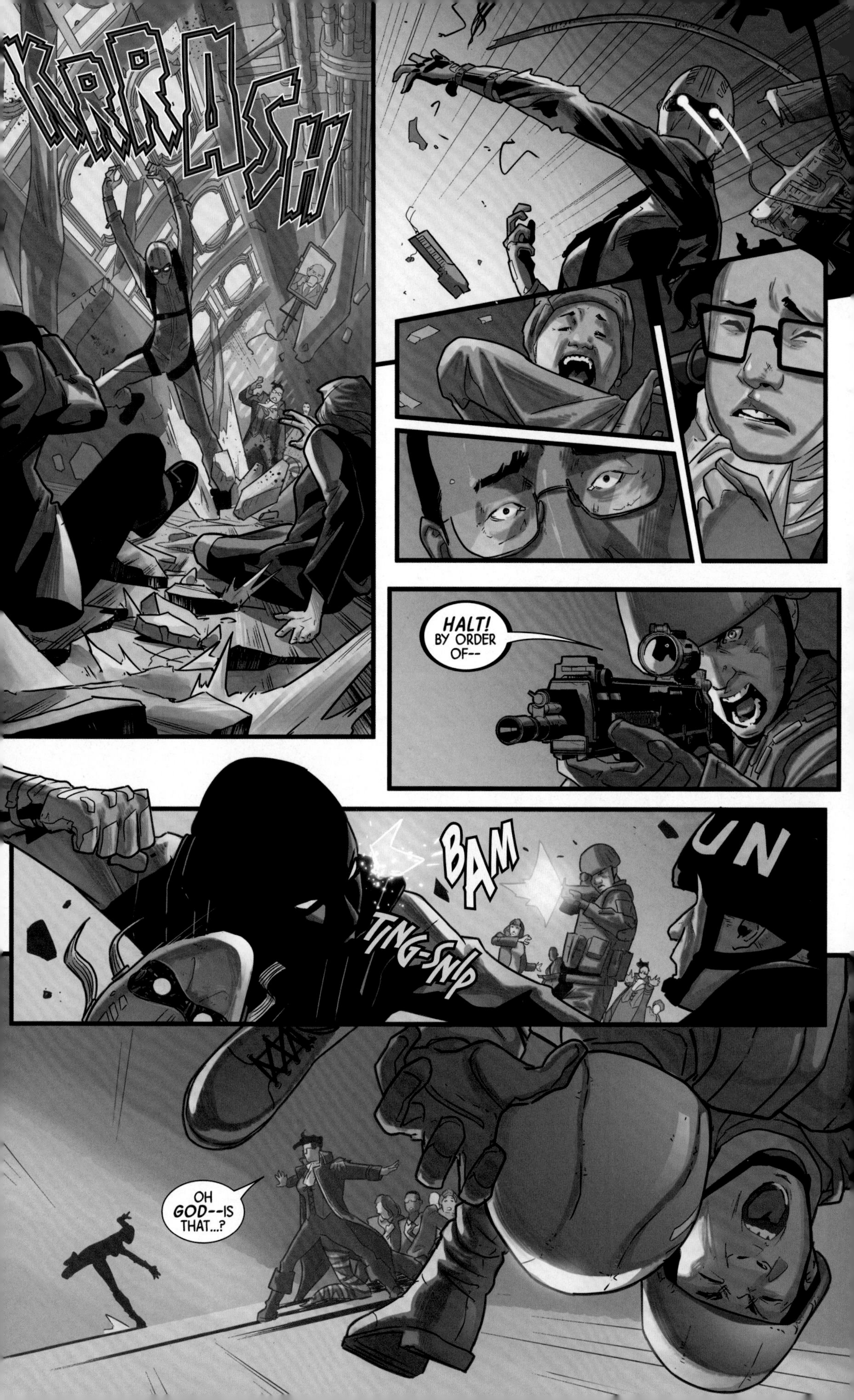
KRRASH
HALT! BY ORDER OF--
BAM
TING-SNIP
UN
OH GOD--IS THAT...?

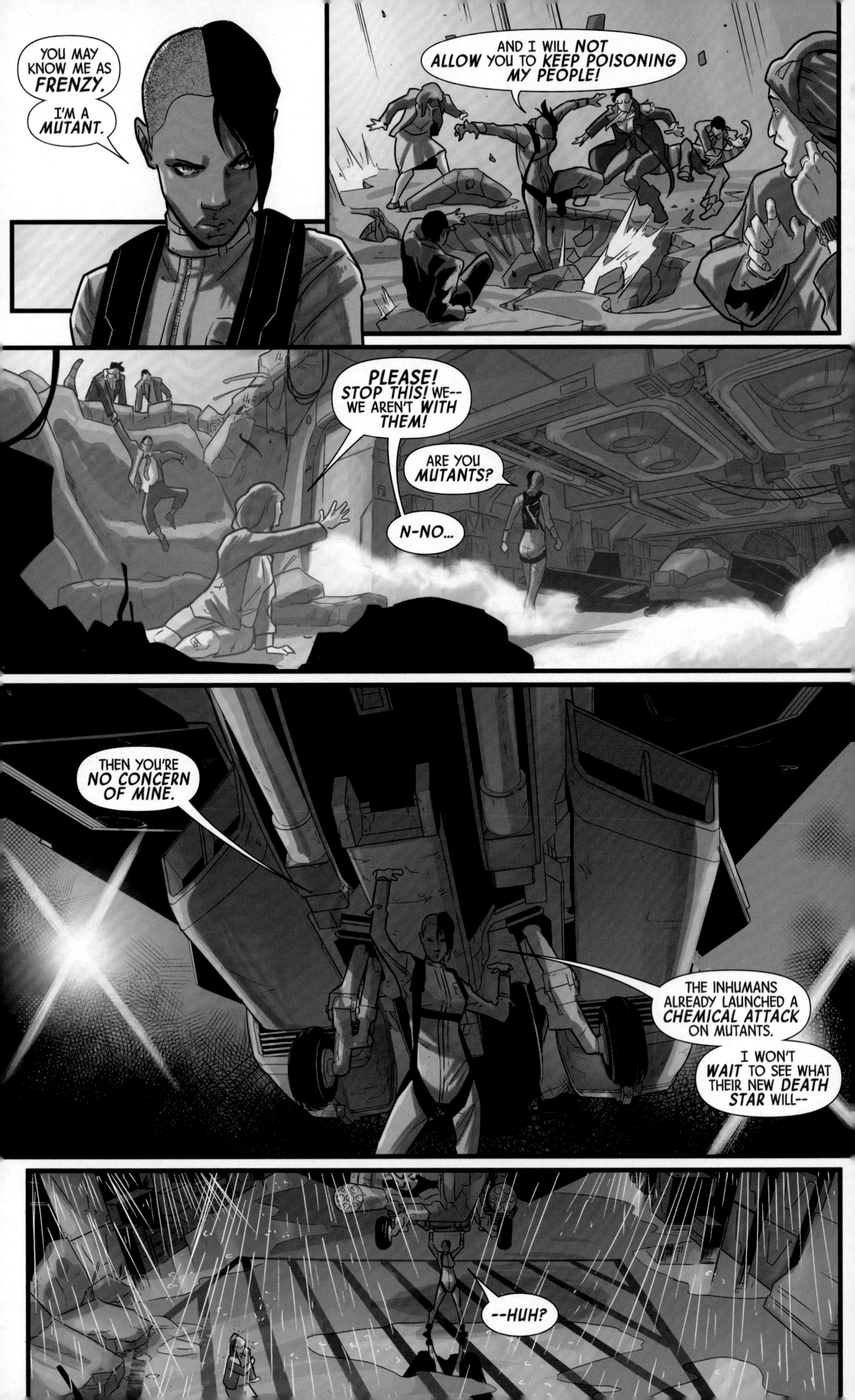
YOU MAY KNOW ME AS FRENZY.
I'M A MUTANT.
AND I WILL NOT ALLOW YOU TO KEEP POISONING MY PEOPLE!
PLEASE! STOP THIS! WE-- WE AREN'T WITH THEM!
ARE YOU MUTANTS?
N-NO...
THEN YOU'RE NO CONCERN OF MINE.
THE INHUMANS ALREADY LAUNCHED A CHEMICAL ATTACK ON MUTANTS.
I WON'T WAIT TO SEE WHAT THEIR NEW DEATH STAR WILL--
--HUH?

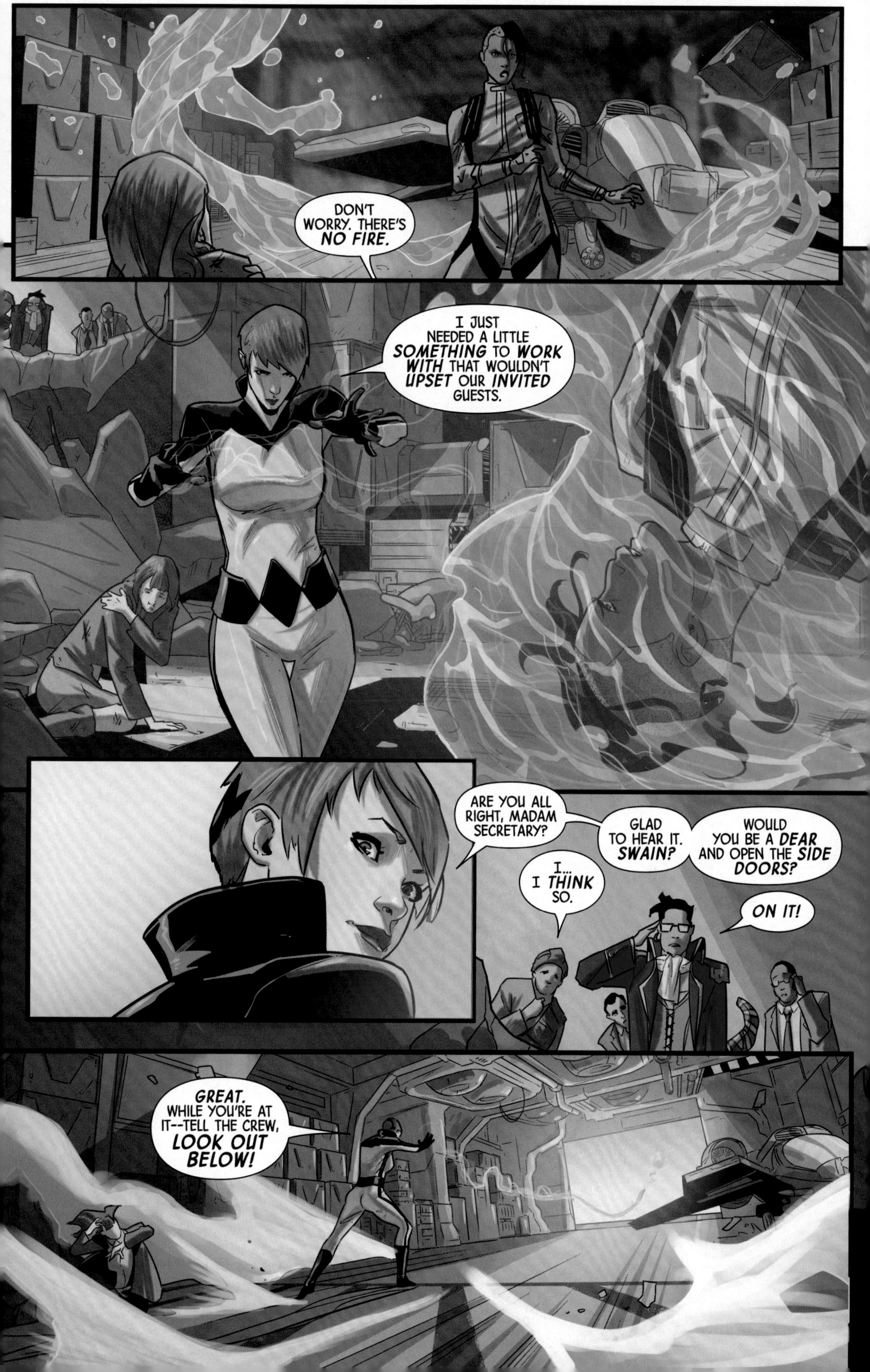

DON'T WORRY. THERE'S NO FIRE.
I JUST NEEDED A LITTLE SOMETHING TO WORK WITH THAT WOULDN'T UPSET OUR INVITED GUESTS.
ARE YOU ALL RIGHT, MADAM SECRETARY?
I... I THINK SO.
GLAD TO HEAR IT. SWAIN?
WOULD YOU BE A DEAR AND OPEN THE SIDE DOORS?
ON IT!
GREAT. WHILE YOU'RE AT IT--TELL THE CREW, LOOK OUT BELOW!

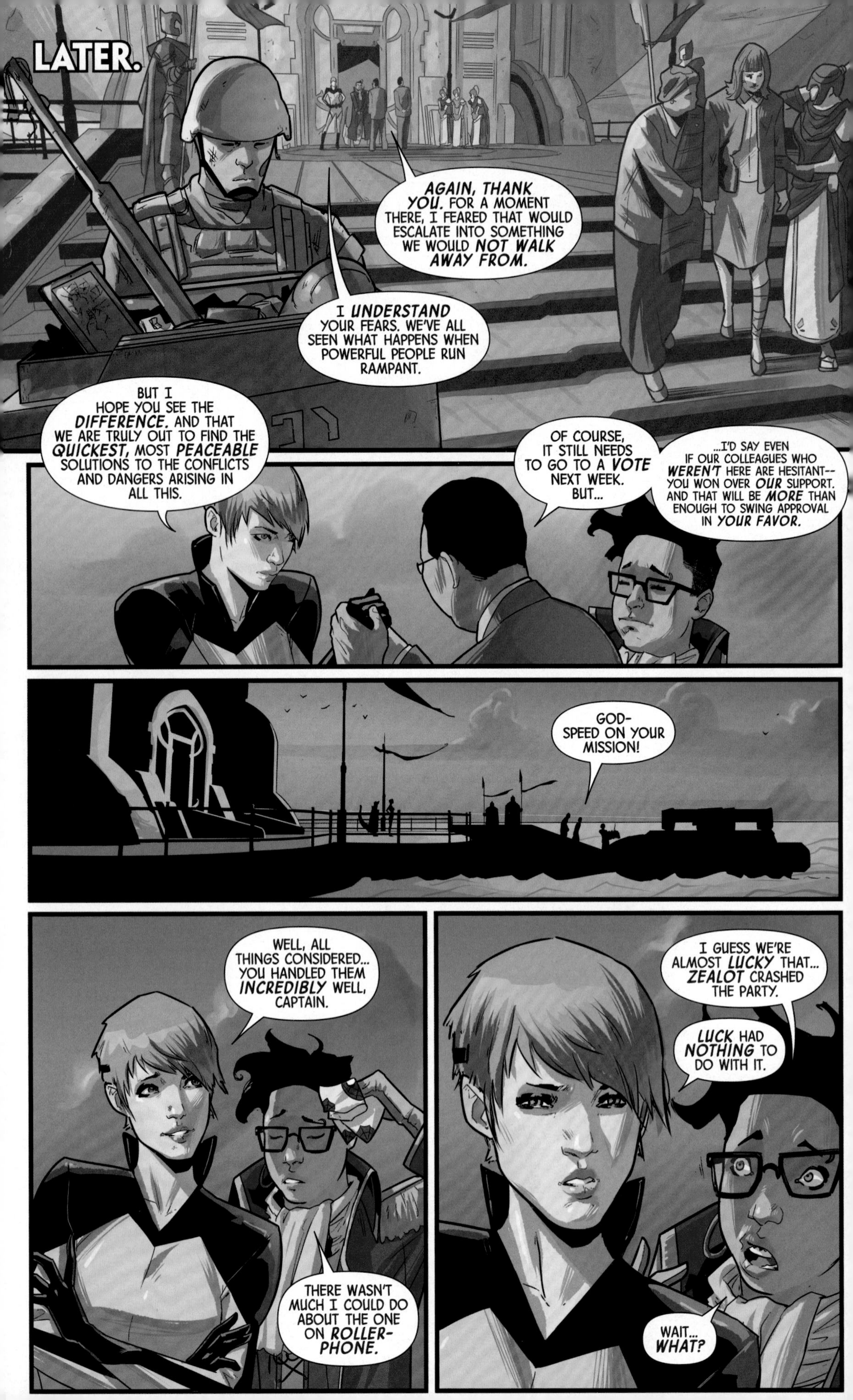
LATER.
AGAIN, THANK YOU. FOR A MOMENT THERE, I FEARED THAT WOULD ESCALATE INTO SOMETHING WE WOULD NOT WALK AWAY FROM.
I UNDERSTAND YOUR FEARS. WE'VE ALL SEEN WHAT HAPPENS WHEN POWERFUL PEOPLE RUN RAMPANT.
BUT I HOPE YOU SEE THE DIFFERENCE. AND THAT WE ARE TRULY OUT TO FIND THE QUICKEST, MOST PEACEABLE SOLUTIONS TO THE CONFLICTS AND DANGERS ARISING IN ALL THIS.
OF COURSE, IT STILL NEEDS TO GO TO A VOTE NEXT WEEK. BUT...
...I'D SAY EVEN IF OUR COLLEAGUES WHO WEREN'T HERE ARE HESITANT-- YOU WON OVER OUR SUPPORT. AND THAT WILL BE MORE THAN ENOUGH TO SWING APPROVAL IN YOUR FAVOR.
GOD-SPEED ON YOUR MISSION!
WELL, ALL THINGS CONSIDERED... YOU HANDLED THEM INCREDIBLY WELL, CAPTAIN.
THERE WASN'T MUCH I COULD DO ABOUT THE ONE ON ROLLER-PHONE.
I GUESS WE'RE ALMOST LUCKY THAT... ZEALOT CRASHED THE PARTY.
LUCK HAD NOTHING TO DO WITH IT.
WAIT... WHAT?

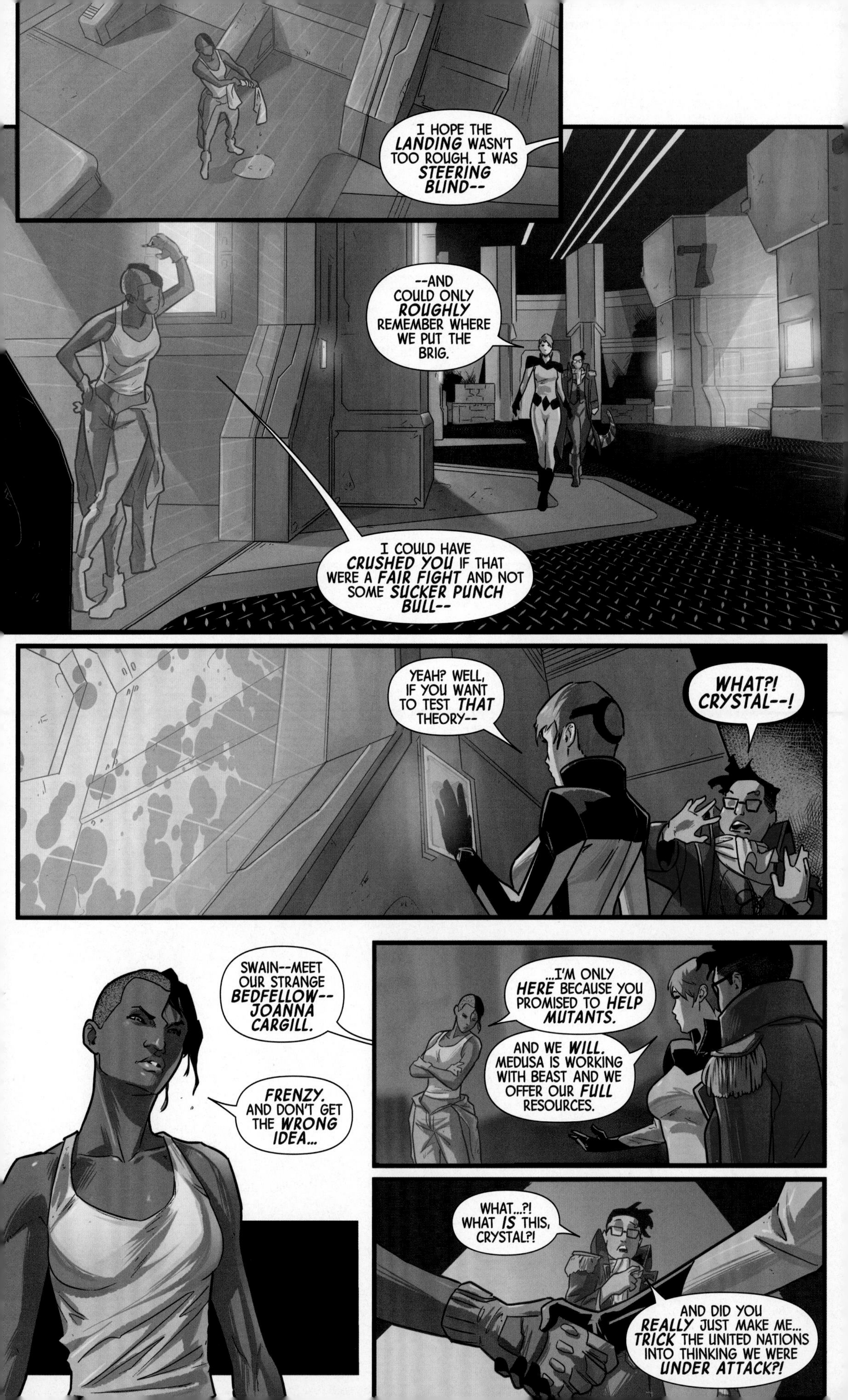
I HOPE THE LANDING WASN'T TOO ROUGH. I WAS STEERING BLIND--
--AND COULD ONLY ROUGHLY REMEMBER WHERE WE PUT THE BRIG.
I COULD HAVE CRUSHED YOU IF THAT WERE A FAIR FIGHT AND NOT SOME SUCKER PUNCH BULL--
YEAH? WELL, IF YOU WANT TO TEST THAT THEORY--
WHAT?! CRYSTAL--!
SWAIN--MEET OUR STRANGE BEDFELLOW-- JOANNA CARGILL.
FRENZY. AND DON'T GET THE WRONG IDEA...
...I'M ONLY HERE BECAUSE YOU PROMISED TO HELP MUTANTS.
AND WE WILL. MEDUSA IS WORKING WITH BEAST AND WE OFFER OUR FULL RESOURCES.
WHAT...?! WHAT IS THIS, CRYSTAL?!
AND DID YOU REALLY JUST MAKE ME... TRICK THE UNITED NATIONS INTO THINKING WE WERE UNDER ATTACK?!

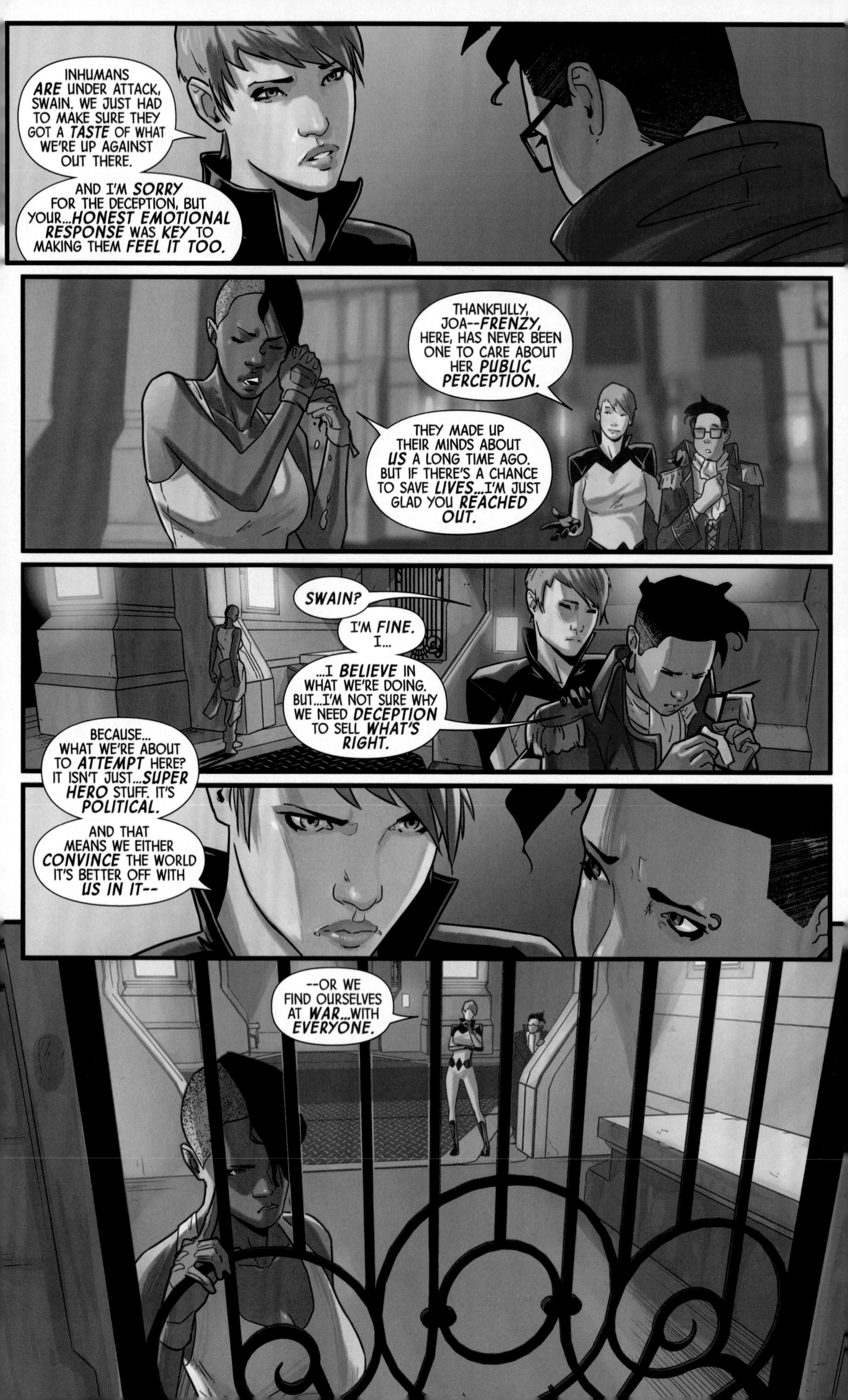
INHUMANS ARE UNDER ATTACK, SWAIN. WE JUST HAD TO MAKE SURE THEY GOT A TASTE OF WHAT WE'RE UP AGAINST OUT THERE.
AND I'M SORRY FOR THE DECEPTION, BUT YOUR...HONEST EMOTIONAL RESPONSE WAS KEY TO MAKING THEM FEEL IT TOO.
THANKFULLY, JOA--FRENZY, HERE, HAS NEVER BEEN ONE TO CARE ABOUT HER PUBLIC PERCEPTION.
THEY MADE UP THEIR MINDS ABOUT US A LONG TIME AGO. BUT IF THERE'S A CHANCE TO SAVE LIVES...I'M JUST GLAD YOU REACHED OUT.
SWAIN?
I'M FINE. I...
...I BELIEVE IN WHAT WE'RE DOING. BUT...I'M NOT SURE WHY WE NEED DECEPTION TO SELL WHAT'S RIGHT.
BECAUSE... WHAT WE'RE ABOUT TO ATTEMPT HERE? IT ISN'T JUST...SUPER HERO STUFF. IT'S POLITICAL.
AND THAT MEANS WE EITHER CONVINCE THE WORLD IT'S BETTER OFF WITH US IN IT--
--OR WE FIND OURSELVES AT WAR...WITH EVERYONE.

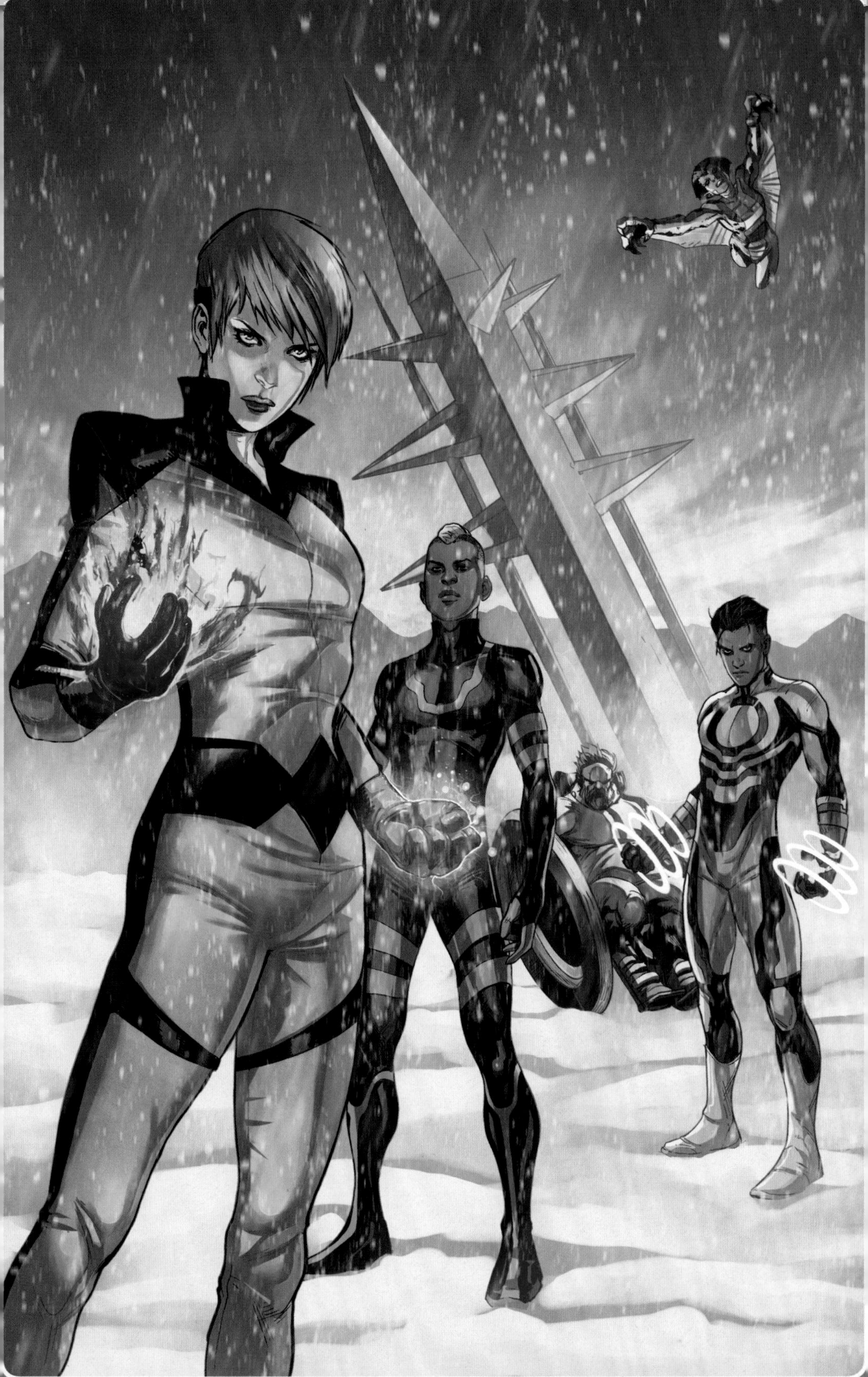

#1 VARIANT BY
STEFANO CASELLI & ANDRES MOSSA

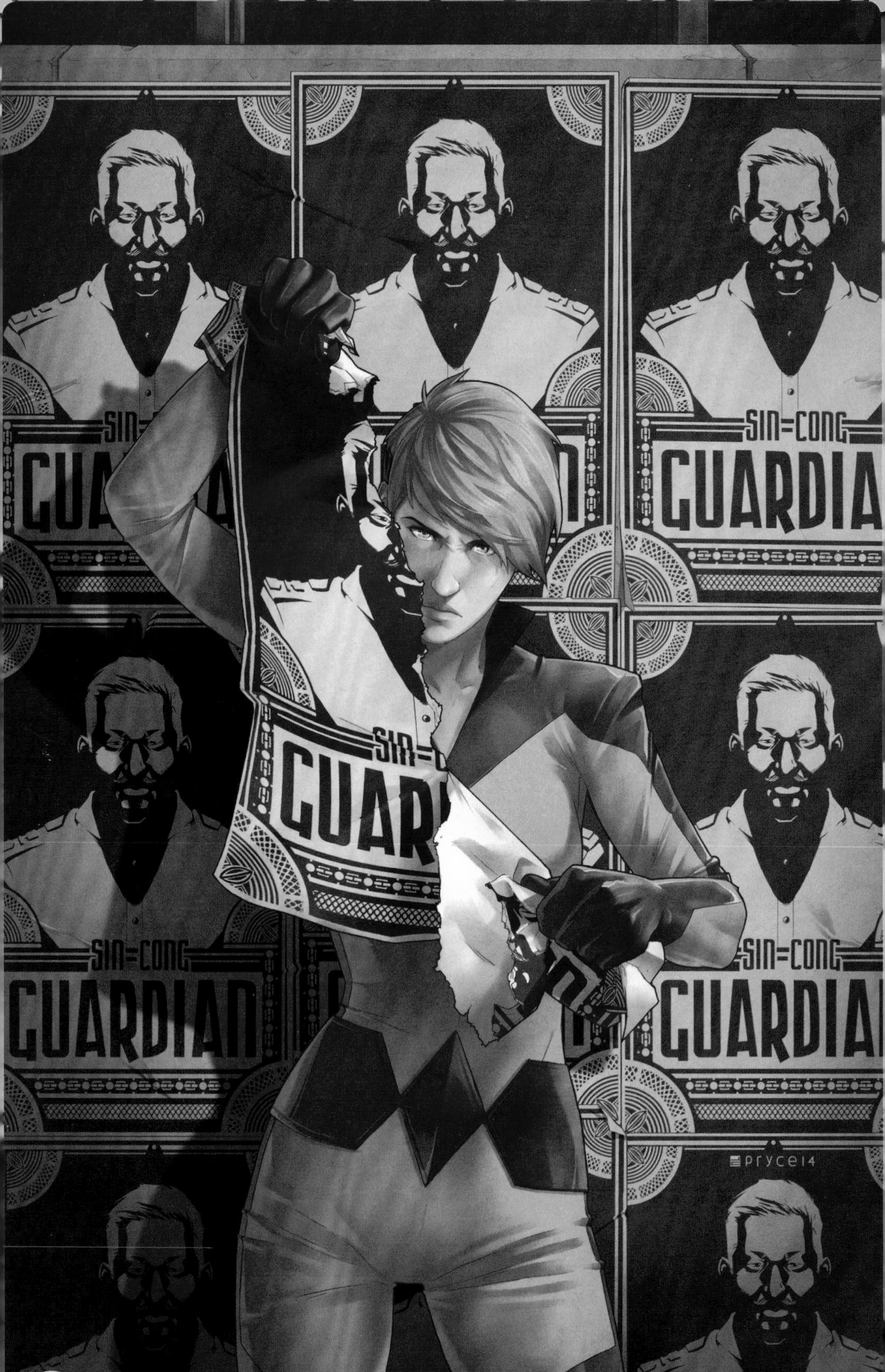
SIN=CONG
GUARDIAN
SIN=CONG
GUARDIAN
SIN=CONG
GUARDIAN
pryce14

2

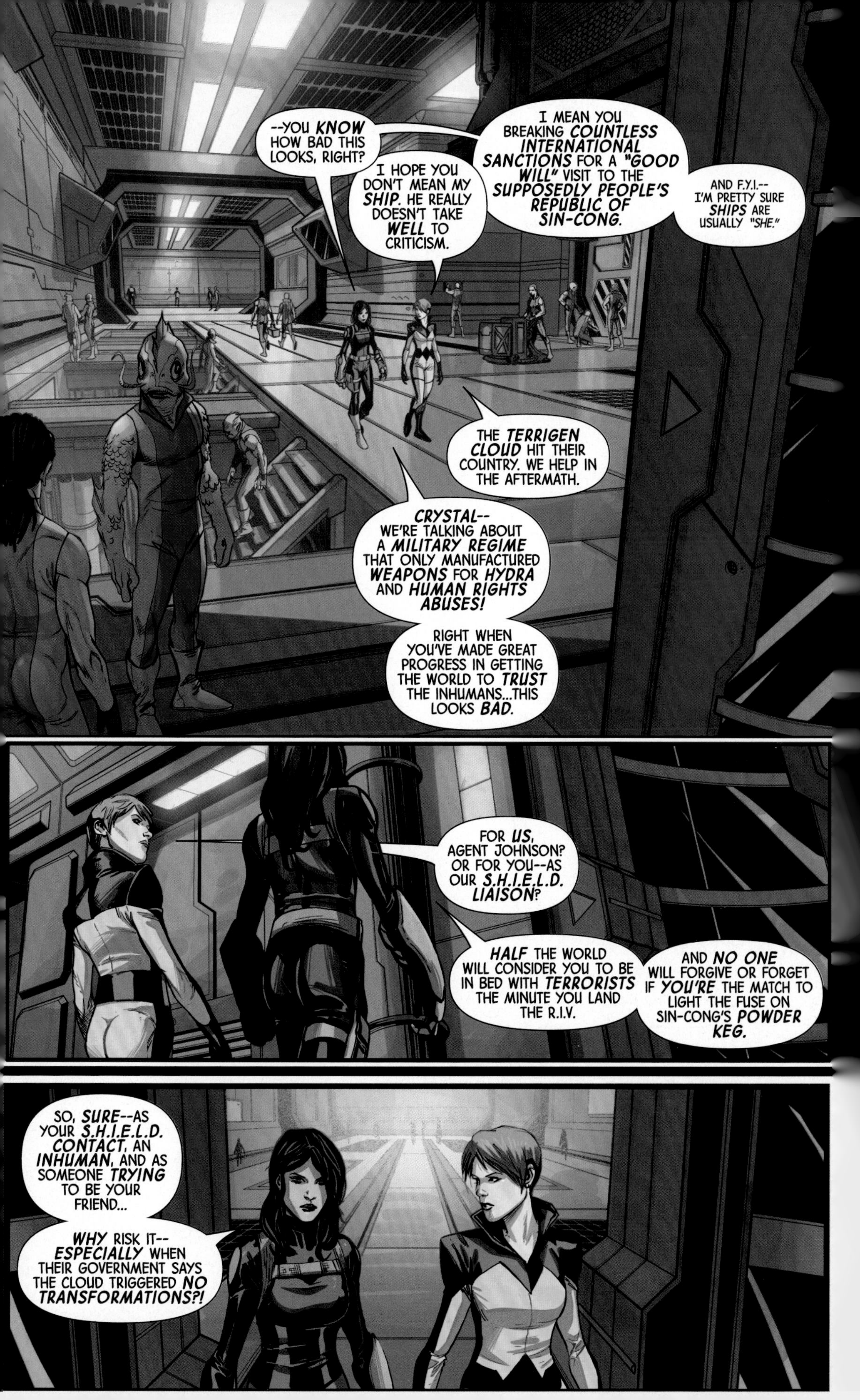
--YOU KNOW HOW BAD THIS LOOKS, RIGHT?
I HOPE YOU DON'T MEAN MY SHIP. HE REALLY DOESN'T TAKE WELL TO CRITICISM.
I MEAN YOU BREAKING COUNTLESS INTERNATIONAL SANCTIONS FOR A "GOOD WILL" VISIT TO THE SUPPOSEDLY PEOPLE'S REPUBLIC OF SIN-CONG.
AND F.Y.I.-- I'M PRETTY SURE SHIPS ARE USUALLY "SHE."
THE TERRIGEN CLOUD HIT THEIR COUNTRY. WE HELP IN THE AFTERMATH.
CRYSTAL-- WE'RE TALKING ABOUT A MILITARY REGIME THAT ONLY MANUFACTURED WEAPONS FOR HYDRA AND HUMAN RIGHTS ABUSES!
RIGHT WHEN YOU'VE MADE GREAT PROGRESS IN GETTING THE WORLD TO TRUST THE INHUMANS...THIS LOOKS BAD.
FOR US, AGENT JOHNSON? OR FOR YOU--AS OUR S.H.I.E.L.D. LIAISON?
HALF THE WORLD WILL CONSIDER YOU TO BE IN BED WITH TERRORISTS THE MINUTE YOU LAND THE R.I.V.
AND NO ONE WILL FORGIVE OR FORGET IF YOU'RE THE MATCH TO LIGHT THE FUSE ON SIN-CONG'S POWDER KEG.
SO, SURE--AS YOUR S.H.I.E.L.D. CONTACT, AN INHUMAN, AND AS SOMEONE TRYING TO BE YOUR FRIEND...
WHY RISK IT-- ESPECIALLY WHEN THEIR GOVERNMENT SAYS THE CLOUD TRIGGERED NO TRANSFORMATIONS?!

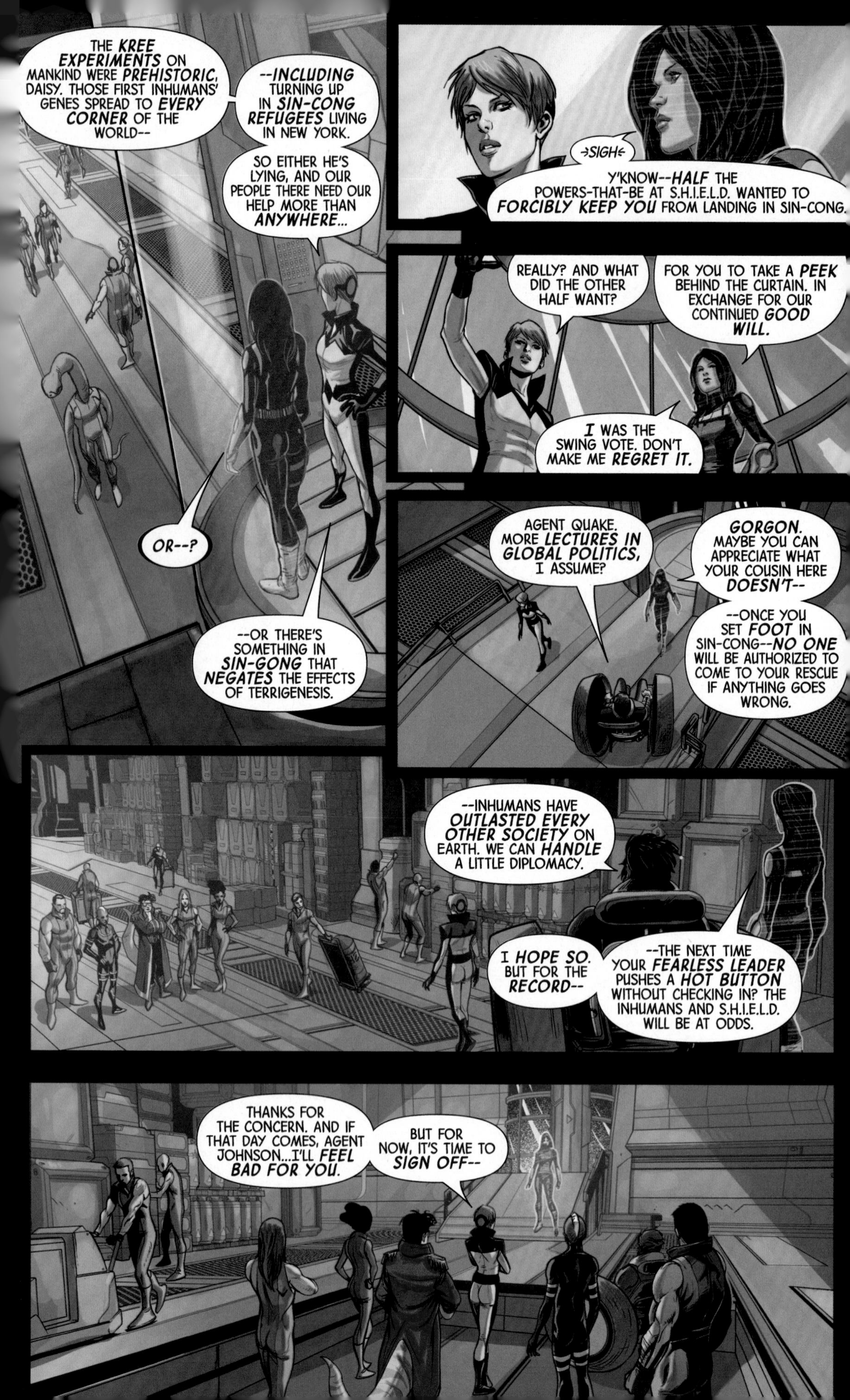
THE KREE EXPERIMENTS ON MANKIND WERE PREHISTORIC, DAISY. THOSE FIRST INHUMANS' GENES SPREAD TO EVERY CORNER OF THE WORLD--
--INCLUDING TURNING UP IN SIN-CONG REFUGEES LIVING IN NEW YORK.
SO EITHER HE'S LYING, AND OUR PEOPLE THERE NEED OUR HELP MORE THAN ANYWHERE...
OR--?
--OR THERE'S SOMETHING IN SIN-GONG THAT NEGATES THE EFFECTS OF TERRIGENESIS.
→SIGH←
Y'KNOW--HALF THE POWERS-THAT-BE AT S.H.I.E.L.D. WANTED TO FORCIBLY KEEP YOU FROM LANDING IN SIN-CONG.
REALLY? AND WHAT DID THE OTHER HALF WANT?
FOR YOU TO TAKE A PEEK BEHIND THE CURTAIN. IN EXCHANGE FOR OUR CONTINUED GOOD WILL.
I WAS THE SWING VOTE. DON'T MAKE ME REGRET IT.
AGENT QUAKE. MORE LECTURES IN GLOBAL POLITICS, I ASSUME?
GORGON. MAYBE YOU CAN APPRECIATE WHAT YOUR COUSIN HERE DOESN'T--
--ONCE YOU SET FOOT IN SIN-CONG--NO ONE WILL BE AUTHORIZED TO COME TO YOUR RESCUE IF ANYTHING GOES WRONG.
--INHUMANS HAVE OUTLASTED EVERY OTHER SOCIETY ON EARTH. WE CAN HANDLE A LITTLE DIPLOMACY.
I HOPE SO. BUT FOR THE RECORD--
--THE NEXT TIME YOUR FEARLESS LEADER PUSHES A HOT BUTTON WITHOUT CHECKING IN? THE INHUMANS AND S.H.I.E.L.D. WILL BE AT ODDS.
THANKS FOR THE CONCERN. AND IF THAT DAY COMES, AGENT JOHNSON...I'LL FEEL BAD FOR YOU.
BUT FOR NOW, IT'S TIME TO SIGN OFF--

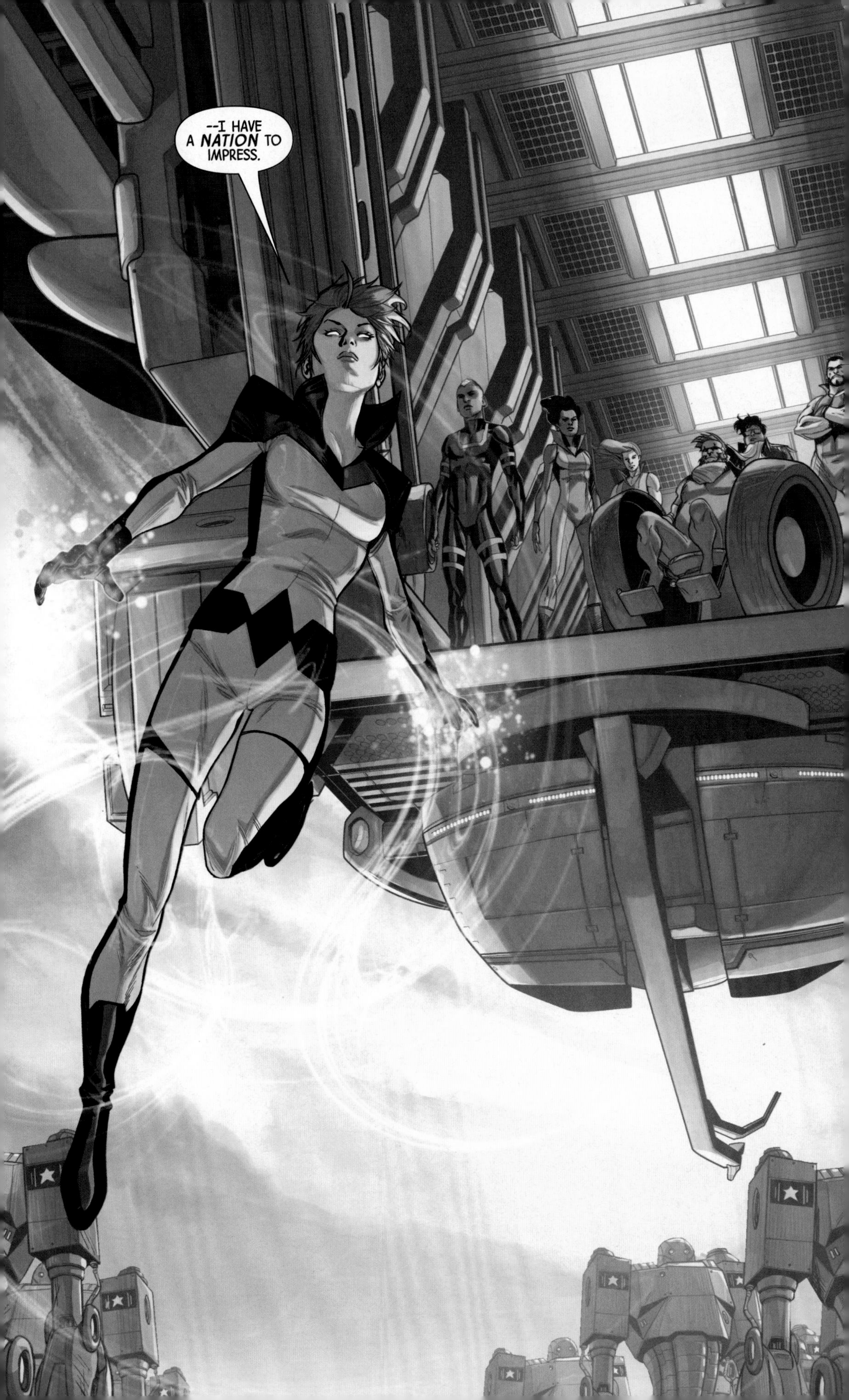
--I HAVE A NATION TO IMPRESS.

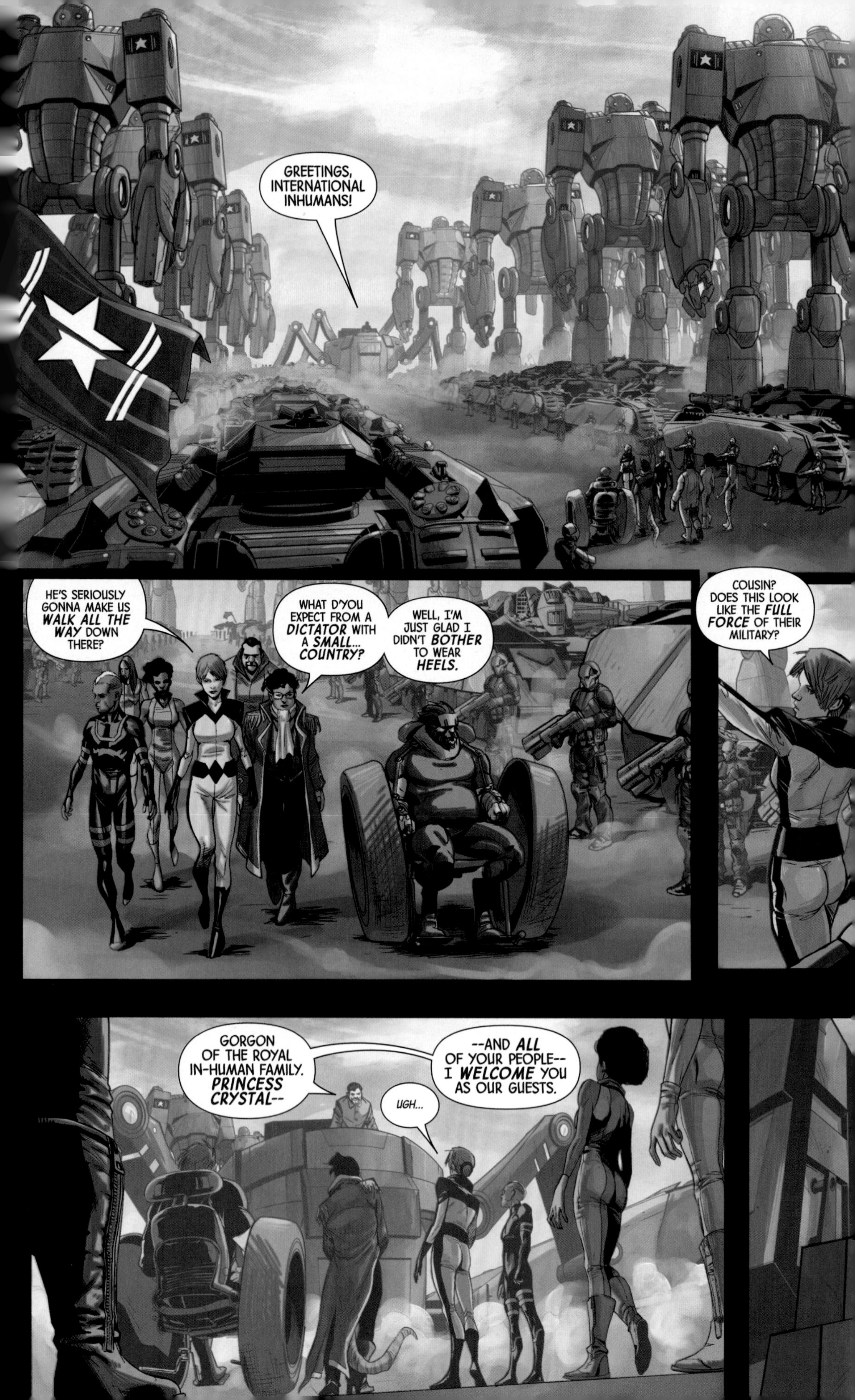
GREETINGS, INTERNATIONAL INHUMANS!
HE'S SERIOUSLY GONNA MAKE US WALK ALL THE WAY DOWN THERE?
WHAT D'YOU EXPECT FROM A DICTATOR WITH A SMALL... COUNTRY?
WELL, I'M JUST GLAD I DIDN'T BOTHER TO WEAR HEELS.
COUSIN? DOES THIS LOOK LIKE THE FULL FORCE OF THEIR MILITARY?
GORGON OF THE ROYAL IN-HUMAN FAMILY. PRINCESS CRYSTAL--
--AND ALL OF YOUR PEOPLE-- I WELCOME YOU AS OUR GUESTS.
UGH...

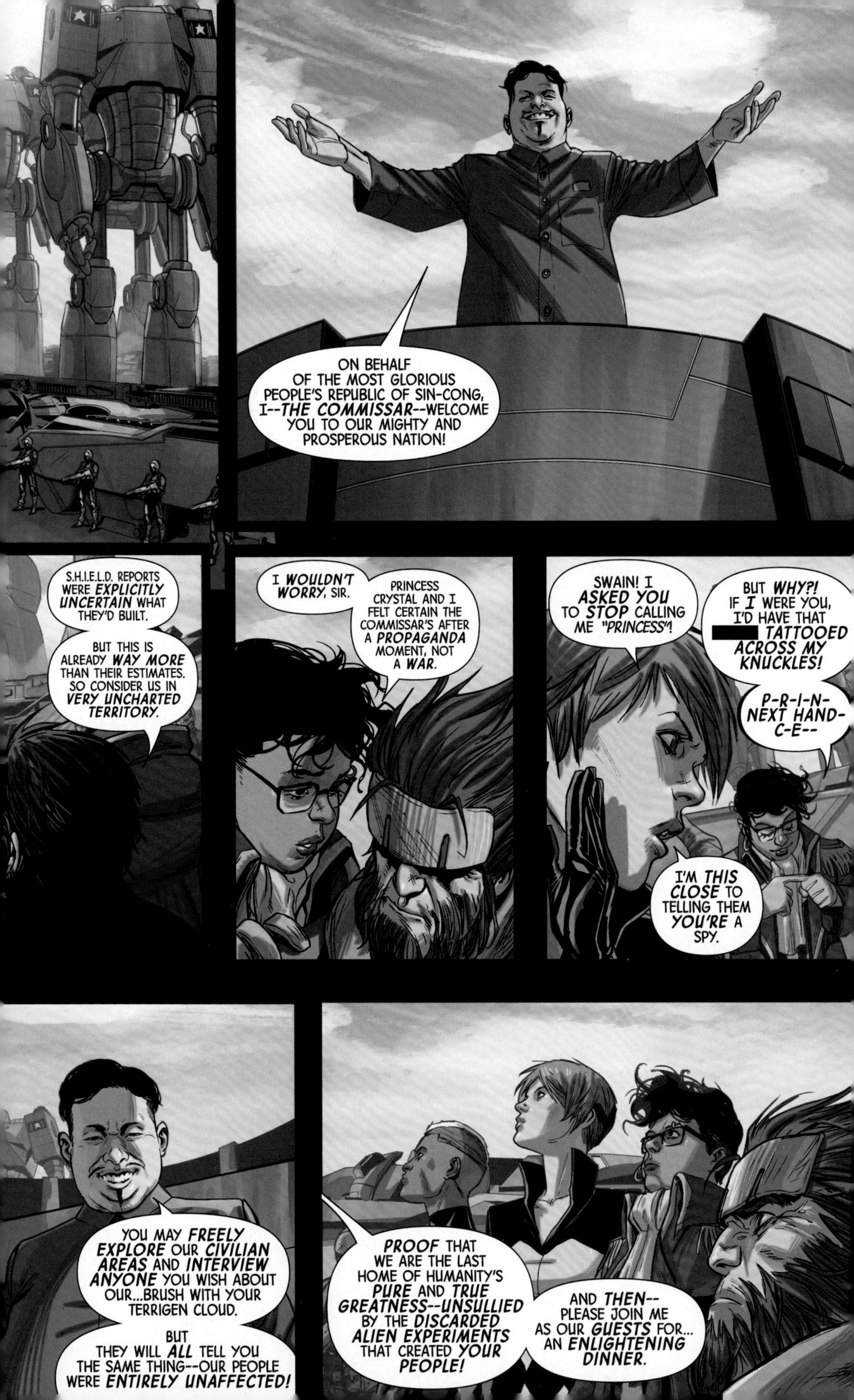
ON BEHALF OF THE MOST GLORIOUS PEOPLE'S REPUBLIC OF SIN-CONG, I--THE COMMISSAR--WELCOME YOU TO OUR MIGHTY AND PROSPEROUS NATION!
S.H.I.E.L.D. REPORTS WERE EXPLICITLY UNCERTAIN WHAT THEY'D BUILT.
BUT THIS IS ALREADY WAY MORE THAN THEIR ESTIMATES. SO CONSIDER US IN VERY UNCHARTED TERRITORY.
I WOULDN'T WORRY, SIR.
PRINCESS CRYSTAL AND I FELT CERTAIN THE COMMISSAR'S AFTER A PROPAGANDA MOMENT, NOT A WAR.
SWAIN! I ASKED YOU TO STOP CALLING ME "PRINCESS"!
BUT WHY?! IF I WERE YOU, I'D HAVE THAT [redacted] TATTOOED ACROSS MY KNUCKLES!
P-R-I-N- NEXT HAND- C-E--
I'M THIS CLOSE TO TELLING THEM YOU'RE A SPY.
YOU MAY FREELY EXPLORE OUR CIVILIAN AREAS AND INTERVIEW ANYONE YOU WISH ABOUT OUR...BRUSH WITH YOUR TERRIGEN CLOUD.
BUT THEY WILL ALL TELL YOU THE SAME THING--OUR PEOPLE WERE ENTIRELY UNAFFECTED!
PROOF THAT WE ARE THE LAST HOME OF HUMANITY'S PURE AND TRUE GREATNESS--UNSULLIED BY THE DISCARDED ALIEN EXPERIMENTS THAT CREATED YOUR PEOPLE!
AND THEN-- PLEASE JOIN ME AS OUR GUESTS FOR... AN ENLIGHTENING DINNER.

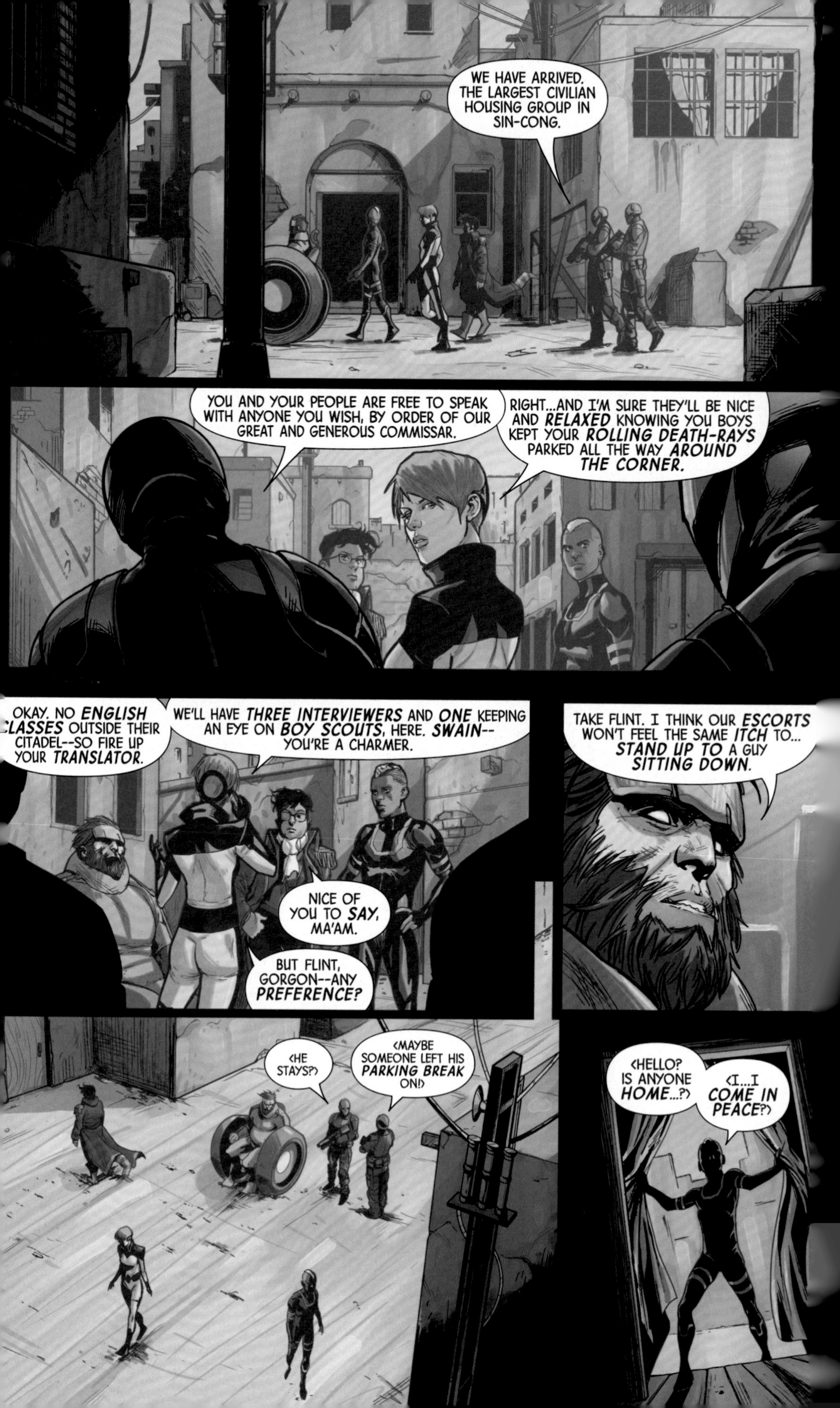
WE HAVE ARRIVED. THE LARGEST CIVILIAN HOUSING GROUP IN SIN-CONG.
YOU AND YOUR PEOPLE ARE FREE TO SPEAK WITH ANYONE YOU WISH, BY ORDER OF OUR GREAT AND GENEROUS COMMISSAR.
RIGHT...AND I'M SURE THEY'LL BE NICE AND RELAXED KNOWING YOU BOYS KEPT YOUR ROLLING DEATH-RAYS PARKED ALL THE WAY AROUND THE CORNER.
OKAY. NO ENGLISH CLASSES OUTSIDE THEIR CITADEL--SO FIRE UP YOUR TRANSLATOR.
WE'LL HAVE THREE INTERVIEWERS AND ONE KEEPING AN EYE ON BOY SCOUTS, HERE. SWAIN-- YOU'RE A CHARMER.
NICE OF YOU TO SAY, MA'AM.
BUT FLINT, GORGON--ANY PREFERENCE?
TAKE FLINT. I THINK OUR ESCORTS WON'T FEEL THE SAME ITCH TO... STAND UP TO A GUY SITTING DOWN.
‹HE STAYS?›
‹MAYBE SOMEONE LEFT HIS PARKING BREAK ON!›
‹HELLO? IS ANYONE HOME...?›
‹I...I COME IN PEACE?›

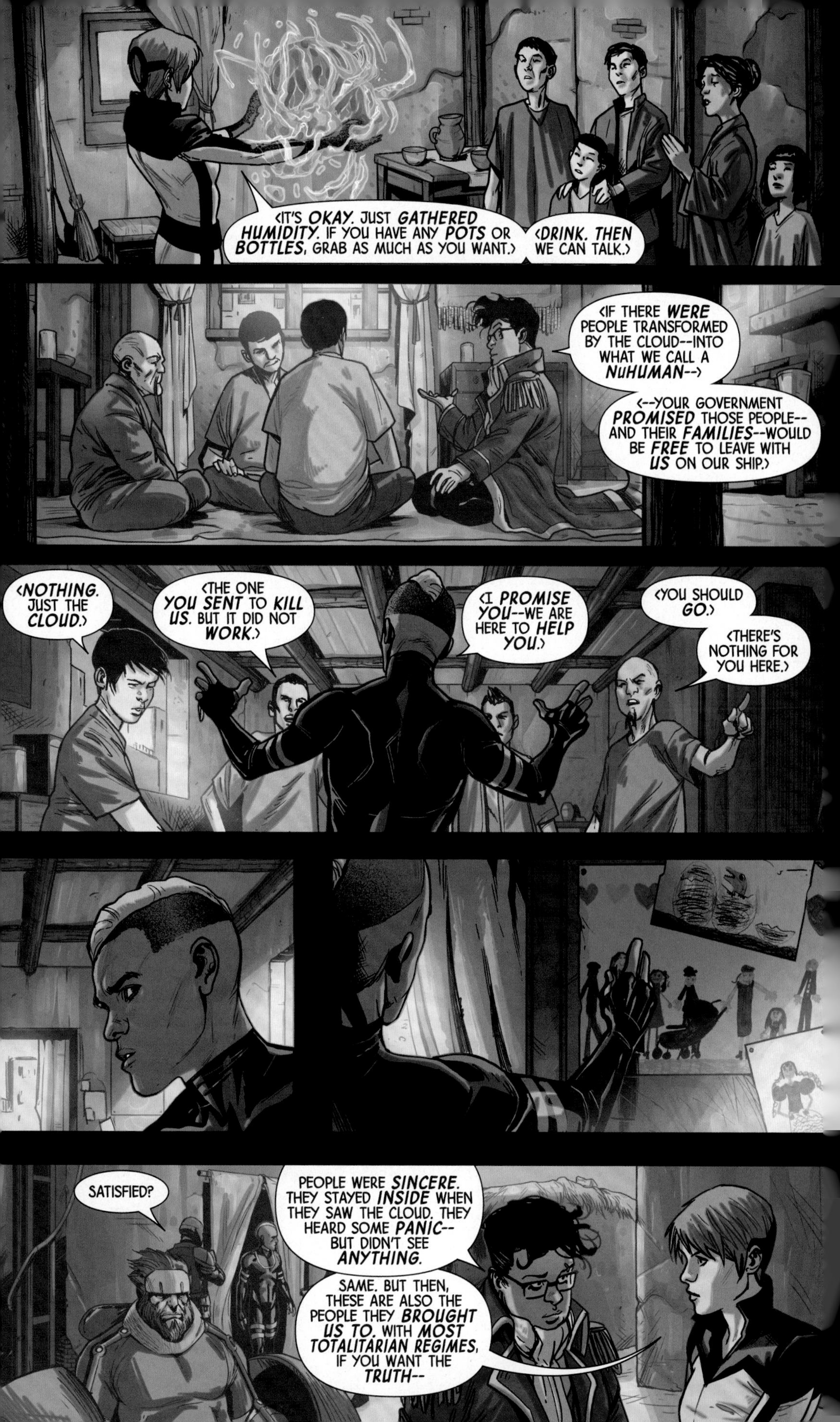

<IT'S OKAY. JUST GATHERED HUMIDITY. IF YOU HAVE ANY POTS OR BOTTLES, GRAB AS MUCH AS YOU WANT.>
<DRINK. THEN WE CAN TALK.>
<IF THERE WERE PEOPLE TRANSFORMED BY THE CLOUD--INTO WHAT WE CALL A NuHUMAN-->
<--YOUR GOVERNMENT PROMISED THOSE PEOPLE--AND THEIR FAMILIES--WOULD BE FREE TO LEAVE WITH US ON OUR SHIP.>
<NOTHING. JUST THE CLOUD.>
<THE ONE YOU SENT TO KILL US. BUT IT DID NOT WORK.>
<I PROMISE YOU--WE ARE HERE TO HELP YOU.>
<YOU SHOULD GO.>
<THERE'S NOTHING FOR YOU HERE.>
SATISFIED?
PEOPLE WERE SINCERE. THEY STAYED INSIDE WHEN THEY SAW THE CLOUD. THEY HEARD SOME PANIC--BUT DIDN'T SEE ANYTHING.
SAME. BUT THEN, THESE ARE ALSO THE PEOPLE THEY BROUGHT US TO. WITH MOST TOTALITARIAN REGIMES, IF YOU WANT THE TRUTH--

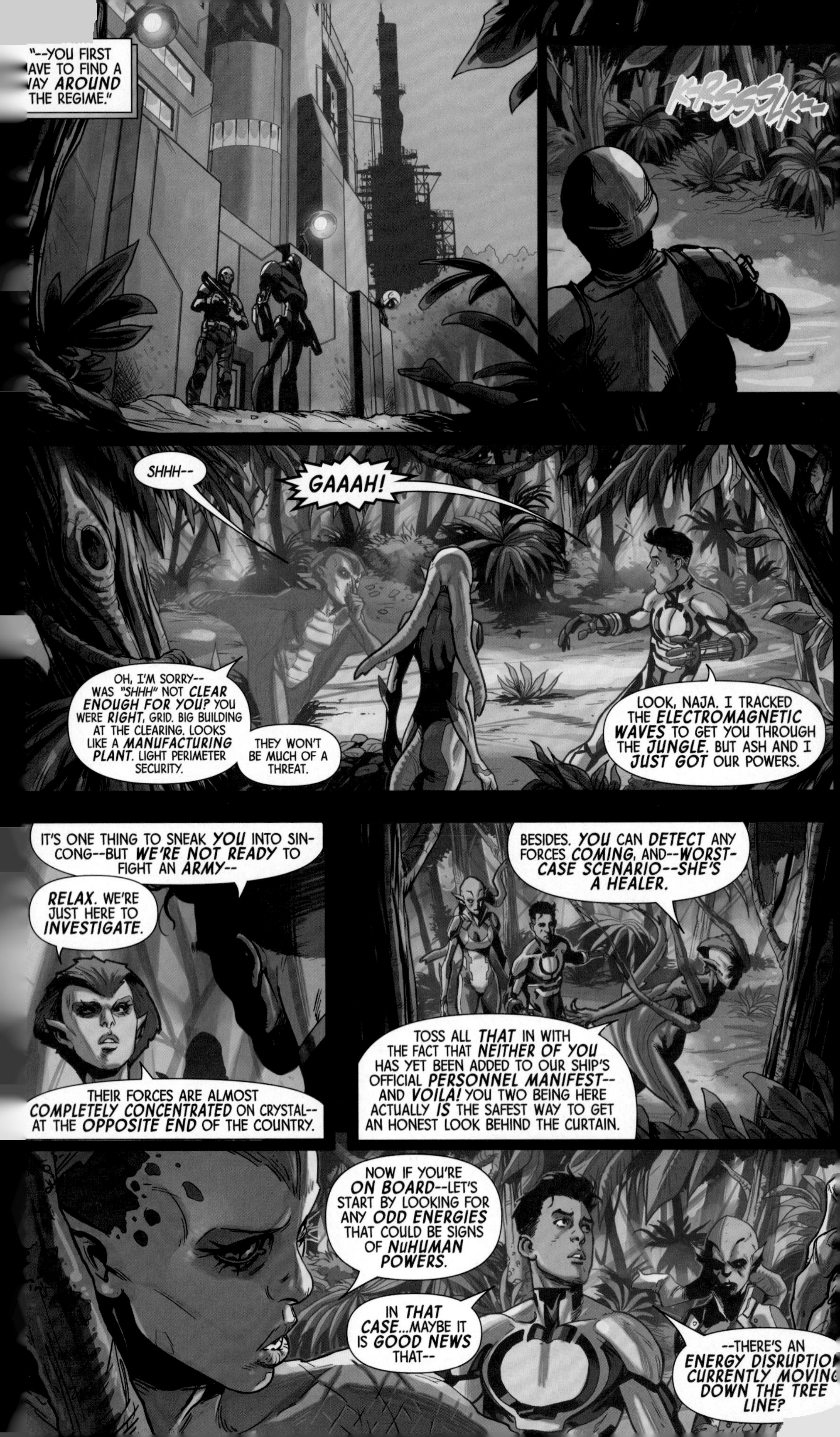
"--YOU FIRST
HAVE TO FIND A
WAY AROUND
THE REGIME."
K-RSSSLK--
SHHH--
GAAAH!
OH, I'M SORRY-- WAS "SHHH" NOT CLEAR ENOUGH FOR YOU? YOU WERE RIGHT, GRID. BIG BUILDING AT THE CLEARING. LOOKS LIKE A MANUFACTURING PLANT. LIGHT PERIMETER SECURITY.
THEY WON'T BE MUCH OF A THREAT.
LOOK, NAJA. I TRACKED THE ELECTROMAGNETIC WAVES TO GET YOU THROUGH THE JUNGLE. BUT ASH AND I JUST GOT OUR POWERS.
IT'S ONE THING TO SNEAK YOU INTO SIN-CONG--BUT WE'RE NOT READY TO FIGHT AN ARMY--
RELAX. WE'RE JUST HERE TO INVESTIGATE.
THEIR FORCES ARE ALMOST COMPLETELY CONCENTRATED ON CRYSTAL--AT THE OPPOSITE END OF THE COUNTRY.
BESIDES. YOU CAN DETECT ANY FORCES COMING, AND--WORST-CASE SCENARIO--SHE'S A HEALER.
TOSS ALL THAT IN WITH THE FACT THAT NEITHER OF YOU HAS YET BEEN ADDED TO OUR SHIP'S OFFICIAL PERSONNEL MANIFEST--AND VOILA! YOU TWO BEING HERE ACTUALLY IS THE SAFEST WAY TO GET AN HONEST LOOK BEHIND THE CURTAIN.
NOW IF YOU'RE ON BOARD--LET'S START BY LOOKING FOR ANY ODD ENERGIES THAT COULD BE SIGNS OF NUHUMAN POWERS.
IN THAT CASE...MAYBE IT IS GOOD NEWS THAT--
--THERE'S AN ENERGY DISRUPTION CURRENTLY MOVING DOWN THE TREE LINE?

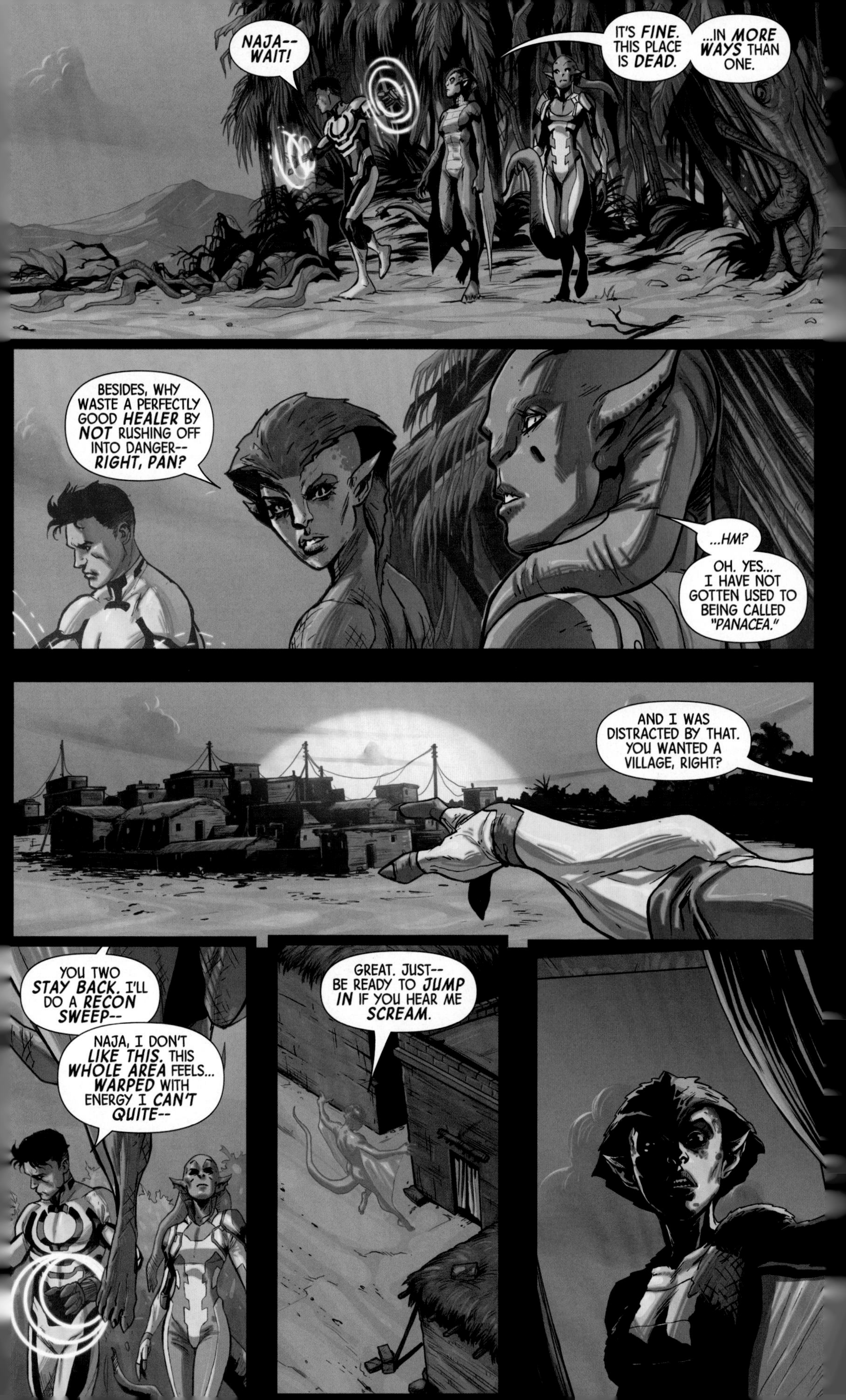
NAJA-- WAIT!
IT'S FINE. THIS PLACE IS DEAD.
...IN MORE WAYS THAN ONE.
BESIDES, WHY WASTE A PERFECTLY GOOD HEALER BY NOT RUSHING OFF INTO DANGER-- RIGHT, PAN?
...HM?
OH. YES... I HAVE NOT GOTTEN USED TO BEING CALLED "PANACEA."
AND I WAS DISTRACTED BY THAT. YOU WANTED A VILLAGE, RIGHT?
YOU TWO STAY BACK. I'LL DO A RECON SWEEP--
NAJA, I DON'T LIKE THIS. THIS WHOLE AREA FEELS... WARPED WITH ENERGY I CAN'T QUITE--
GREAT. JUST-- BE READY TO JUMP IN IF YOU HEAR ME SCREAM.

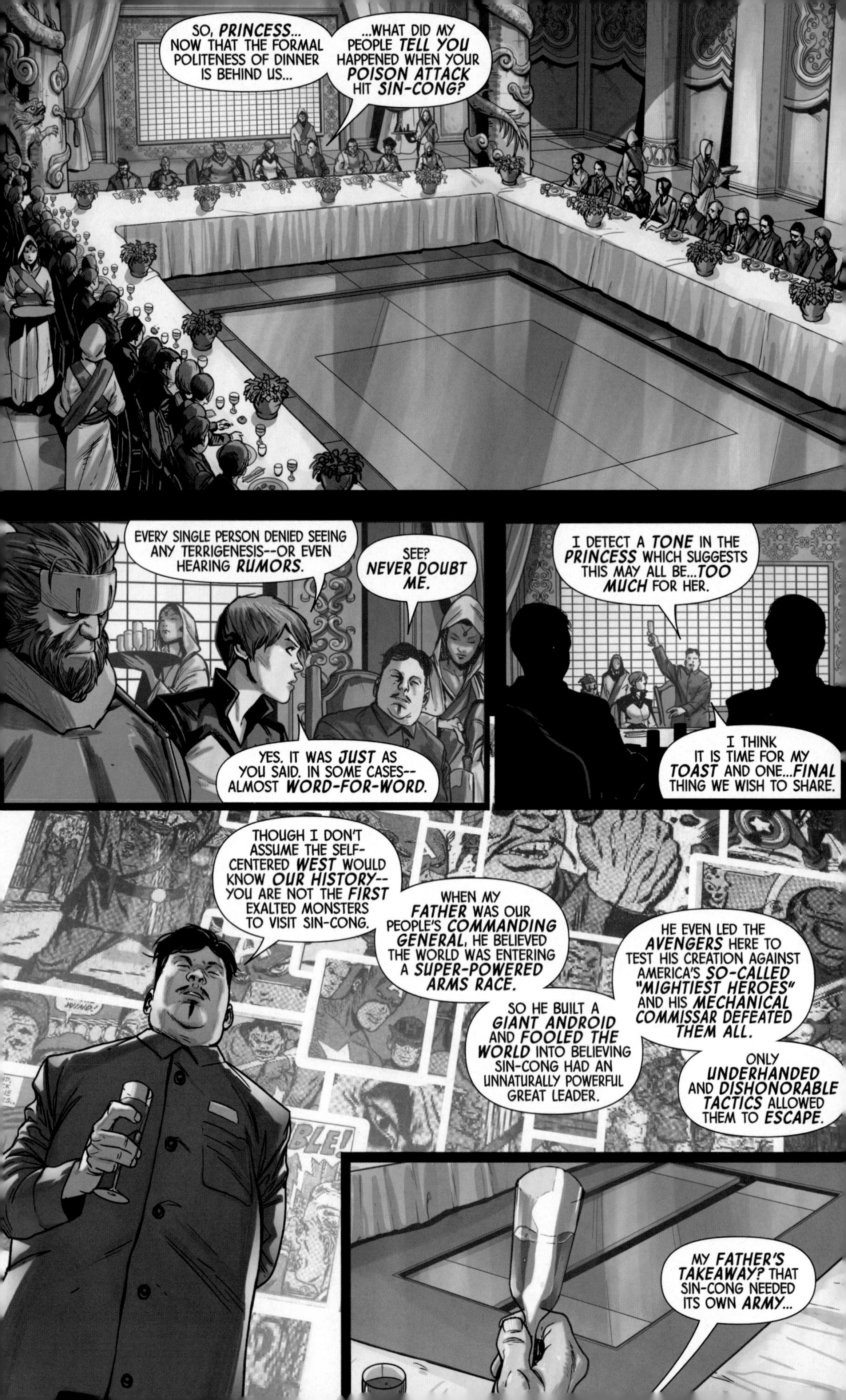
SO, PRINCESS... NOW THAT THE FORMAL POLITENESS OF DINNER IS BEHIND US...
...WHAT DID MY PEOPLE TELL YOU HAPPENED WHEN YOUR POISON ATTACK HIT SIN-CONG?
EVERY SINGLE PERSON DENIED SEEING ANY TERRIGENESIS--OR EVEN HEARING RUMORS.
SEE? NEVER DOUBT ME.
YES. IT WAS JUST AS YOU SAID. IN SOME CASES--ALMOST WORD-FOR-WORD.
I DETECT A TONE IN THE PRINCESS WHICH SUGGESTS THIS MAY ALL BE...TOO MUCH FOR HER.
I THINK IT IS TIME FOR MY TOAST AND ONE...FINAL THING WE WISH TO SHARE.
THOUGH I DON'T ASSUME THE SELF-CENTERED WEST WOULD KNOW OUR HISTORY--YOU ARE NOT THE FIRST EXALTED MONSTERS TO VISIT SIN-CONG.
WHEN MY FATHER WAS OUR PEOPLE'S COMMANDING GENERAL, HE BELIEVED THE WORLD WAS ENTERING A SUPER-POWERED ARMS RACE.
SO HE BUILT A GIANT ANDROID AND FOOLED THE WORLD INTO BELIEVING SIN-CONG HAD AN UNNATURALLY POWERFUL GREAT LEADER.
HE EVEN LED THE AVENGERS HERE TO TEST HIS CREATION AGAINST AMERICA'S SO-CALLED "MIGHTIEST HEROES" AND HIS MECHANICAL COMMISSAR DEFEATED THEM ALL.
ONLY UNDERHANDED AND DISHONORABLE TACTICS ALLOWED THEM TO ESCAPE.
MY FATHER'S TAKEAWAY? THAT SIN-CONG NEEDED ITS OWN ARMY...

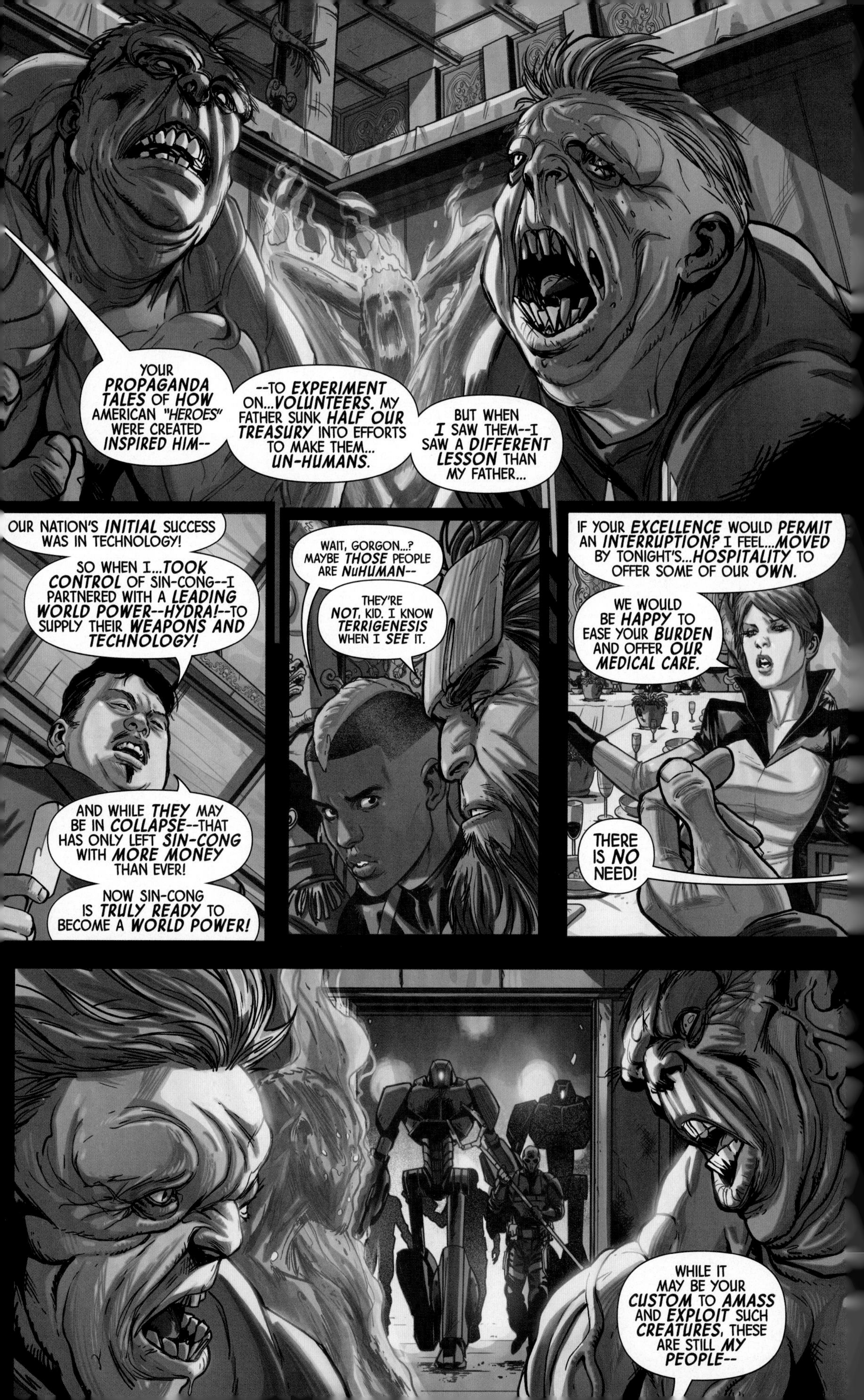

YOUR PROPAGANDA TALES OF HOW AMERICAN "HEROES" WERE CREATED INSPIRED HIM--
--TO EXPERIMENT ON...VOLUNTEERS. MY FATHER SUNK HALF OUR TREASURY INTO EFFORTS TO MAKE THEM... UN-HUMANS.
BUT WHEN I SAW THEM--I SAW A DIFFERENT LESSON THAN MY FATHER...
OUR NATION'S INITIAL SUCCESS WAS IN TECHNOLOGY!
SO WHEN I...TOOK CONTROL OF SIN-CONG--I PARTNERED WITH A LEADING WORLD POWER--HYDRA!--TO SUPPLY THEIR WEAPONS AND TECHNOLOGY!
AND WHILE THEY MAY BE IN COLLAPSE--THAT HAS ONLY LEFT SIN-CONG WITH MORE MONEY THAN EVER!
NOW SIN-CONG IS TRULY READY TO BECOME A WORLD POWER!
WAIT, GORGON...? MAYBE THOSE PEOPLE ARE NuHUMAN--
THEY'RE NOT, KID. I KNOW TERRIGENESIS WHEN I SEE IT.
IF YOUR EXCELLENCE WOULD PERMIT AN INTERRUPTION? I FEEL...MOVED BY TONIGHT'S...HOSPITALITY TO OFFER SOME OF OUR OWN.
WE WOULD BE HAPPY TO EASE YOUR BURDEN AND OFFER OUR MEDICAL CARE.
THERE IS NO NEED!
WHILE IT MAY BE YOUR CUSTOM TO AMASS AND EXPLOIT SUCH CREATURES, THESE ARE STILL MY PEOPLE--

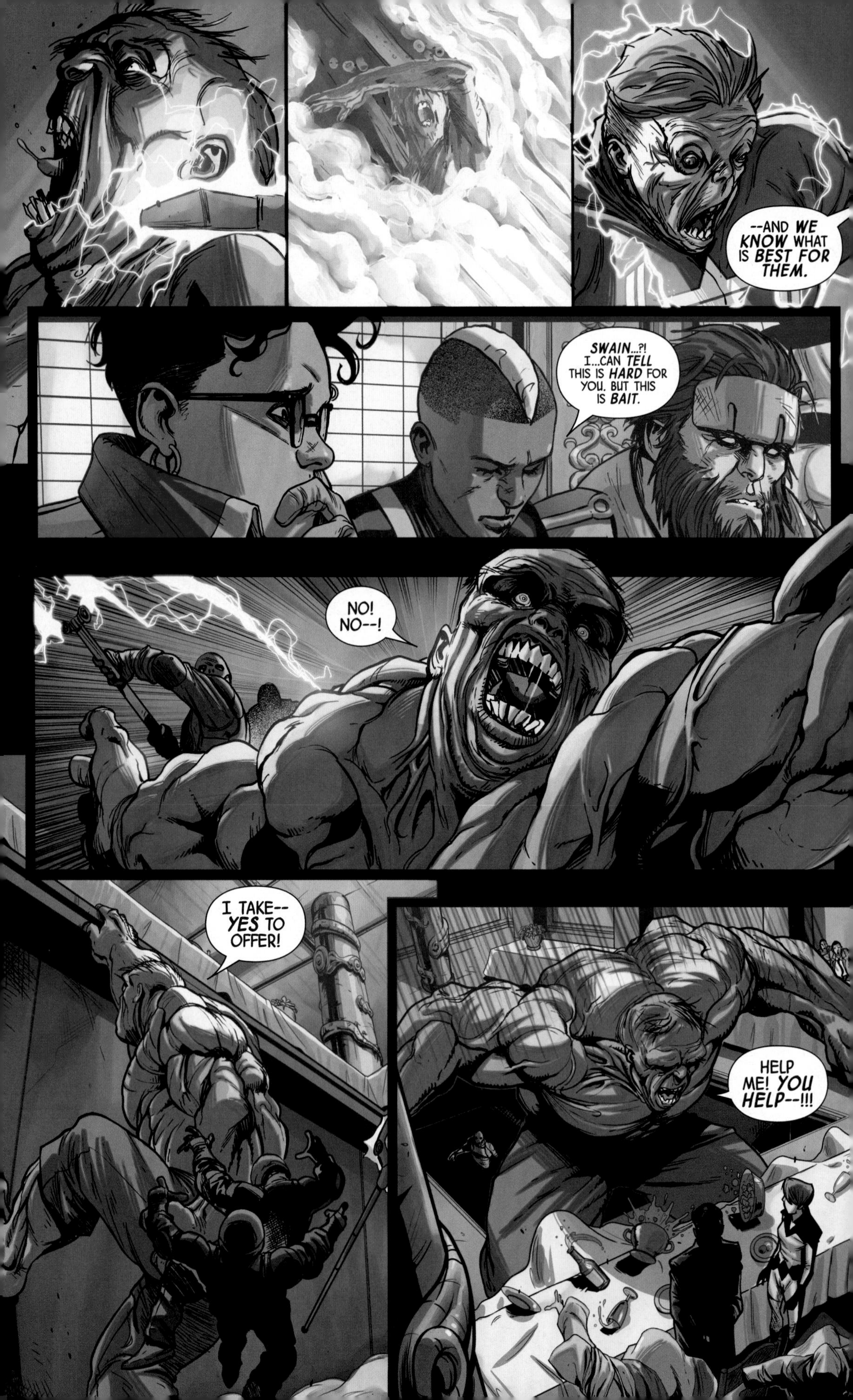
--AND WE KNOW WHAT IS BEST FOR THEM.
SWAIN...?! I...CAN TELL THIS IS HARD FOR YOU. BUT THIS IS BAIT.
NO! NO--!
I TAKE-- YES TO OFFER!
HELP ME! YOU HELP--!!!

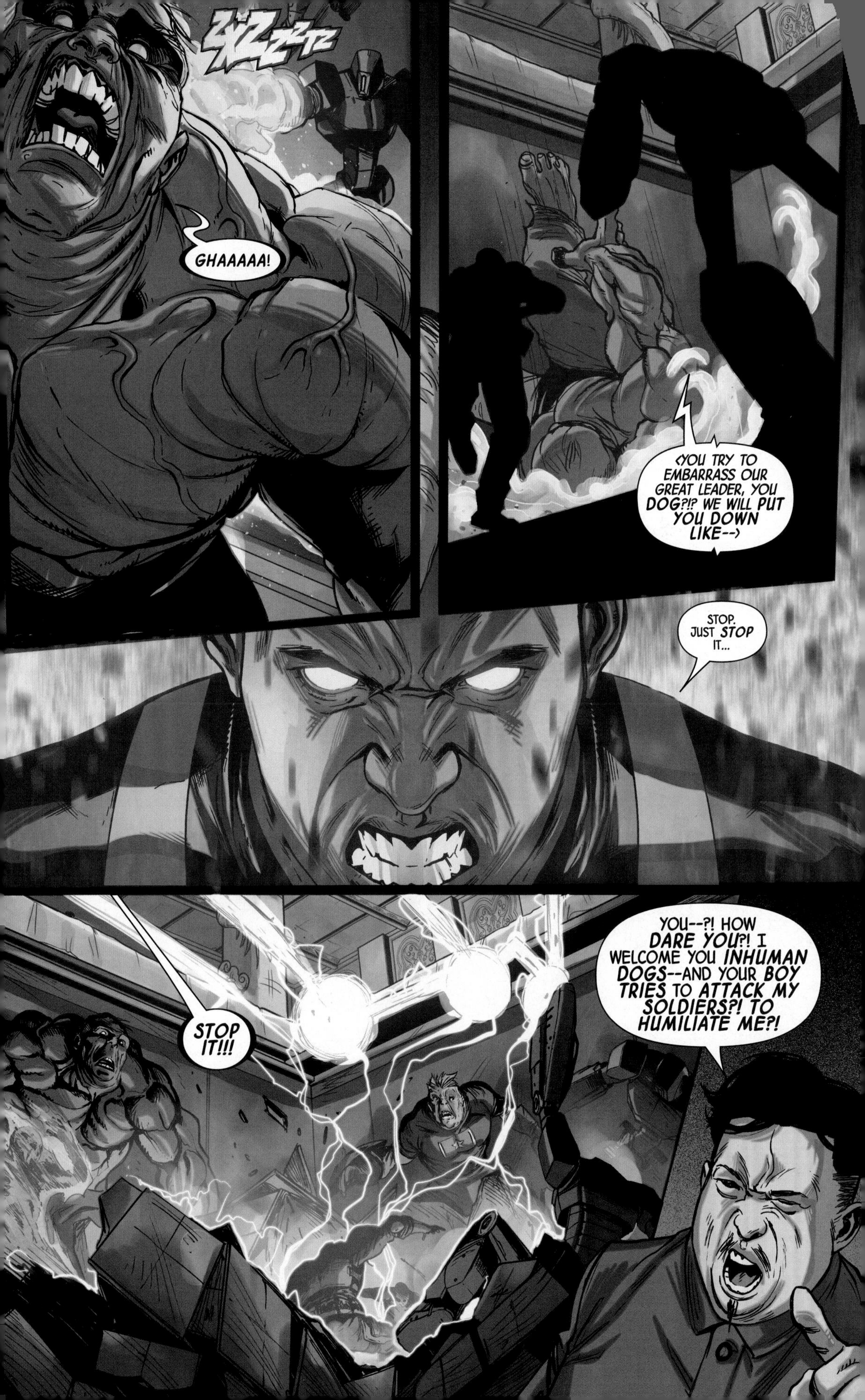

ZZZZZZT
GHAAAAA!
<YOU TRY TO EMBARRASS OUR GREAT LEADER, YOU DOG?!? WE WILL PUT YOU DOWN LIKE-->
STOP. JUST STOP IT...
STOP IT!!!
YOU--?! HOW DARE YOU?! I WELCOME YOU INHUMAN DOGS--AND YOUR BOY TRIES TO ATTACK MY SOLDIERS?! TO HUMILIATE ME?!

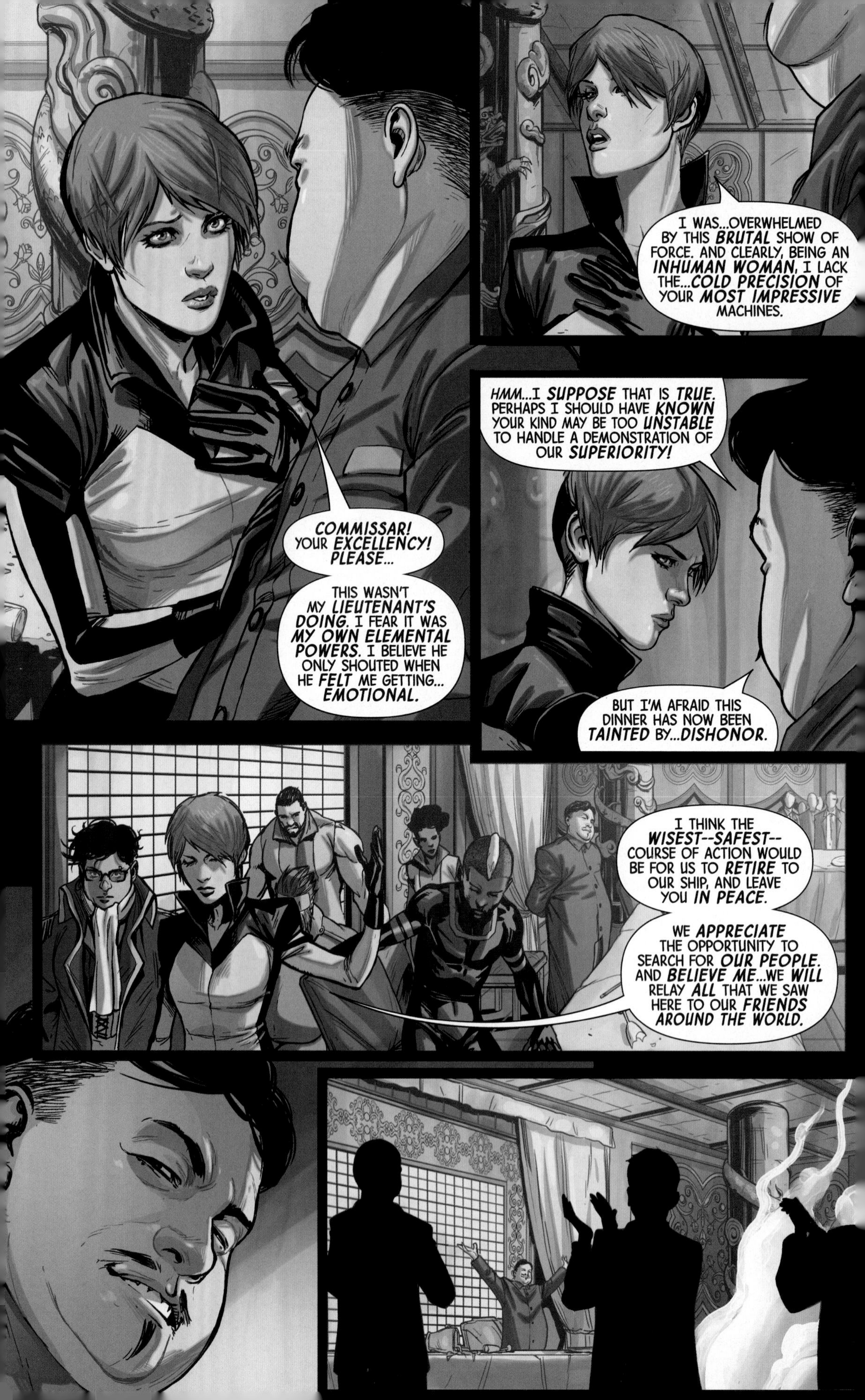
COMMISSAR! YOUR EXCELLENCY! PLEASE...
THIS WASN'T MY LIEUTENANT'S DOING. I FEAR IT WAS MY OWN ELEMENTAL POWERS. I BELIEVE HE ONLY SHOUTED WHEN HE FELT ME GETTING... EMOTIONAL.
I WAS...OVERWHELMED BY THIS BRUTAL SHOW OF FORCE. AND CLEARLY, BEING AN INHUMAN WOMAN, I LACK THE...COLD PRECISION OF YOUR MOST IMPRESSIVE MACHINES.
HMM...I SUPPOSE THAT IS TRUE. PERHAPS I SHOULD HAVE KNOWN YOUR KIND MAY BE TOO UNSTABLE TO HANDLE A DEMONSTRATION OF OUR SUPERIORITY!
BUT I'M AFRAID THIS DINNER HAS NOW BEEN TAINTED BY...DISHONOR.
I THINK THE WISEST--SAFEST--COURSE OF ACTION WOULD BE FOR US TO RETIRE TO OUR SHIP, AND LEAVE YOU IN PEACE.
WE APPRECIATE THE OPPORTUNITY TO SEARCH FOR OUR PEOPLE. AND BELIEVE ME...WE WILL RELAY ALL THAT WE SAW HERE TO OUR FRIENDS AROUND THE WORLD.

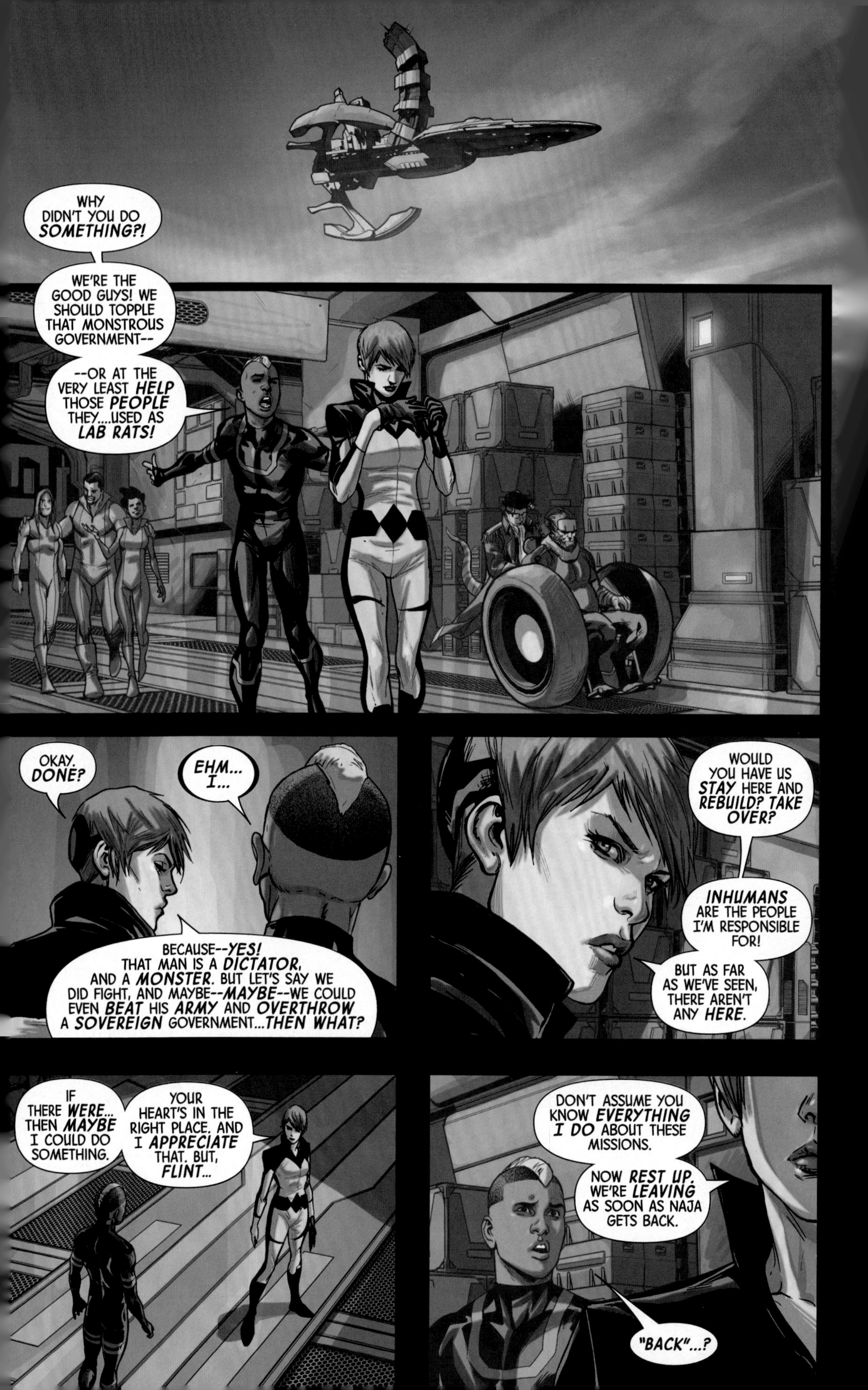
WHY DIDN'T YOU DO SOMETHING?!
WE'RE THE GOOD GUYS! WE SHOULD TOPPLE THAT MONSTROUS GOVERNMENT--
--OR AT THE VERY LEAST HELP THOSE PEOPLE THEY...USED AS LAB RATS!
OKAY. DONE?
EHM... I...
BECAUSE--YES! THAT MAN IS A DICTATOR, AND A MONSTER. BUT LET'S SAY WE DID FIGHT, AND MAYBE--MAYBE--WE COULD EVEN BEAT HIS ARMY AND OVERTHROW A SOVEREIGN GOVERNMENT...THEN WHAT?
WOULD YOU HAVE US STAY HERE AND REBUILD? TAKE OVER?
INHUMANS ARE THE PEOPLE I'M RESPONSIBLE FOR!
BUT AS FAR AS WE'VE SEEN, THERE AREN'T ANY HERE.
IF THERE WERE... THEN MAYBE I COULD DO SOMETHING.
YOUR HEART'S IN THE RIGHT PLACE, AND I APPRECIATE THAT. BUT, FLINT...
DON'T ASSUME YOU KNOW EVERYTHING I DO ABOUT THESE MISSIONS.
NOW REST UP. WE'RE LEAVING AS SOON AS NAJA GETS BACK.
"BACK"...?

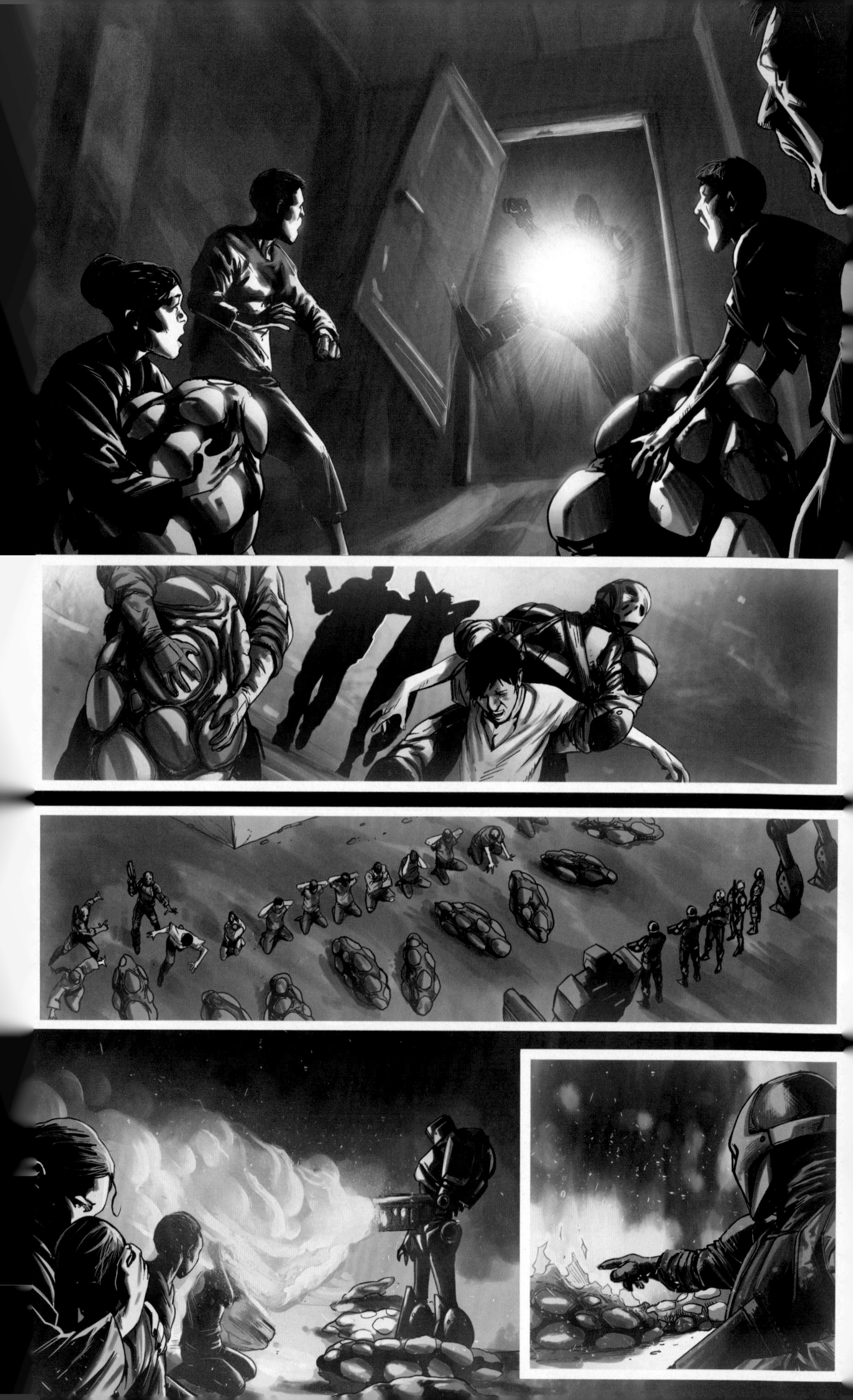

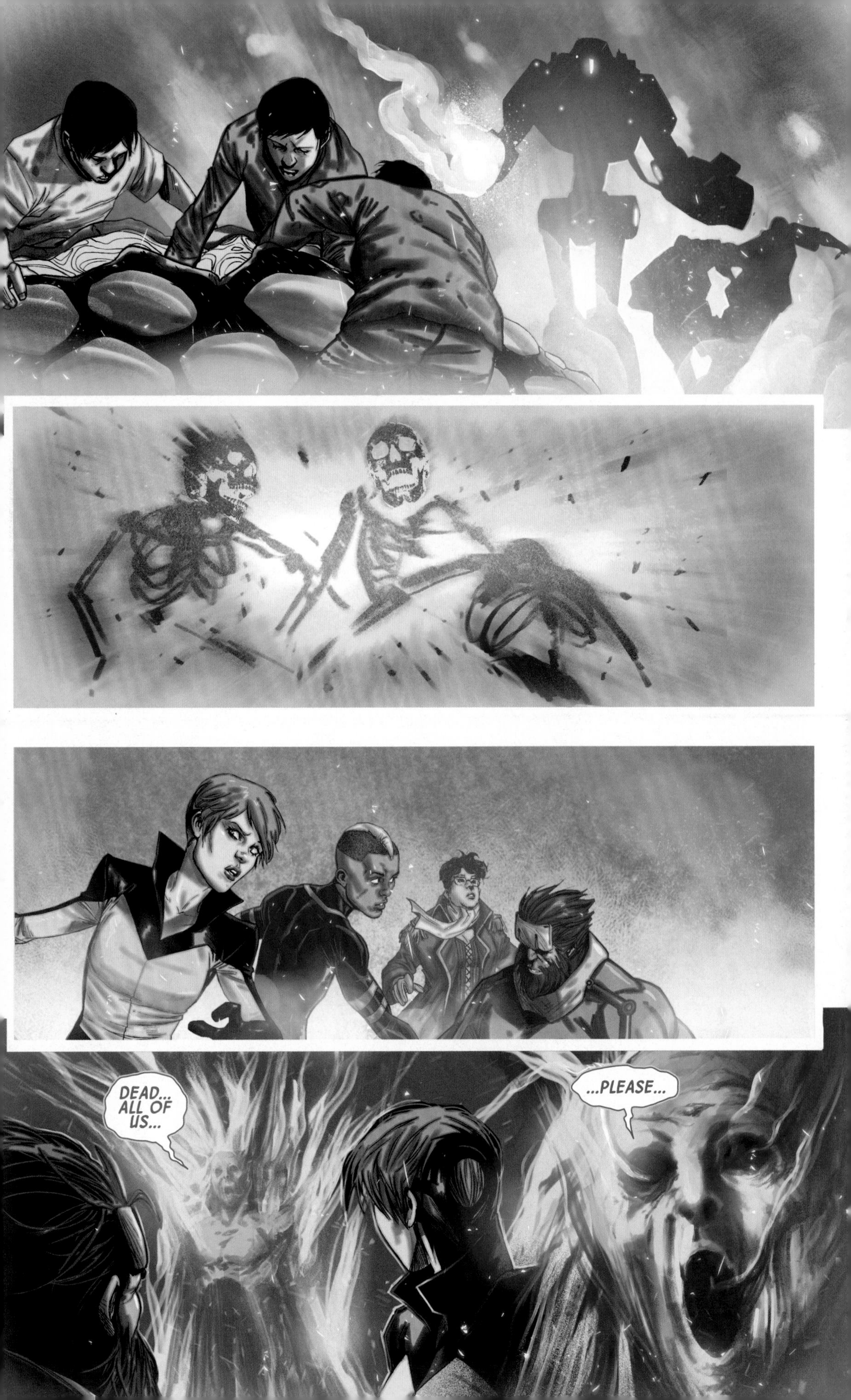
DEAD... ALL OF US...
...PLEASE...

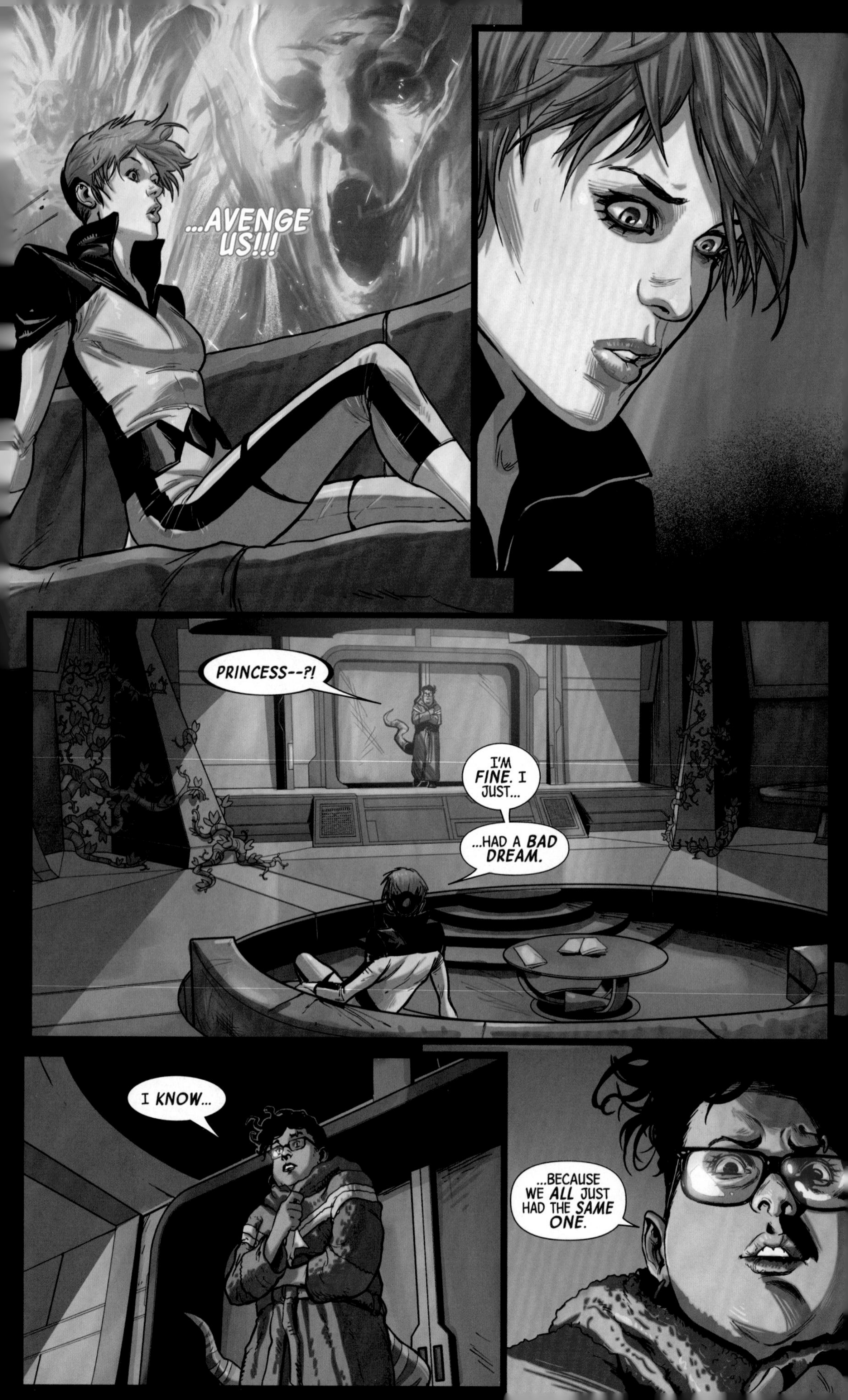
...AVENGE US!!!
PRINCESS--?!
I'M FINE. I JUST...
...HAD A BAD DREAM.
I KNOW...
...BECAUSE WE ALL JUST HAD THE SAME ONE.

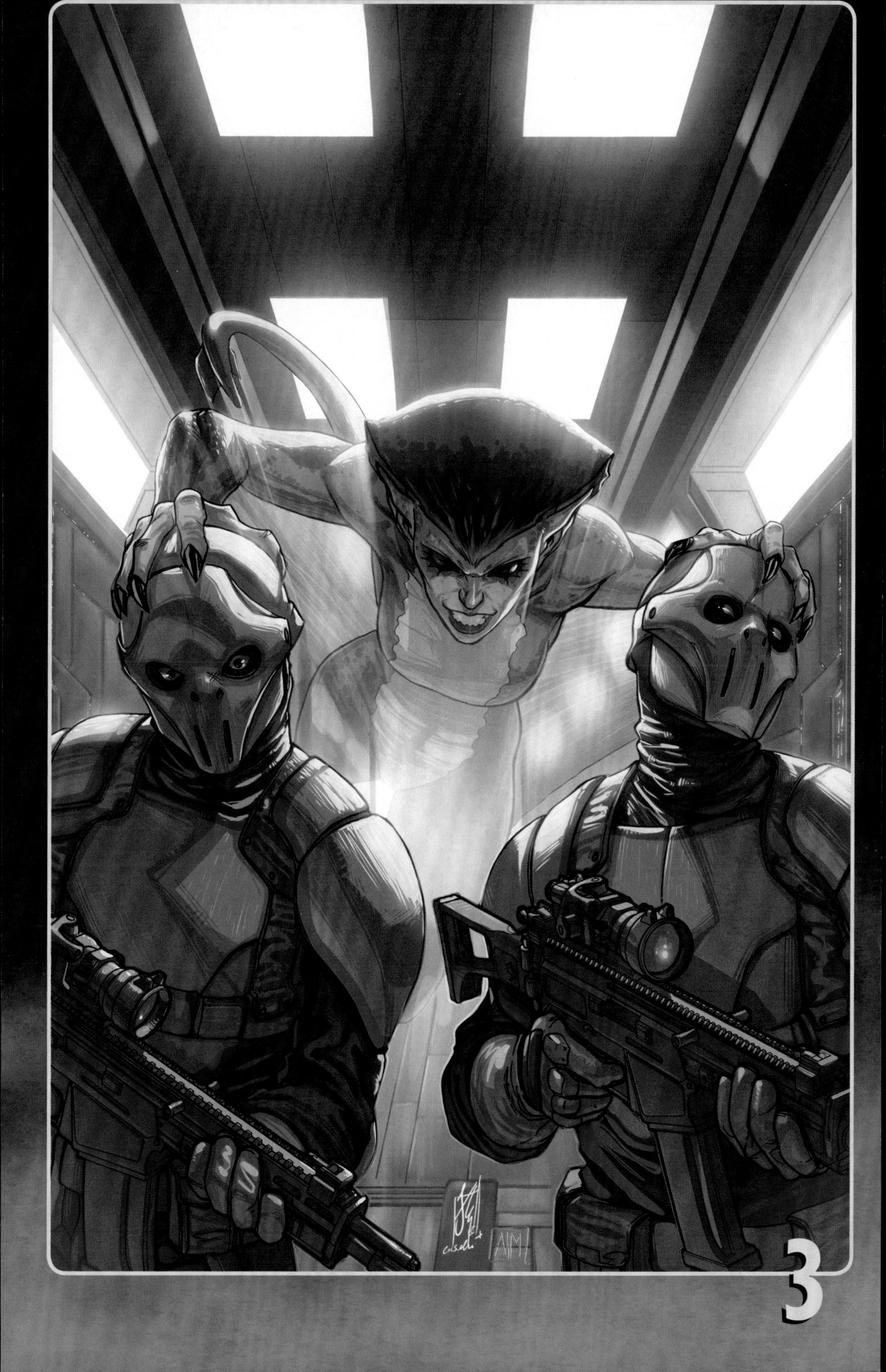

3

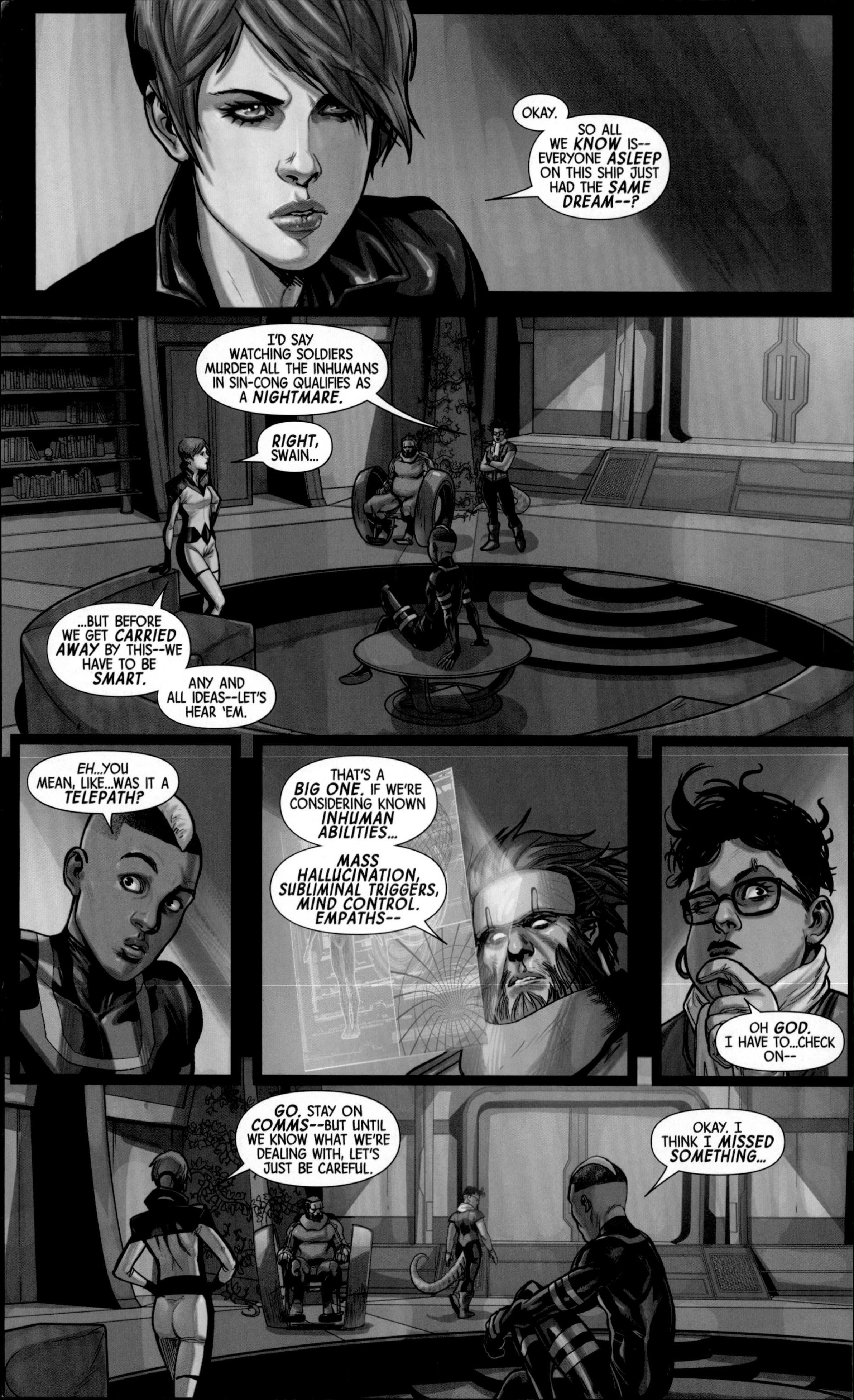
OKAY.
SO ALL WE KNOW IS-- EVERYONE ASLEEP ON THIS SHIP JUST HAD THE SAME DREAM--?
I'D SAY WATCHING SOLDIERS MURDER ALL THE INHUMANS IN SIN-CONG QUALIFIES AS A NIGHTMARE.
RIGHT, SWAIN...
...BUT BEFORE WE GET CARRIED AWAY BY THIS--WE HAVE TO BE SMART.
ANY AND ALL IDEAS--LET'S HEAR 'EM.
EH...YOU MEAN, LIKE...WAS IT A TELEPATH?
THAT'S A BIG ONE. IF WE'RE CONSIDERING KNOWN INHUMAN ABILITIES...
MASS HALLUCINATION, SUBLIMINAL TRIGGERS, MIND CONTROL. EMPATHS--
OH GOD. I HAVE TO...CHECK ON--
GO. STAY ON COMMS--BUT UNTIL WE KNOW WHAT WE'RE DEALING WITH, LET'S JUST BE CAREFUL.
OKAY. I THINK I MISSED SOMETHING...

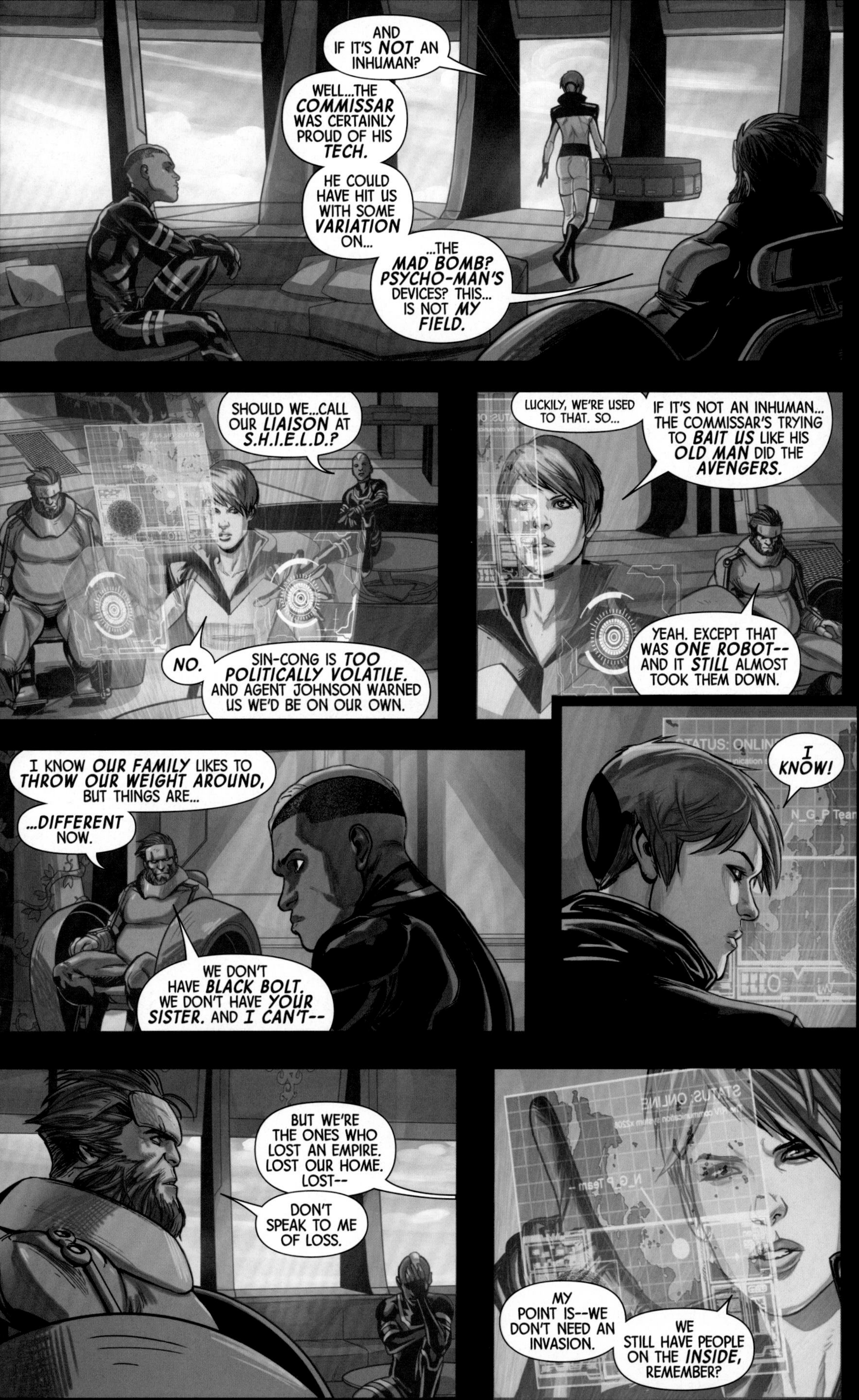

AND IF IT'S NOT AN INHUMAN?
WELL...THE COMMISSAR WAS CERTAINLY PROUD OF HIS TECH.
HE COULD HAVE HIT US WITH SOME VARIATION ON...
...THE MAD BOMB? PSYCHO-MAN'S DEVICES? THIS... IS NOT MY FIELD.
SHOULD WE...CALL OUR LIAISON AT S.H.I.E.L.D.?
NO.
SIN-CONG IS TOO POLITICALLY VOLATILE. AND AGENT JOHNSON WARNED US WE'D BE ON OUR OWN.
LUCKILY, WE'RE USED TO THAT. SO...
IF IT'S NOT AN INHUMAN... THE COMMISSAR'S TRYING TO BAIT US LIKE HIS OLD MAN DID THE AVENGERS.
YEAH. EXCEPT THAT WAS ONE ROBOT-- AND IT STILL ALMOST TOOK THEM DOWN.
I KNOW OUR FAMILY LIKES TO THROW OUR WEIGHT AROUND, BUT THINGS ARE...
...DIFFERENT NOW.
WE DON'T HAVE BLACK BOLT. WE DON'T HAVE YOUR SISTER. AND I CAN'T--
I KNOW!
STATUS: ONLINE
BUT WE'RE THE ONES WHO LOST AN EMPIRE. LOST OUR HOME. LOST--
DON'T SPEAK TO ME OF LOSS.
MY POINT IS--WE DON'T NEED AN INVASION.
WE STILL HAVE PEOPLE ON THE INSIDE, REMEMBER?

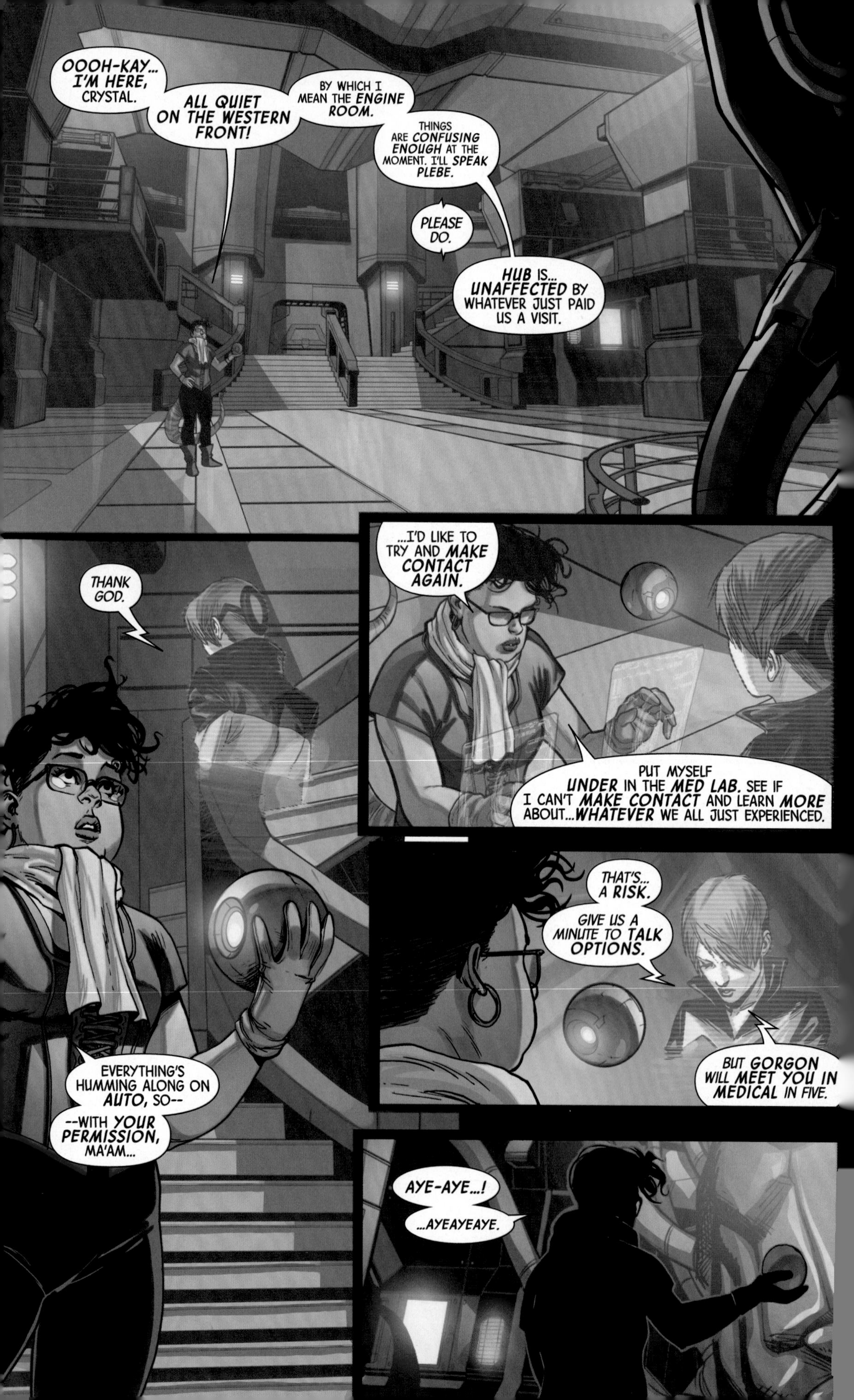
OOOH-KAY... I'M HERE, CRYSTAL.
ALL QUIET ON THE WESTERN FRONT!
BY WHICH I MEAN THE ENGINE ROOM.
THINGS ARE CONFUSING ENOUGH AT THE MOMENT. I'LL SPEAK PLEBE.
PLEASE DO.
HUB IS... UNAFFECTED BY WHATEVER JUST PAID US A VISIT.
THANK GOD.
EVERYTHING'S HUMMING ALONG ON AUTO, SO--
--WITH YOUR PERMISSION, MA'AM...
...I'D LIKE TO TRY AND MAKE CONTACT AGAIN.
PUT MYSELF UNDER IN THE MED LAB. SEE IF I CAN'T MAKE CONTACT AND LEARN MORE ABOUT...WHATEVER WE ALL JUST EXPERIENCED.
THAT'S... A RISK.
GIVE US A MINUTE TO TALK OPTIONS.
BUT GORGON WILL MEET YOU IN MEDICAL IN FIVE.
AYE-AYE...!
...AYEAYEAYE.

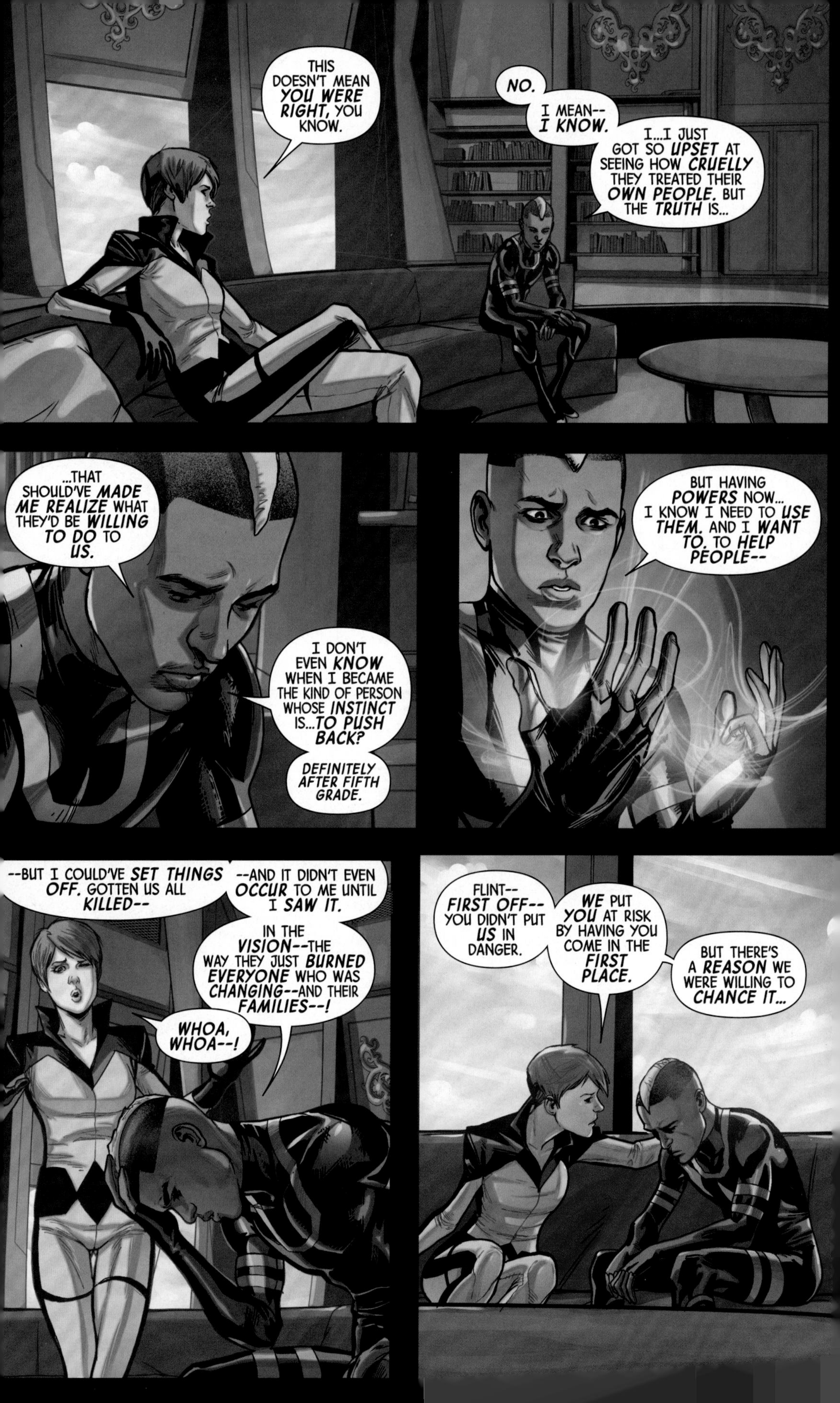
THIS DOESN'T MEAN YOU WERE RIGHT, YOU KNOW.
NO.
I MEAN-- I KNOW.
I...I JUST GOT SO UPSET AT SEEING HOW CRUELLY THEY TREATED THEIR OWN PEOPLE. BUT THE TRUTH IS...
...THAT SHOULD'VE MADE ME REALIZE WHAT THEY'D BE WILLING TO DO TO US.
I DON'T EVEN KNOW WHEN I BECAME THE KIND OF PERSON WHOSE INSTINCT IS...TO PUSH BACK?
DEFINITELY AFTER FIFTH GRADE.
BUT HAVING POWERS NOW... I KNOW I NEED TO USE THEM. AND I WANT TO. TO HELP PEOPLE--
--BUT I COULD'VE SET THINGS OFF. GOTTEN US ALL KILLED--
--AND IT DIDN'T EVEN OCCUR TO ME UNTIL I SAW IT.
IN THE VISION--THE WAY THEY JUST BURNED EVERYONE WHO WAS CHANGING--AND THEIR FAMILIES--!
WHOA, WHOA--!
FLINT-- FIRST OFF-- YOU DIDN'T PUT US IN DANGER.
WE PUT YOU AT RISK BY HAVING YOU COME IN THE FIRST PLACE.
BUT THERE'S A REASON WE WERE WILLING TO CHANCE IT...

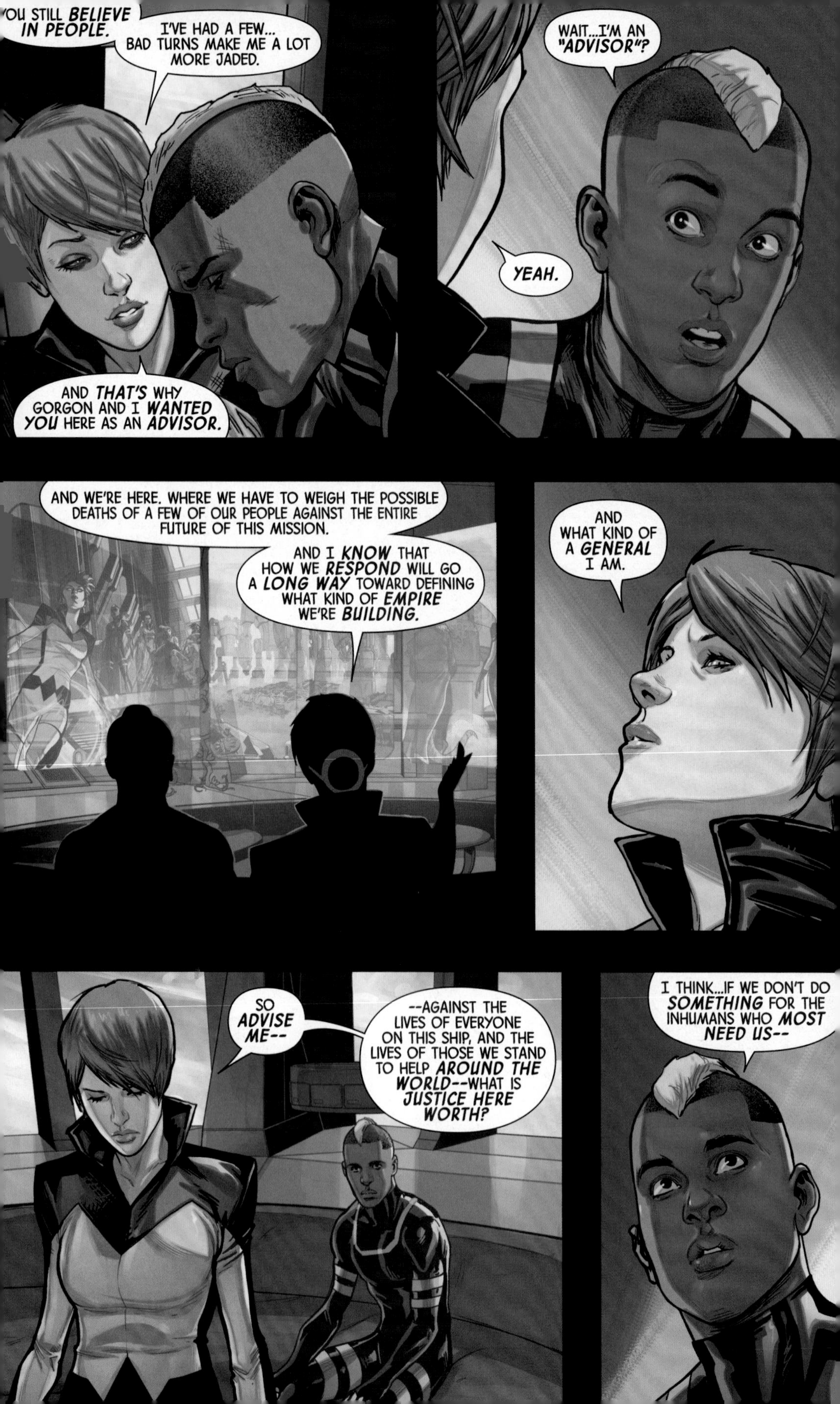
YOU STILL BELIEVE IN PEOPLE.
I'VE HAD A FEW... BAD TURNS MAKE ME A LOT MORE JADED.
AND THAT'S WHY GORGON AND I WANTED YOU HERE AS AN ADVISOR.
WAIT...I'M AN "ADVISOR"?
YEAH.
AND WE'RE HERE. WHERE WE HAVE TO WEIGH THE POSSIBLE DEATHS OF A FEW OF OUR PEOPLE AGAINST THE ENTIRE FUTURE OF THIS MISSION.
AND I KNOW THAT HOW WE RESPOND WILL GO A LONG WAY TOWARD DEFINING WHAT KIND OF EMPIRE WE'RE BUILDING.
AND WHAT KIND OF A GENERAL I AM.
SO ADVISE ME--
--AGAINST THE LIVES OF EVERYONE ON THIS SHIP, AND THE LIVES OF THOSE WE STAND TO HELP AROUND THE WORLD--WHAT IS JUSTICE HERE WORTH?
I THINK...IF WE DON'T DO SOMETHING FOR THE INHUMANS WHO MOST NEED US--

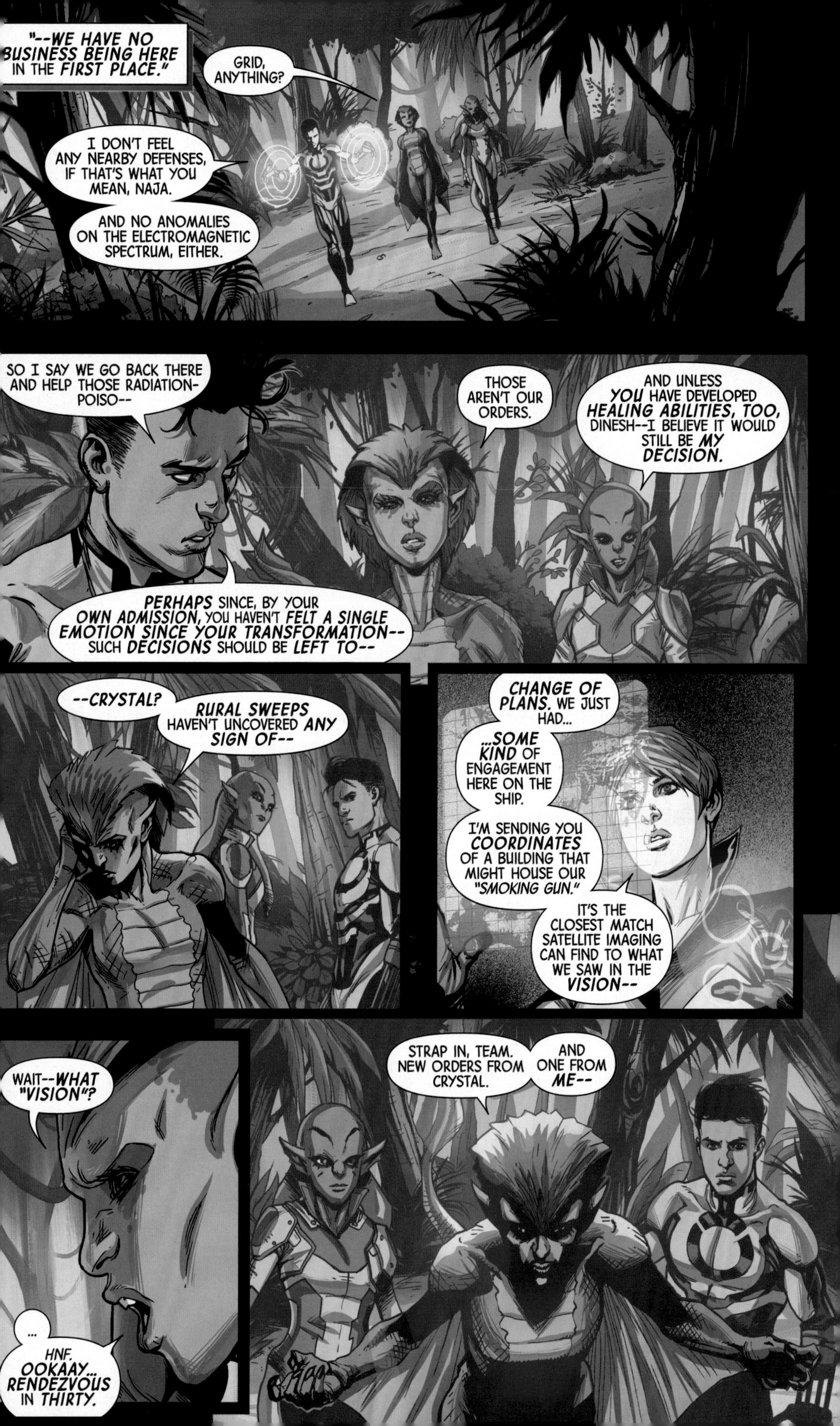

"--WE HAVE NO BUSINESS BEING HERE IN THE FIRST PLACE."
GRID, ANYTHING?
I DON'T FEEL ANY NEARBY DEFENSES, IF THAT'S WHAT YOU MEAN, NAJA.
AND NO ANOMALIES ON THE ELECTROMAGNETIC SPECTRUM, EITHER.
SO I SAY WE GO BACK THERE AND HELP THOSE RADIATION-POISO--
THOSE AREN'T OUR ORDERS.
AND UNLESS YOU HAVE DEVELOPED HEALING ABILITIES, TOO, DINESH--I BELIEVE IT WOULD STILL BE MY DECISION.
PERHAPS SINCE, BY YOUR OWN ADMISSION, YOU HAVEN'T FELT A SINGLE EMOTION SINCE YOUR TRANSFORMATION--SUCH DECISIONS SHOULD BE LEFT TO--
--CRYSTAL?
RURAL SWEEPS HAVEN'T UNCOVERED ANY SIGN OF--
CHANGE OF PLANS. WE JUST HAD...
...SOME KIND OF ENGAGEMENT HERE ON THE SHIP.
I'M SENDING YOU COORDINATES OF A BUILDING THAT MIGHT HOUSE OUR "SMOKING GUN."
IT'S THE CLOSEST MATCH SATELLITE IMAGING CAN FIND TO WHAT WE SAW IN THE VISION--
WAIT--WHAT "VISION"?
...
HNF. OOKAAY... RENDEZVOUS IN THIRTY.
STRAP IN, TEAM. NEW ORDERS FROM CRYSTAL.
AND ONE FROM ME--

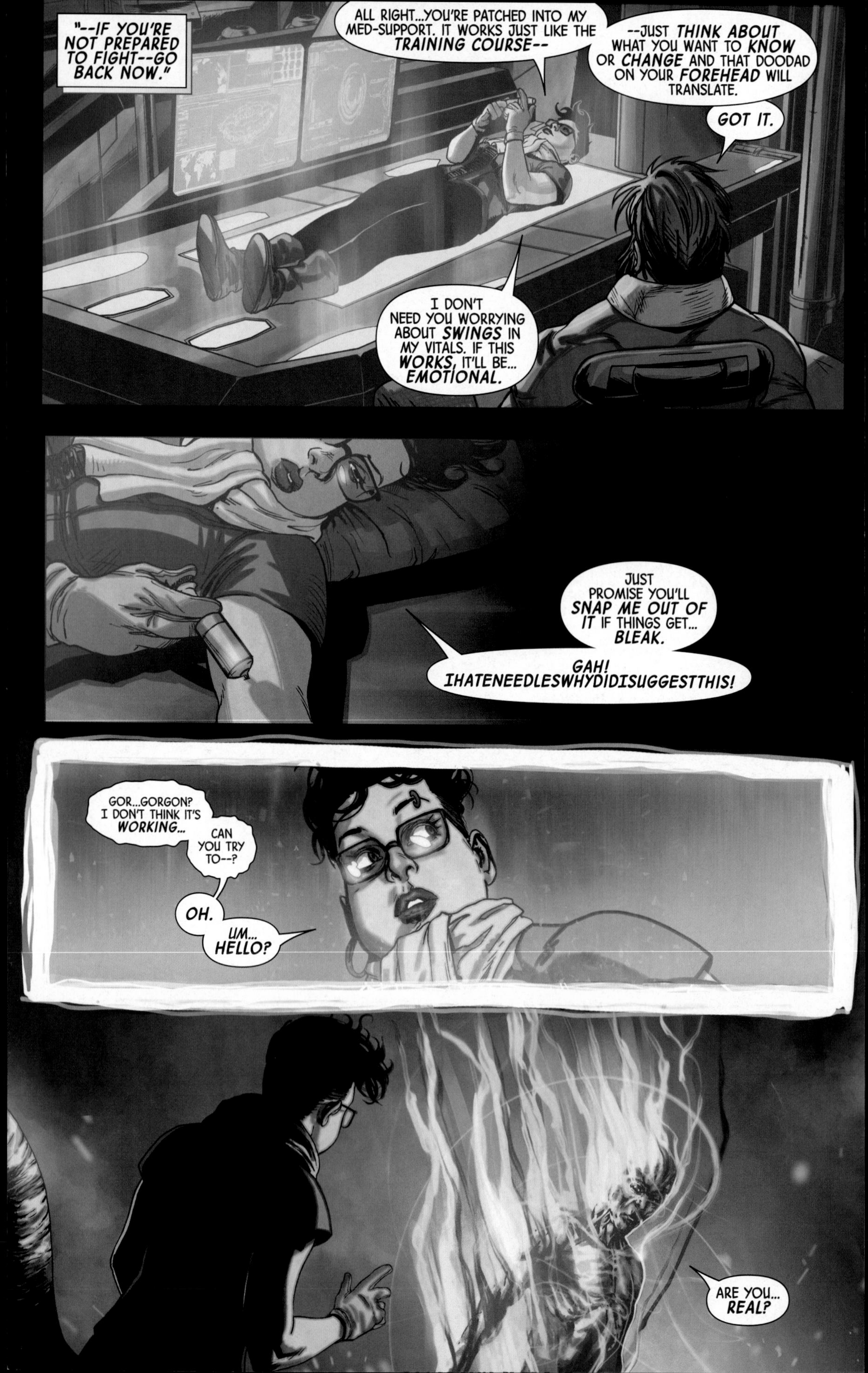
"--IF YOU'RE NOT PREPARED TO FIGHT--GO BACK NOW."
ALL RIGHT...YOU'RE PATCHED INTO MY MED-SUPPORT. IT WORKS JUST LIKE THE TRAINING COURSE--
--JUST THINK ABOUT WHAT YOU WANT TO KNOW OR CHANGE AND THAT DOODAD ON YOUR FOREHEAD WILL TRANSLATE.
GOT IT.
I DON'T NEED YOU WORRYING ABOUT SWINGS IN MY VITALS. IF THIS WORKS, IT'LL BE... EMOTIONAL.
JUST PROMISE YOU'LL SNAP ME OUT OF IT IF THINGS GET... BLEAK.
GAH! IHATENEEDLESWHYDIDISUGGESTTHIS!
GOR...GORGON? I DON'T THINK IT'S WORKING...
CAN YOU TRY TO--?
OH.
UM... HELLO?
ARE YOU... REAL?

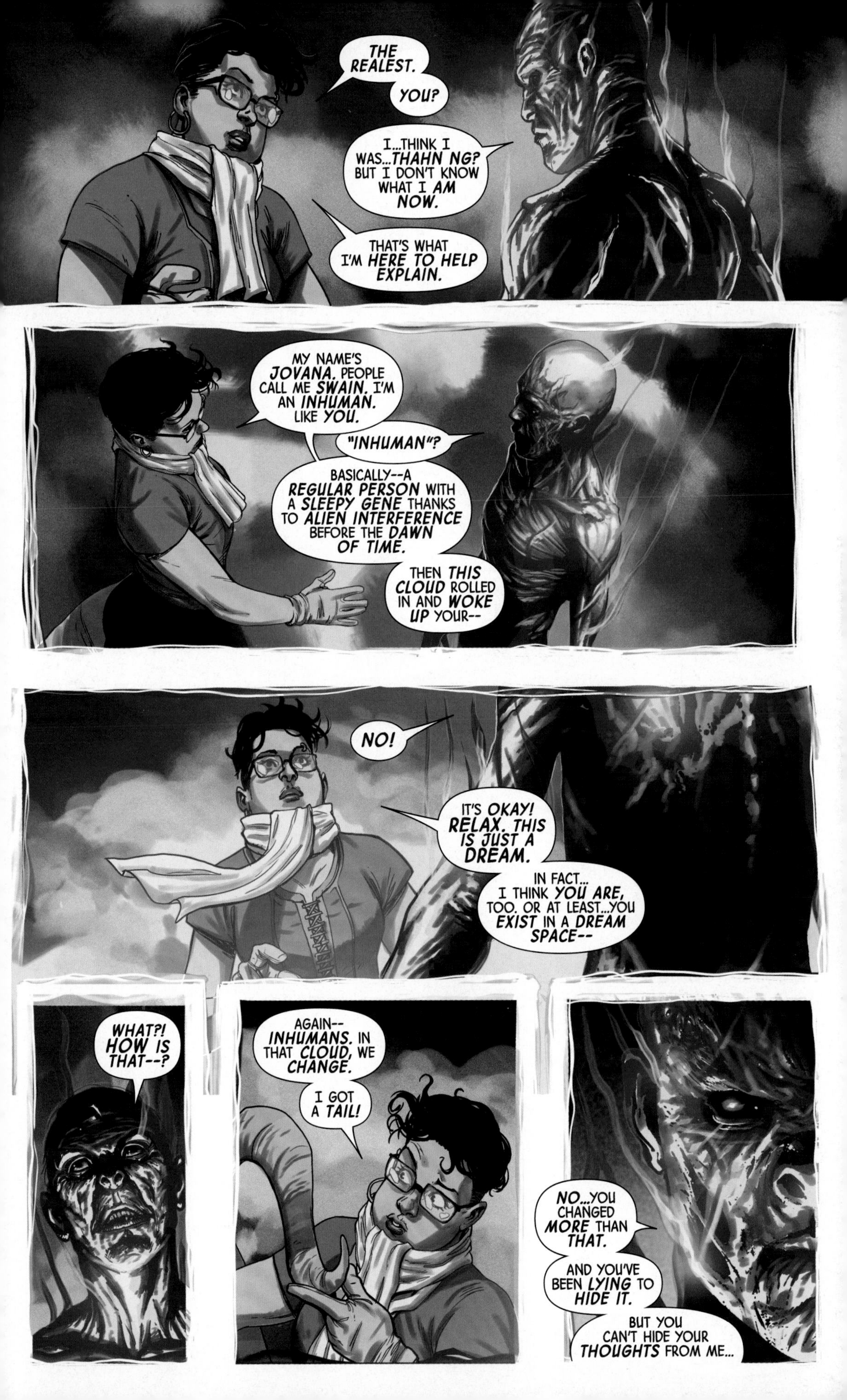
THE REALEST.
YOU?
I...THINK I WAS...THAHN NG? BUT I DON'T KNOW WHAT I AM NOW.
THAT'S WHAT I'M HERE TO HELP EXPLAIN.
MY NAME'S JOVANA. PEOPLE CALL ME SWAIN. I'M AN INHUMAN. LIKE YOU.
"INHUMAN"?
BASICALLY--A REGULAR PERSON WITH A SLEEPY GENE THANKS TO ALIEN INTERFERENCE BEFORE THE DAWN OF TIME.
THEN THIS CLOUD ROLLED IN AND WOKE UP YOUR--
NO!
IT'S OKAY! RELAX. THIS IS JUST A DREAM.
IN FACT... I THINK YOU ARE, TOO. OR AT LEAST...YOU EXIST IN A DREAM SPACE--
WHAT?! HOW IS THAT--?
AGAIN--INHUMANS. IN THAT CLOUD, WE CHANGE.
I GOT A TAIL!
NO...YOU CHANGED MORE THAN THAT.
AND YOU'VE BEEN LYING TO HIDE IT.
BUT YOU CAN'T HIDE YOUR THOUGHTS FROM ME...

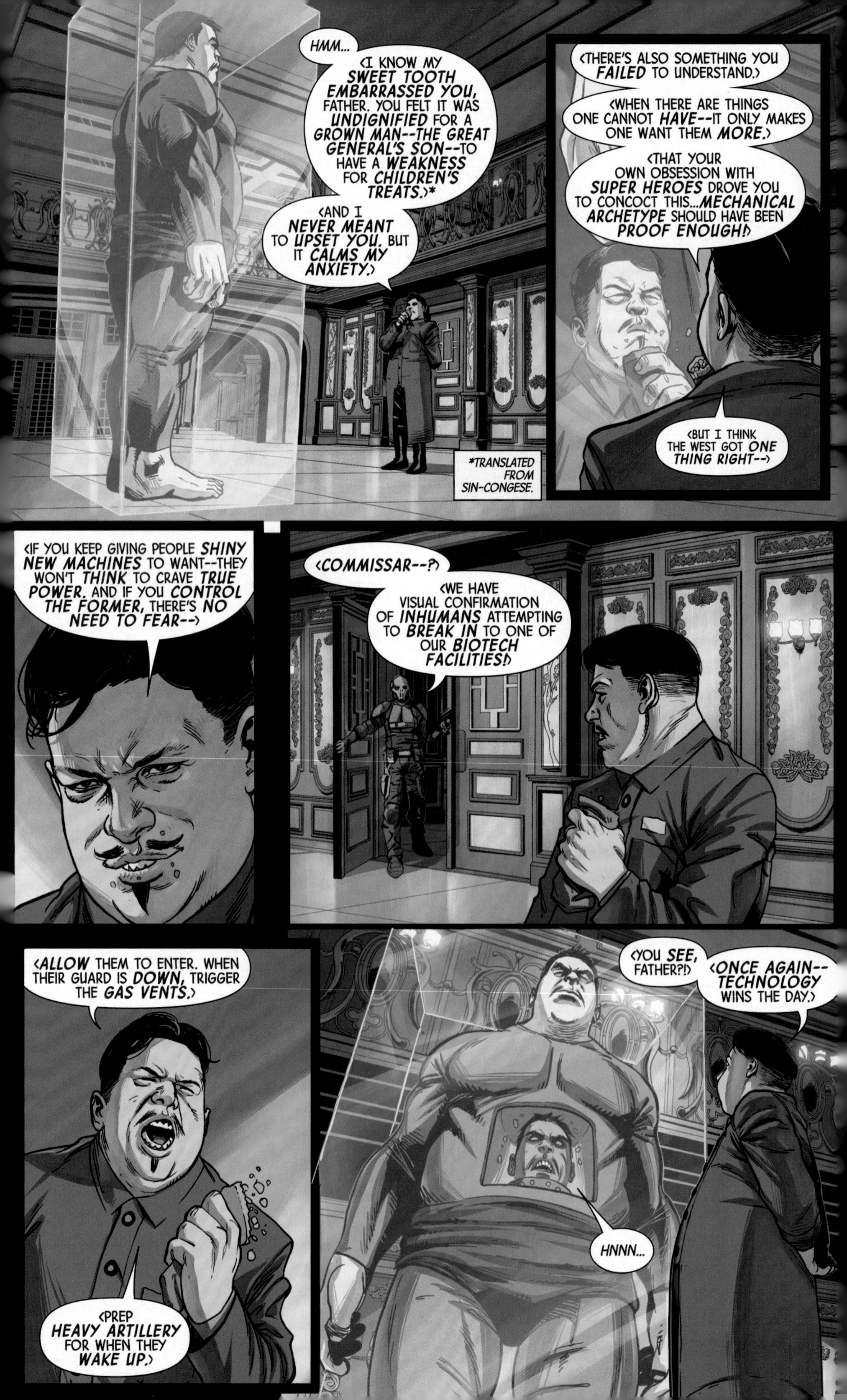
HMM...
<I KNOW MY SWEET TOOTH EMBARRASSED YOU, FATHER. YOU FELT IT WAS UNDIGNIFIED FOR A GROWN MAN--THE GREAT GENERAL'S SON--TO HAVE A WEAKNESS FOR CHILDREN'S TREATS.>*
<AND I NEVER MEANT TO UPSET YOU. BUT IT CALMS MY ANXIETY.>
*TRANSLATED FROM SIN-CONGESE.
<THERE'S ALSO SOMETHING YOU FAILED TO UNDERSTAND.>
<WHEN THERE ARE THINGS ONE CANNOT HAVE--IT ONLY MAKES ONE WANT THEM MORE.>
<THAT YOUR OWN OBSESSION WITH SUPER HEROES DROVE YOU TO CONCOCT THIS...MECHANICAL ARCHETYPE SHOULD HAVE BEEN PROOF ENOUGH!>
<BUT I THINK THE WEST GOT ONE THING RIGHT-->
<IF YOU KEEP GIVING PEOPLE SHINY NEW MACHINES TO WANT--THEY WON'T THINK TO CRAVE TRUE POWER. AND IF YOU CONTROL THE FORMER, THERE'S NO NEED TO FEAR-->
<COMMISSAR--?>
<WE HAVE VISUAL CONFIRMATION OF INHUMANS ATTEMPTING TO BREAK IN TO ONE OF OUR BIOTECH FACILITIES!>
<ALLOW THEM TO ENTER. WHEN THEIR GUARD IS DOWN, TRIGGER THE GAS VENTS.>
<PREP HEAVY ARTILLERY FOR WHEN THEY WAKE UP.>
<YOU SEE, FATHER?!>
<ONCE AGAIN--TECHNOLOGY WINS THE DAY.>
HNNN...

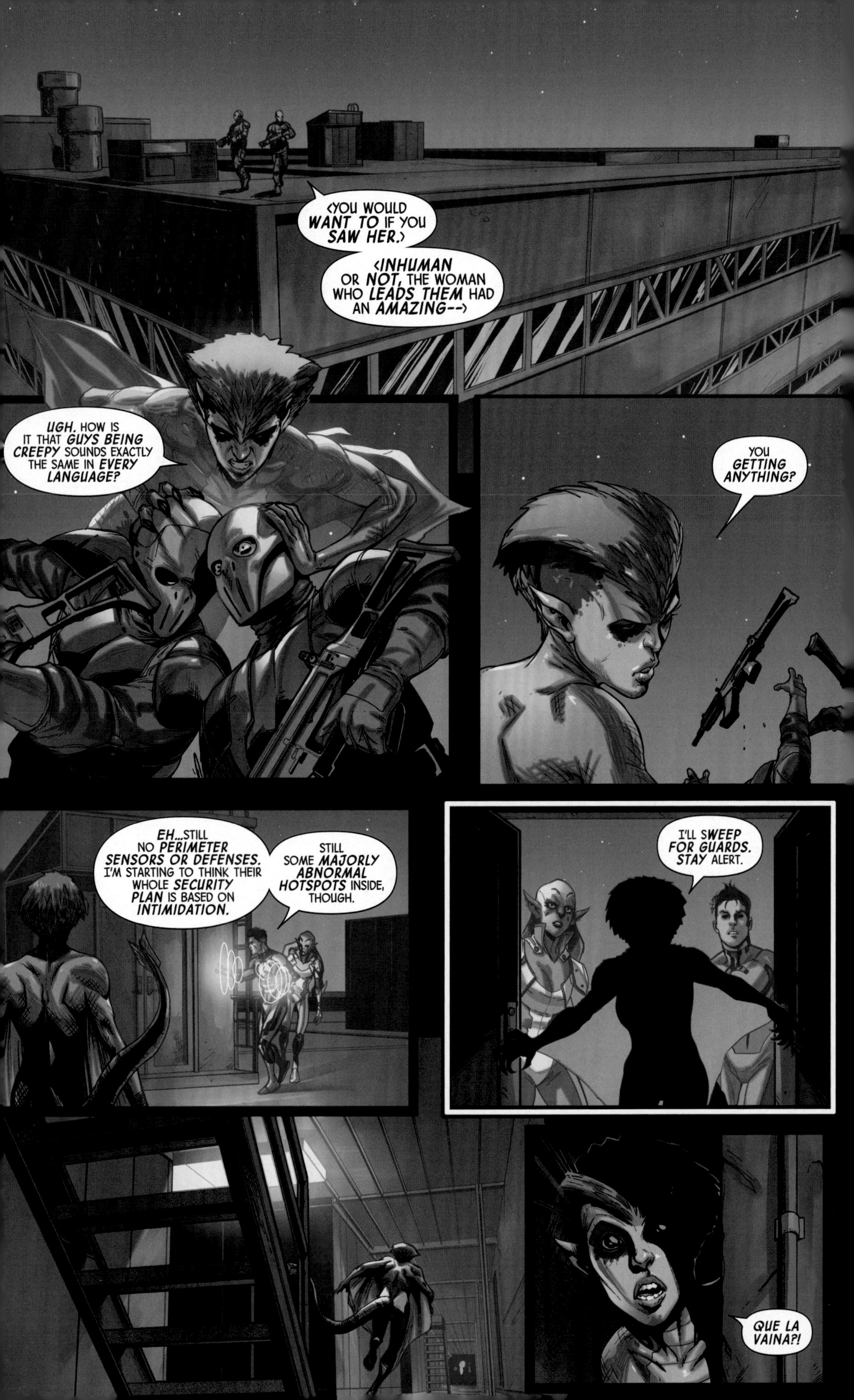
‹YOU WOULD WANT TO IF YOU SAW HER.›
‹INHUMAN OR NOT, THE WOMAN WHO LEADS THEM HAD AN AMAZING--›
UGH. HOW IS IT THAT GUYS BEING CREEPY SOUNDS EXACTLY THE SAME IN EVERY LANGUAGE?
YOU GETTING ANYTHING?
EH...STILL NO PERIMETER SENSORS OR DEFENSES. I'M STARTING TO THINK THEIR WHOLE SECURITY PLAN IS BASED ON INTIMIDATION.
STILL SOME MAJORLY ABNORMAL HOTSPOTS INSIDE, THOUGH.
I'LL SWEEP FOR GUARDS. STAY ALERT.
QUE LA VAINA?!

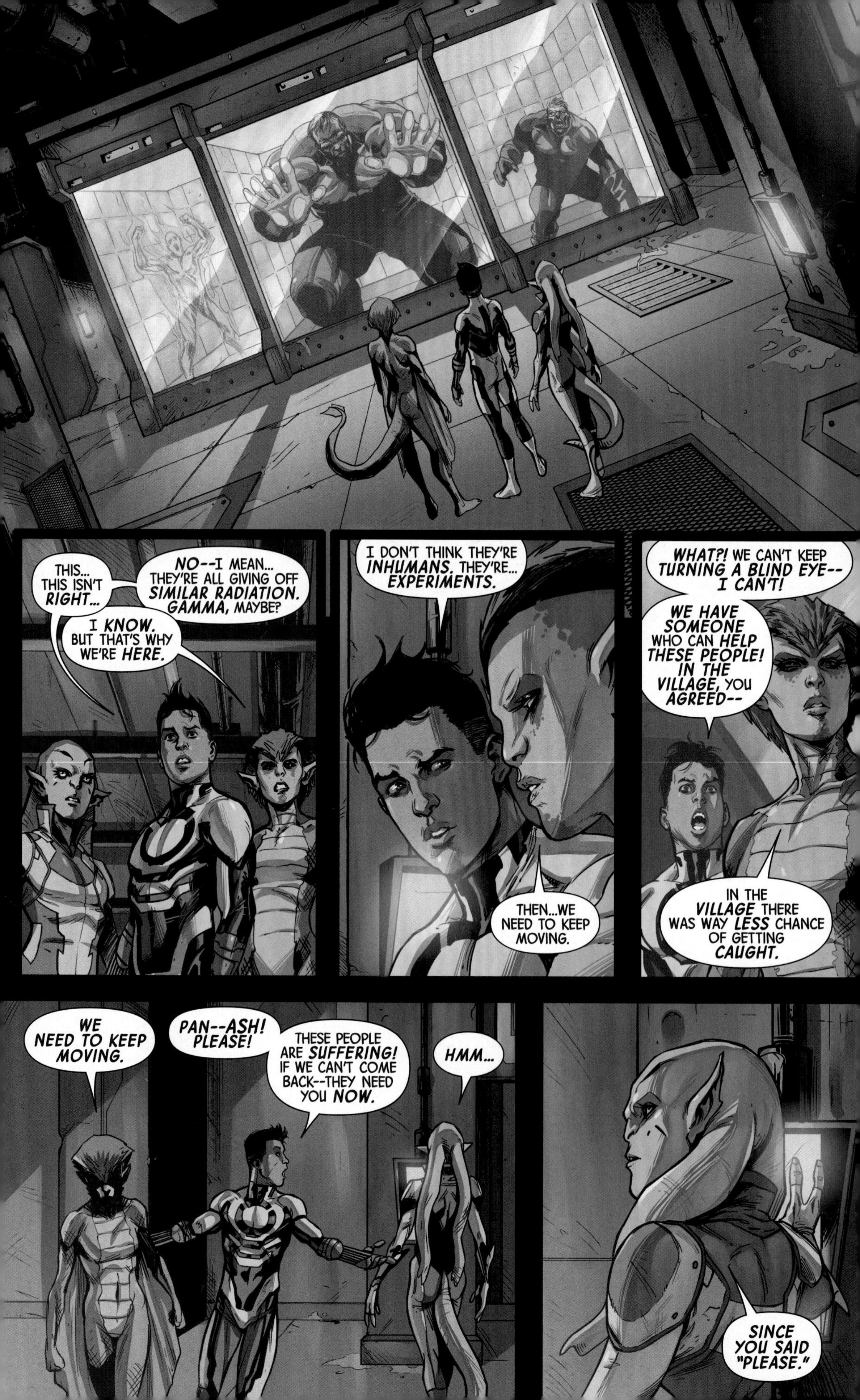
THIS... THIS ISN'T RIGHT...
NO--I MEAN... THEY'RE ALL GIVING OFF SIMILAR RADIATION. GAMMA, MAYBE?
I KNOW. BUT THAT'S WHY WE'RE HERE.
I DON'T THINK THEY'RE INHUMANS. THEY'RE... EXPERIMENTS.
THEN...WE NEED TO KEEP MOVING.
WHAT?! WE CAN'T KEEP TURNING A BLIND EYE-- I CAN'T!
WE HAVE SOMEONE WHO CAN HELP THESE PEOPLE! IN THE VILLAGE, YOU AGREED--
IN THE VILLAGE THERE WAS WAY LESS CHANCE OF GETTING CAUGHT.
WE NEED TO KEEP MOVING.
PAN--ASH! PLEASE!
THESE PEOPLE ARE SUFFERING! IF WE CAN'T COME BACK--THEY NEED YOU NOW.
HMM...
SINCE YOU SAID "PLEASE."

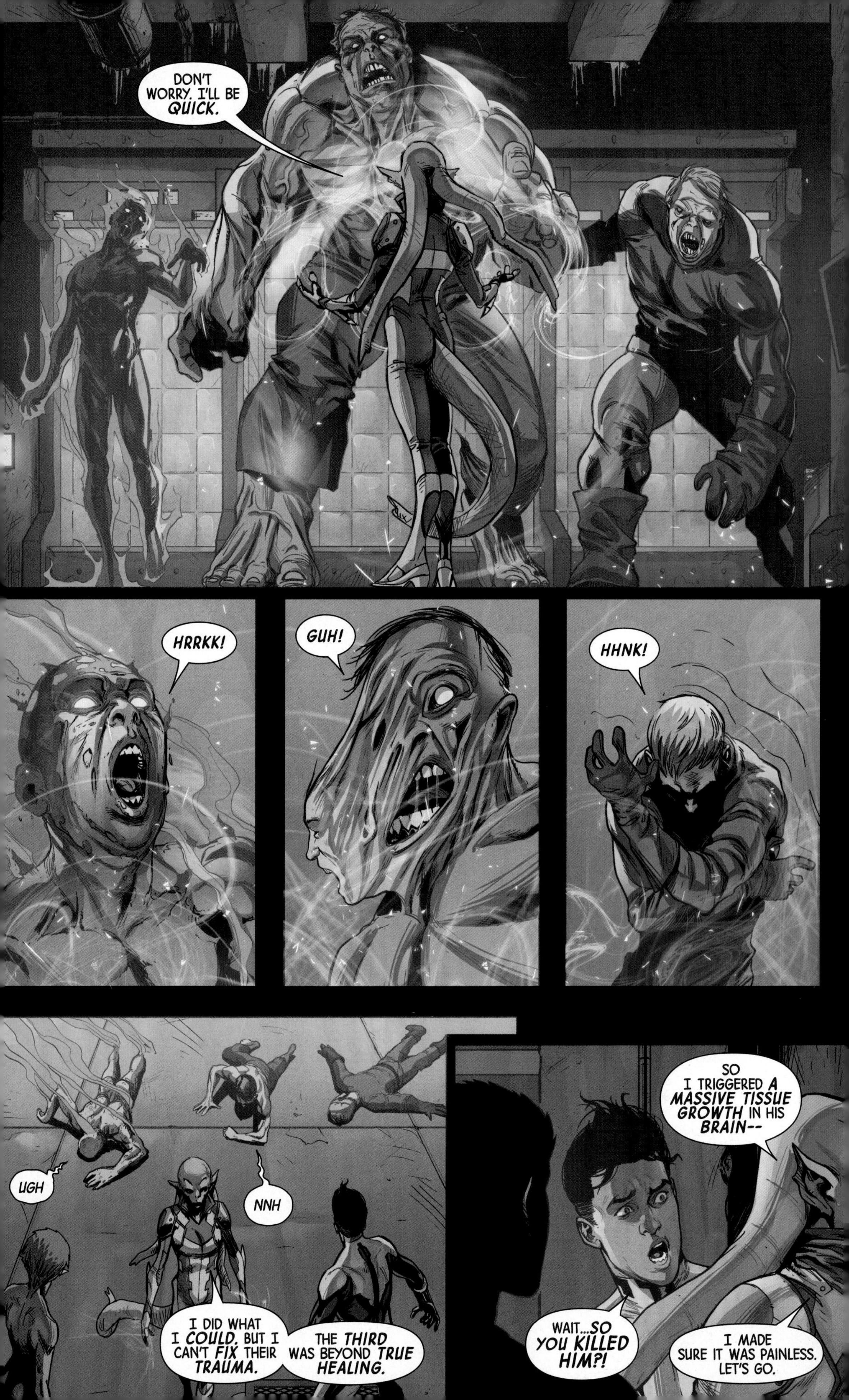
DON'T WORRY. I'LL BE QUICK.
HRRKK!
GUH!
HHNK!
UGH
NNH
I DID WHAT I COULD. BUT I CAN'T FIX THEIR TRAUMA.
THE THIRD WAS BEYOND TRUE HEALING.
SO I TRIGGERED A MASSIVE TISSUE GROWTH IN HIS BRAIN--
WAIT...SO YOU KILLED HIM?!
I MADE SURE IT WAS PAINLESS. LET'S GO.

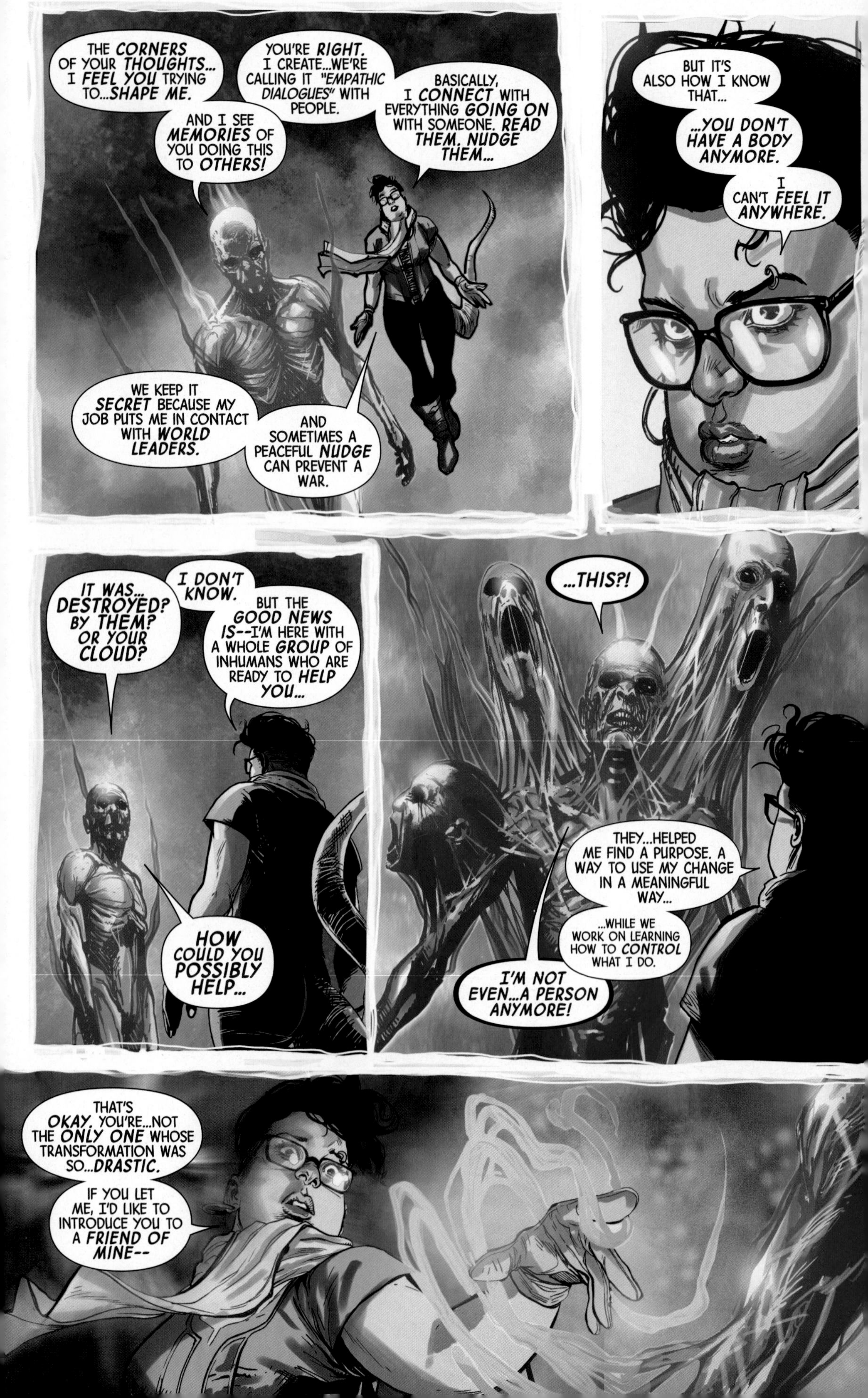
THE CORNERS OF YOUR THOUGHTS... I FEEL YOU TRYING TO...SHAPE ME.
AND I SEE MEMORIES OF YOU DOING THIS TO OTHERS!
YOU'RE RIGHT. I CREATE...WE'RE CALLING IT "EMPATHIC DIALOGUES" WITH PEOPLE.
BASICALLY, I CONNECT WITH EVERYTHING GOING ON WITH SOMEONE. READ THEM. NUDGE THEM...
WE KEEP IT SECRET BECAUSE MY JOB PUTS ME IN CONTACT WITH WORLD LEADERS.
AND SOMETIMES A PEACEFUL NUDGE CAN PREVENT A WAR.
BUT IT'S ALSO HOW I KNOW THAT...
...YOU DON'T HAVE A BODY ANYMORE.
I CAN'T FEEL IT ANYWHERE.
IT WAS... DESTROYED? BY THEM? OR YOUR CLOUD?
I DON'T KNOW.
BUT THE GOOD NEWS IS--I'M HERE WITH A WHOLE GROUP OF INHUMANS WHO ARE READY TO HELP YOU...
HOW COULD YOU POSSIBLY HELP...
...THIS?!
I'M NOT EVEN...A PERSON ANYMORE!
THEY...HELPED ME FIND A PURPOSE. A WAY TO USE MY CHANGE IN A MEANINGFUL WAY...
...WHILE WE WORK ON LEARNING HOW TO CONTROL WHAT I DO.
THAT'S OKAY. YOU'RE...NOT THE ONLY ONE WHOSE TRANSFORMATION WAS SO...DRASTIC.
IF YOU LET ME, I'D LIKE TO INTRODUCE YOU TO A FRIEND OF MINE--

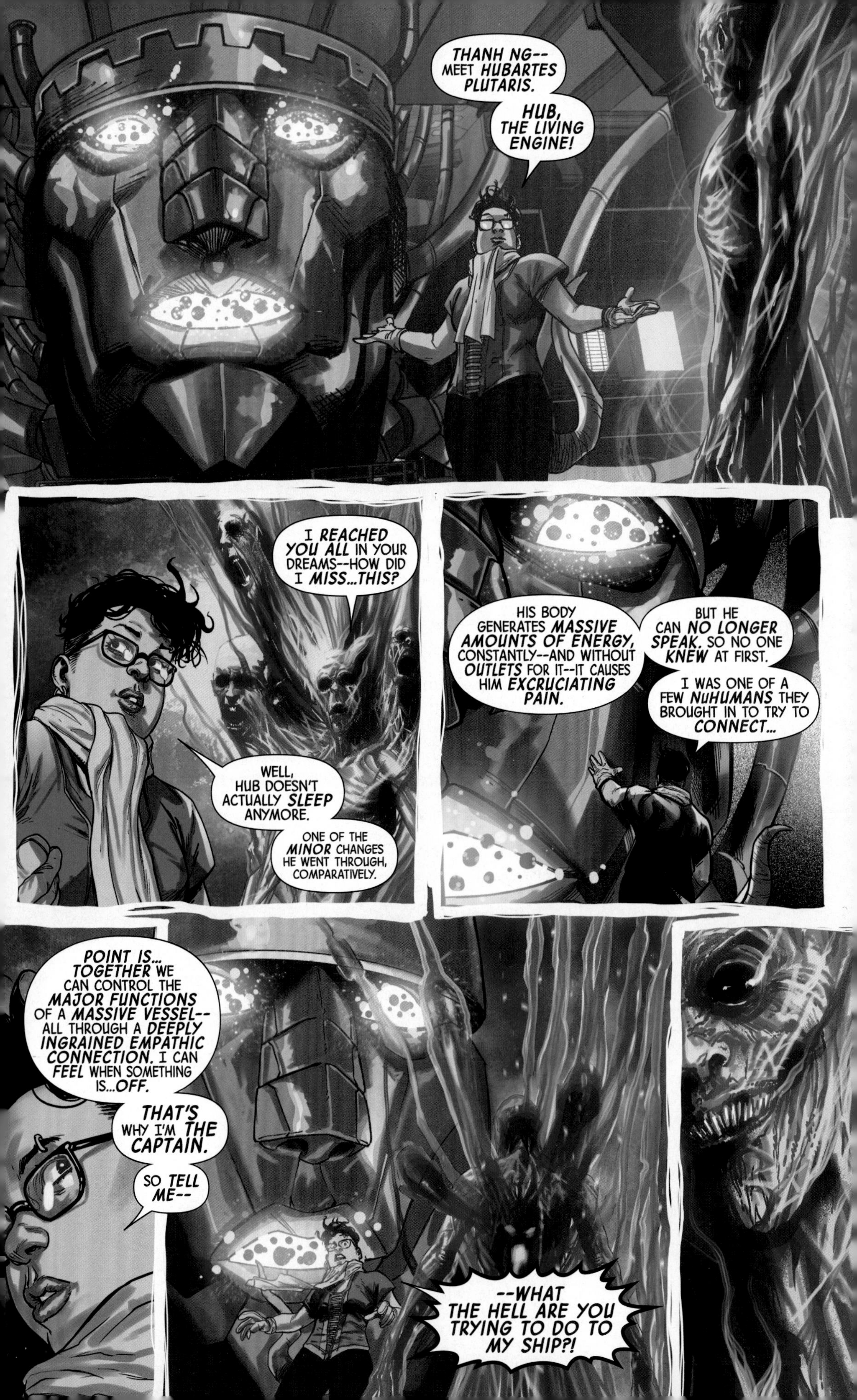
THANH NG--MEET HUBARTES PLUTARIS.
HUB, THE LIVING ENGINE!
I REACHED YOU ALL IN YOUR DREAMS--HOW DID I MISS...THIS?
WELL, HUB DOESN'T ACTUALLY SLEEP ANYMORE.
ONE OF THE MINOR CHANGES HE WENT THROUGH, COMPARATIVELY.
HIS BODY GENERATES MASSIVE AMOUNTS OF ENERGY, CONSTANTLY--AND WITHOUT OUTLETS FOR IT--IT CAUSES HIM EXCRUCIATING PAIN.
BUT HE CAN NO LONGER SPEAK, SO NO ONE KNEW AT FIRST.
I WAS ONE OF A FEW NuHUMANS THEY BROUGHT IN TO TRY TO CONNECT...
POINT IS... TOGETHER WE CAN CONTROL THE MAJOR FUNCTIONS OF A MASSIVE VESSEL--ALL THROUGH A DEEPLY INGRAINED EMPATHIC CONNECTION. I CAN FEEL WHEN SOMETHING IS...OFF.
THAT'S WHY I'M THE CAPTAIN.
SO TELL ME--
--WHAT THE HELL ARE YOU TRYING TO DO TO MY SHIP?!

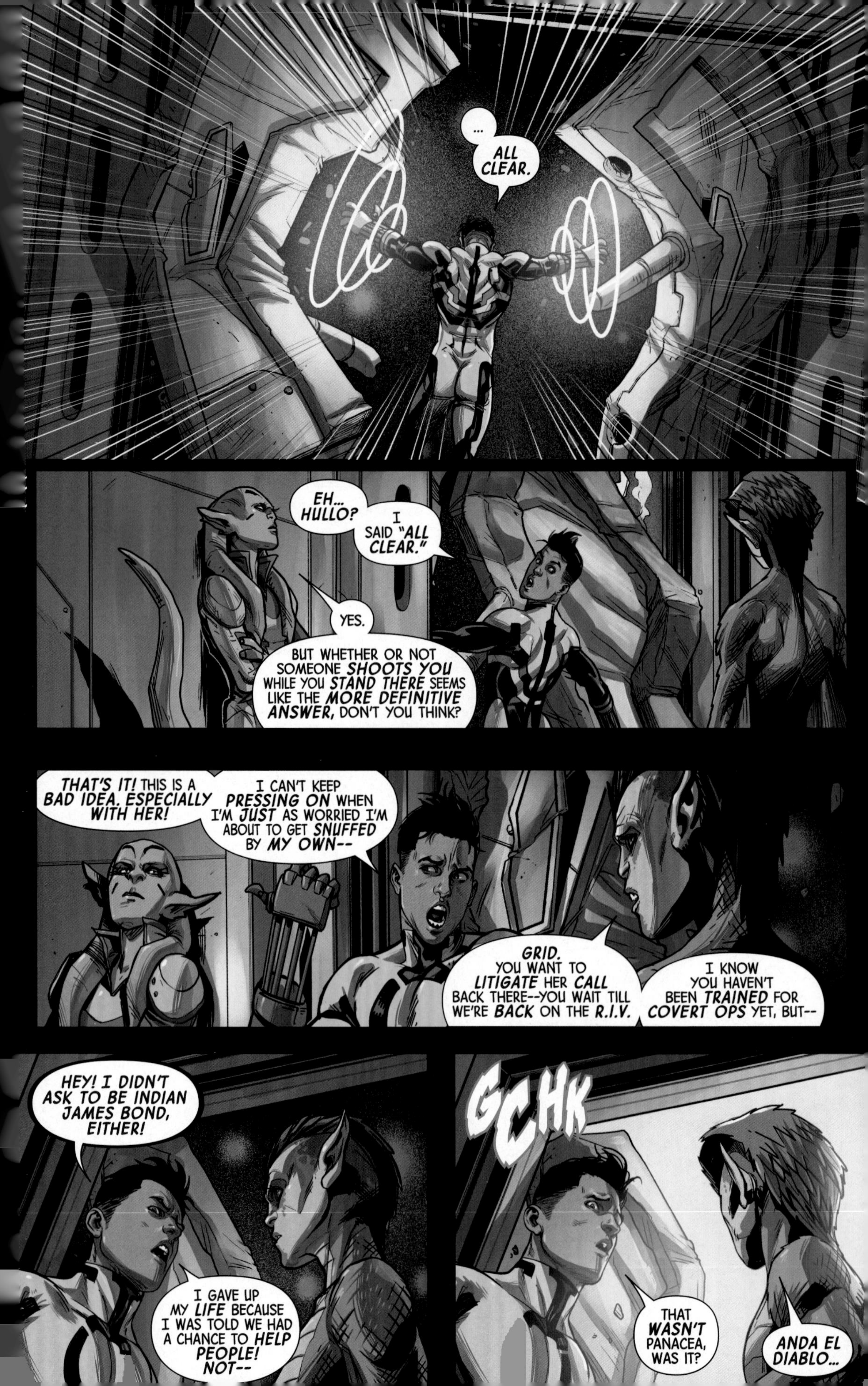

...
ALL CLEAR.
EH... HULLO?
I SAID "ALL CLEAR."
YES.
BUT WHETHER OR NOT SOMEONE SHOOTS YOU WHILE YOU STAND THERE SEEMS LIKE THE MORE DEFINITIVE ANSWER, DON'T YOU THINK?
THAT'S IT! THIS IS A BAD IDEA. ESPECIALLY WITH HER!
I CAN'T KEEP PRESSING ON WHEN I'M JUST AS WORRIED I'M ABOUT TO GET SNUFFED BY MY OWN--
GRID. YOU WANT TO LITIGATE HER CALL BACK THERE--YOU WAIT TILL WE'RE BACK ON THE R.I.V.
I KNOW YOU HAVEN'T BEEN TRAINED FOR COVERT OPS YET, BUT--
HEY! I DIDN'T ASK TO BE INDIAN JAMES BOND, EITHER!
I GAVE UP MY LIFE BECAUSE I WAS TOLD WE HAD A CHANCE TO HELP PEOPLE! NOT--
GCHK
THAT WASN'T PANACEA, WAS IT?
ANDA EL DIABLO...

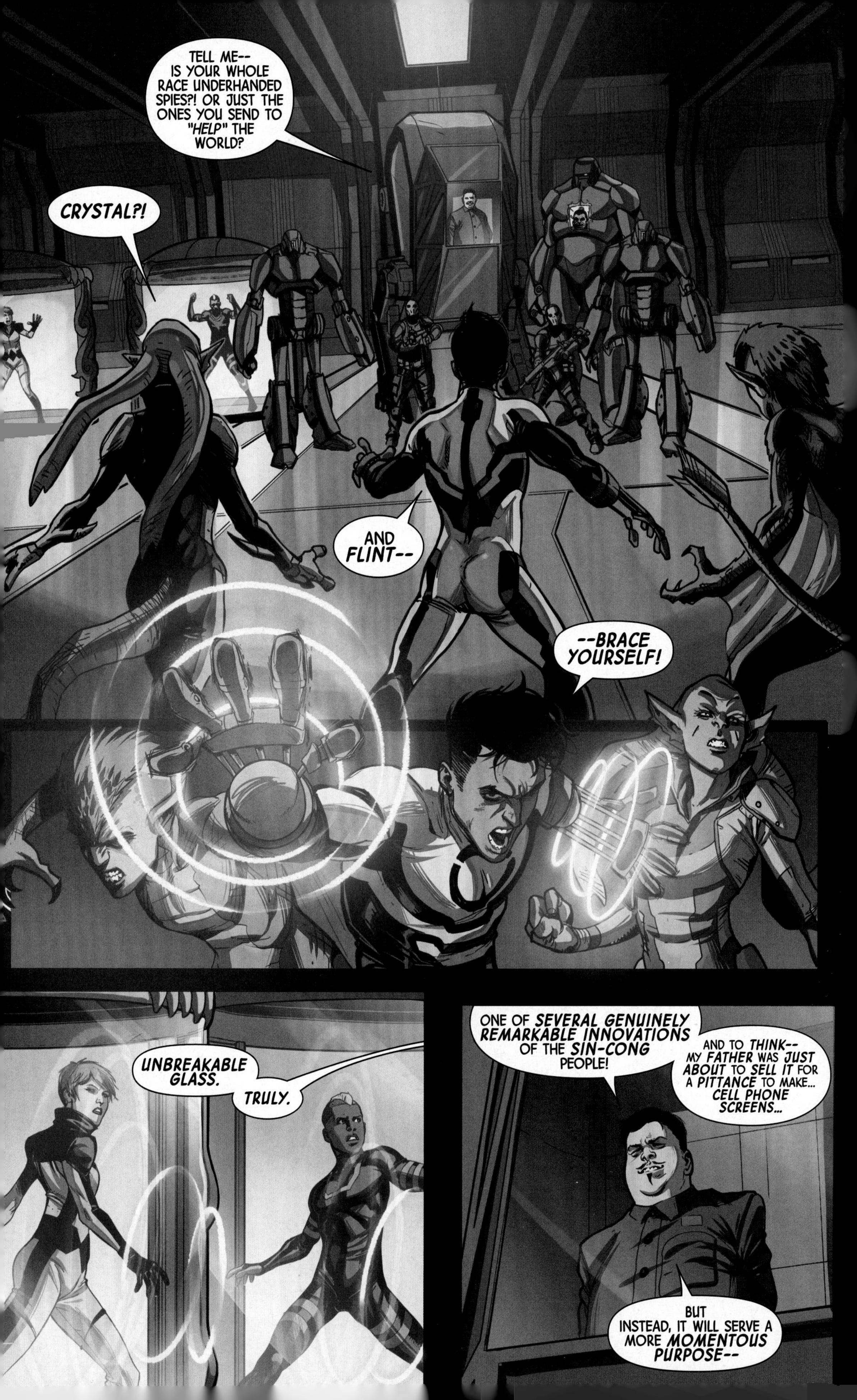
TELL ME-- IS YOUR WHOLE RACE UNDERHANDED SPIES?! OR JUST THE ONES YOU SEND TO "HELP" THE WORLD?
CRYSTAL?!
AND FLINT--
--BRACE YOURSELF!
UNBREAKABLE GLASS.
TRULY.
ONE OF SEVERAL GENUINELY REMARKABLE INNOVATIONS OF THE SIN-CONG PEOPLE!
AND TO THINK-- MY FATHER WAS JUST ABOUT TO SELL IT FOR A PITTANCE TO MAKE... CELL PHONE SCREENS...
BUT INSTEAD, IT WILL SERVE A MORE MOMENTOUS PURPOSE--

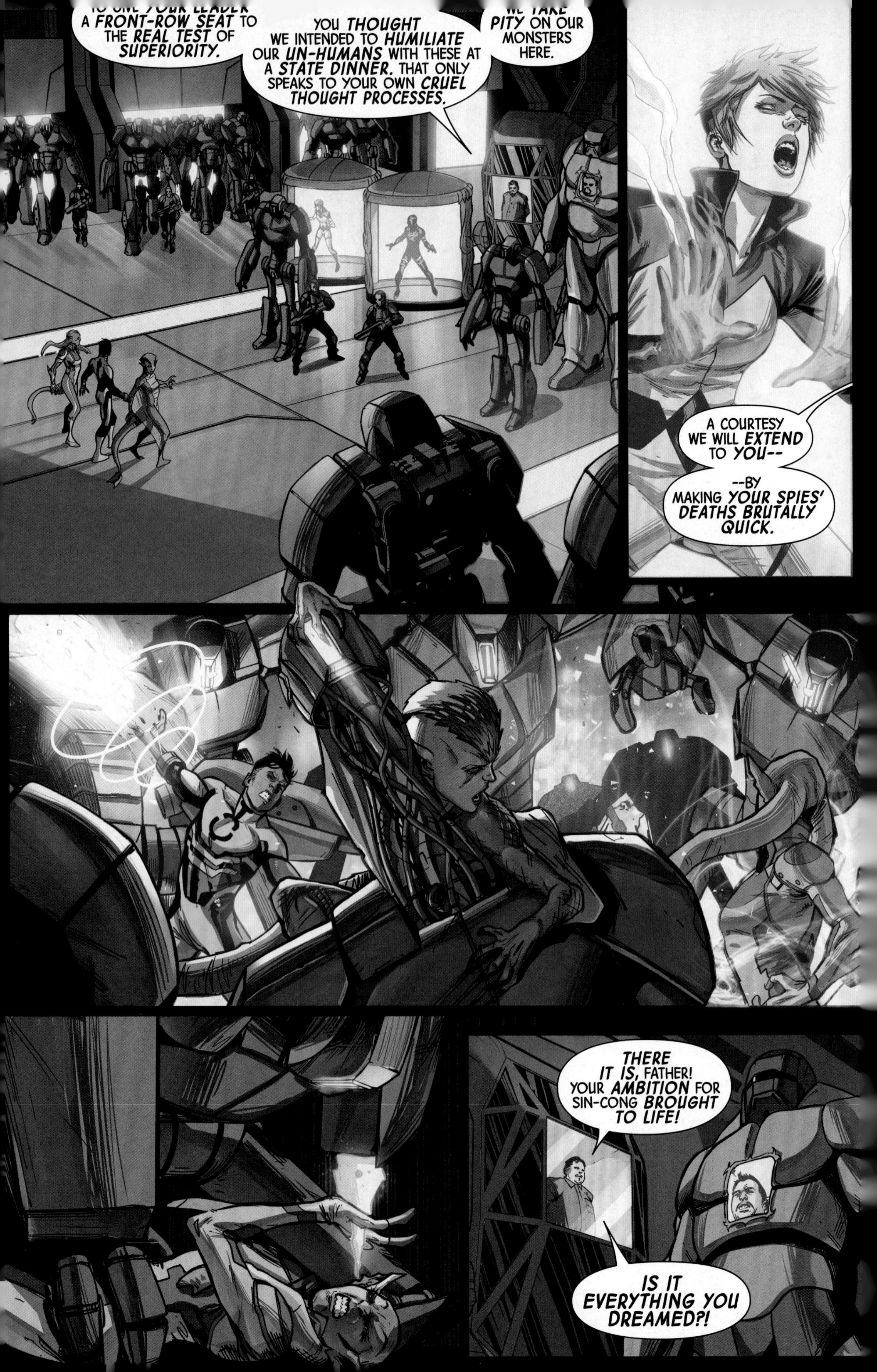
A FRONT-ROW SEAT TO THE REAL TEST OF SUPERIORITY.
YOU THOUGHT WE INTENDED TO HUMILIATE OUR UN-HUMANS WITH THESE AT A STATE DINNER. THAT ONLY SPEAKS TO YOUR OWN CRUEL THOUGHT PROCESSES.
PITY ON OUR MONSTERS HERE.
A COURTESY WE WILL EXTEND TO YOU--
--BY MAKING YOUR SPIES' DEATHS BRUTALLY QUICK.
THERE IT IS, FATHER! YOUR AMBITION FOR SIN-CONG BROUGHT TO LIFE!
IS IT EVERYTHING YOU DREAMED?!

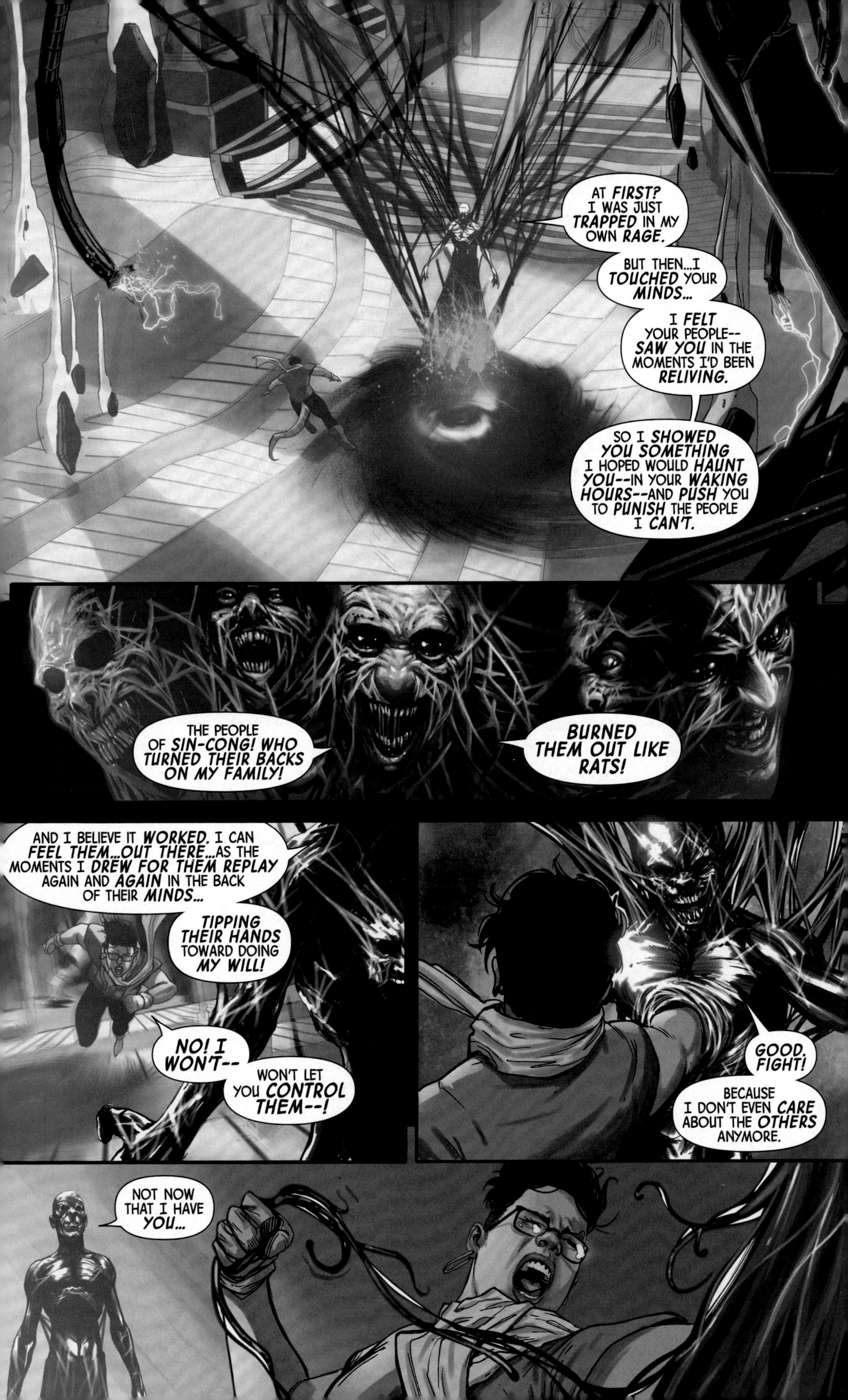
AT FIRST? I WAS JUST TRAPPED IN MY OWN RAGE.
BUT THEN...I TOUCHED YOUR MINDS...
I FELT YOUR PEOPLE-- SAW YOU IN THE MOMENTS I'D BEEN RELIVING.
SO I SHOWED YOU SOMETHING I HOPED WOULD HAUNT YOU--IN YOUR WAKING HOURS--AND PUSH YOU TO PUNISH THE PEOPLE I CAN'T.
THE PEOPLE OF SIN-CONG! WHO TURNED THEIR BACKS ON MY FAMILY!
BURNED THEM OUT LIKE RATS!
AND I BELIEVE IT WORKED. I CAN FEEL THEM...OUT THERE...AS THE MOMENTS I DREW FOR THEM REPLAY AGAIN AND AGAIN IN THE BACK OF THEIR MINDS...
TIPPING THEIR HANDS TOWARD DOING MY WILL!
NO! I WON'T--
WON'T LET YOU CONTROL THEM--!
GOOD. FIGHT!
BECAUSE I DON'T EVEN CARE ABOUT THE OTHERS ANYMORE.
NOT NOW THAT I HAVE YOU...

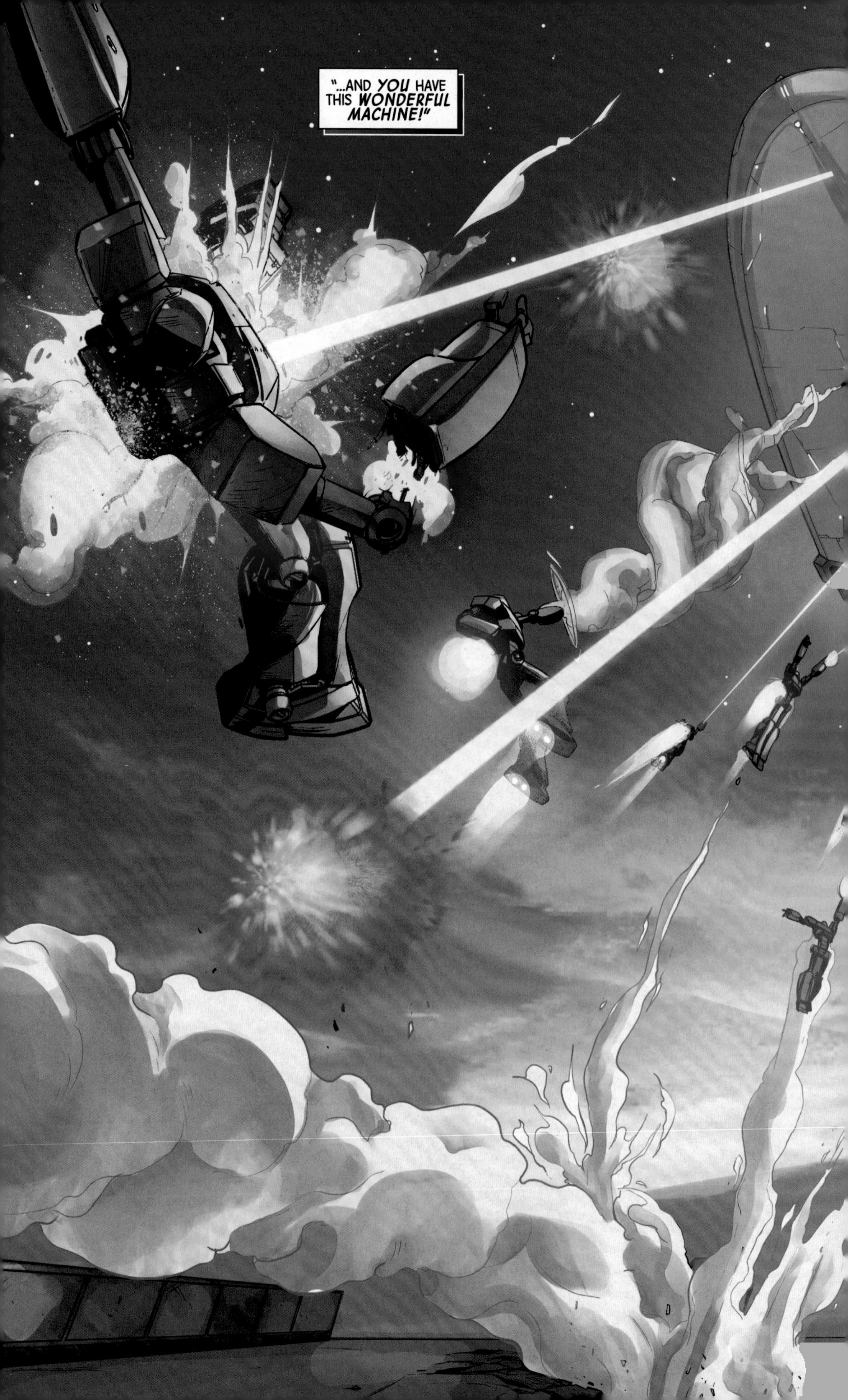
"...AND YOU HAVE THIS WONDERFUL MACHINE!"

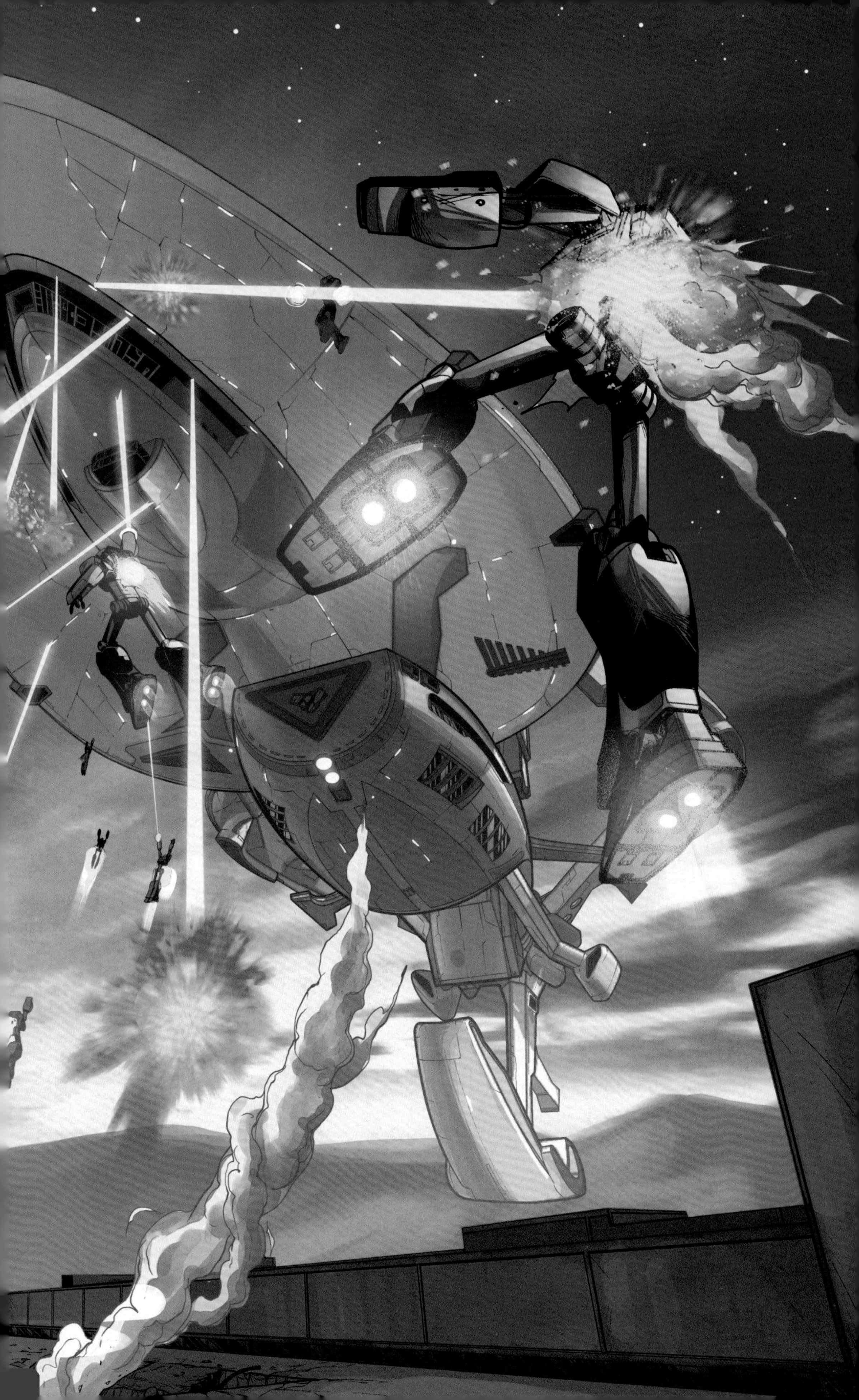

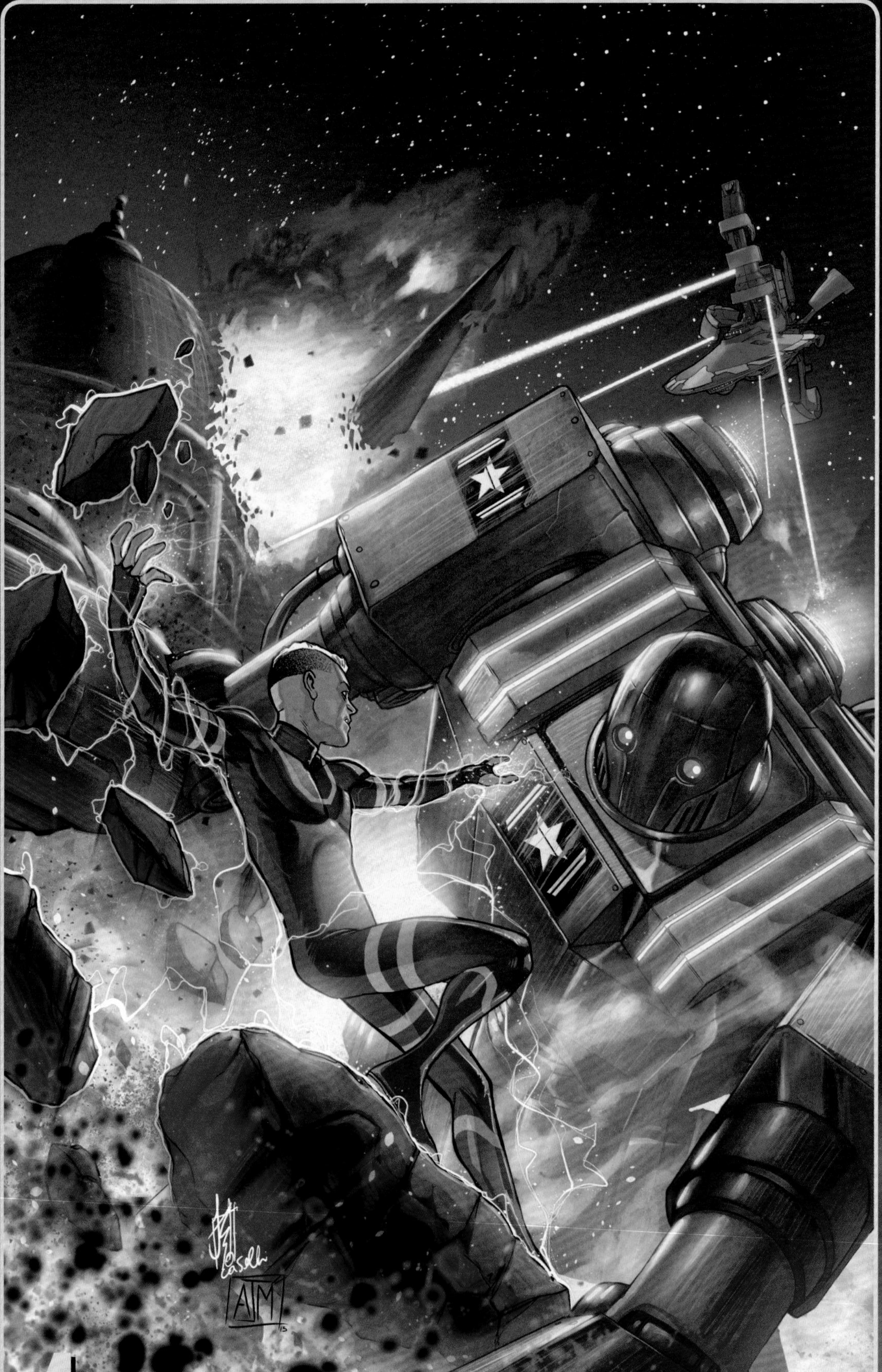

4

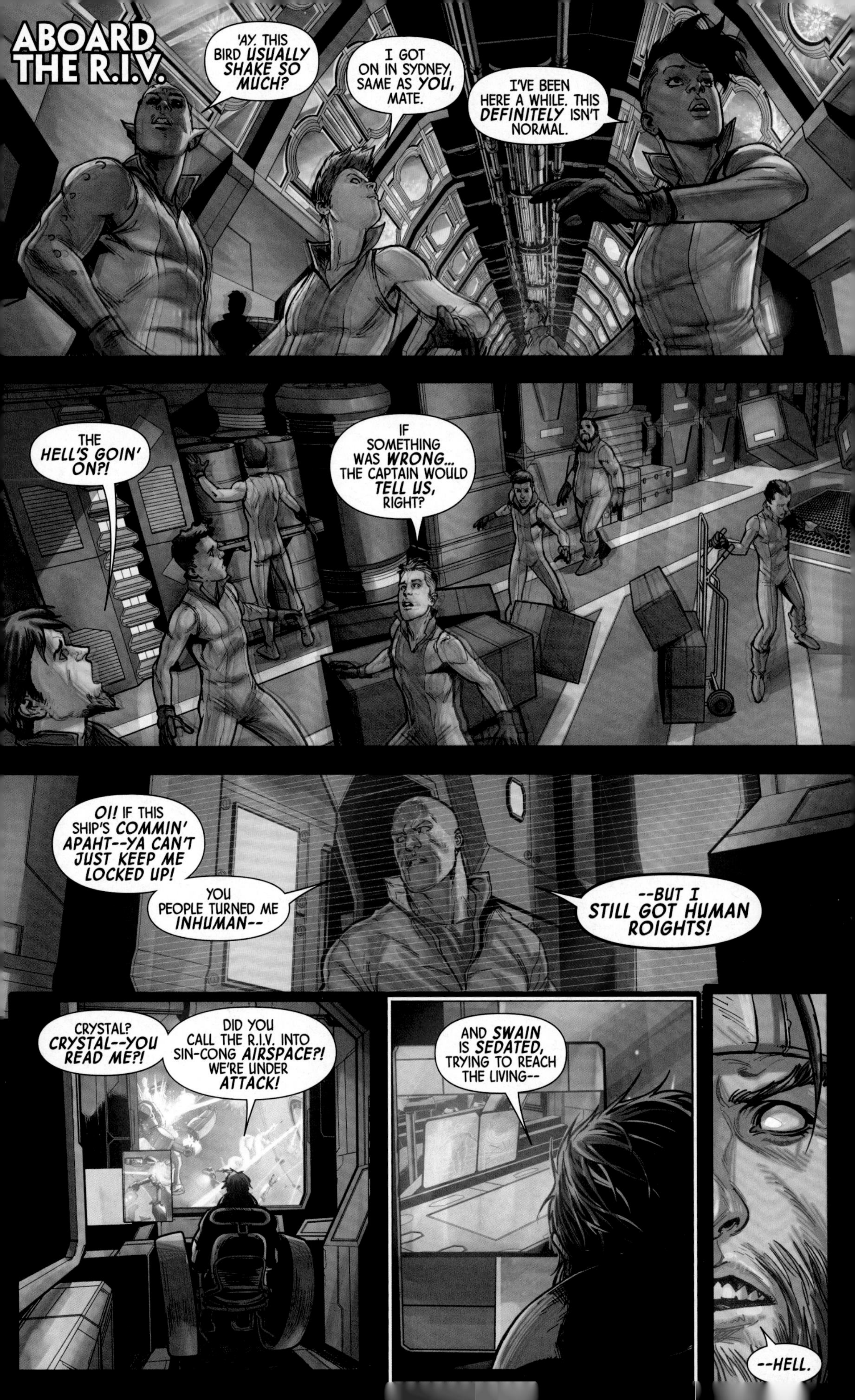
ABOARD THE R.I.V.
'AY. THIS BIRD USUALLY SHAKE SO MUCH?
I GOT ON IN SYDNEY, SAME AS YOU, MATE.
I'VE BEEN HERE A WHILE. THIS DEFINITELY ISN'T NORMAL.
THE HELL'S GOIN' ON?!
IF SOMETHING WAS WRONG... THE CAPTAIN WOULD TELL US, RIGHT?
OI! IF THIS SHIP'S COMMIN' APAHT--YA CAN'T JUST KEEP ME LOCKED UP!
YOU PEOPLE TURNED ME INHUMAN--
--BUT I STILL GOT HUMAN ROIGHTS!
CRYSTAL? CRYSTAL--YOU READ ME?!
DID YOU CALL THE R.I.V. INTO SIN-CONG AIRSPACE?! WE'RE UNDER ATTACK!
AND SWAIN IS SEDATED, TRYING TO REACH THE LIVING--
--HELL.

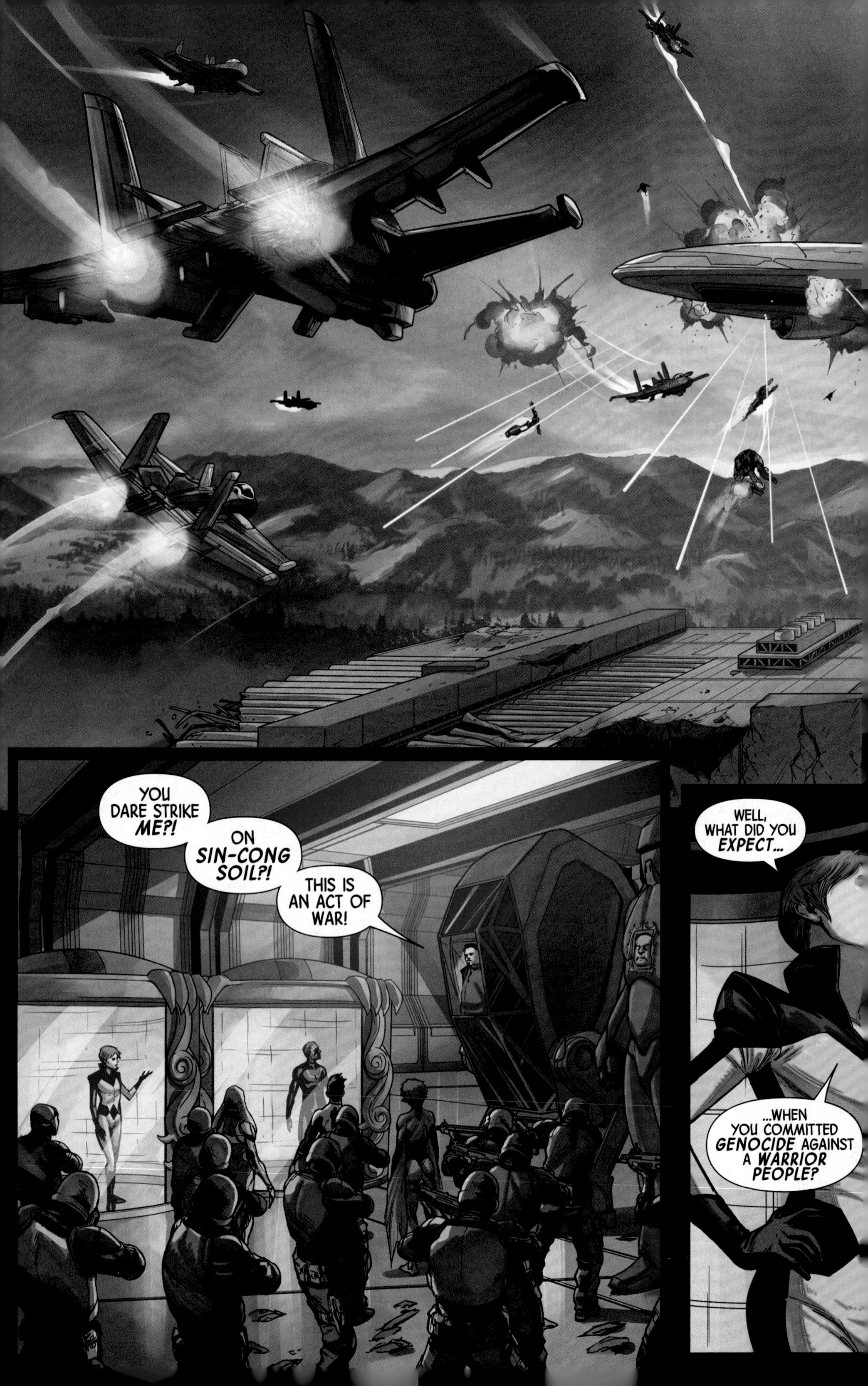
YOU DARE STRIKE ME?!
ON SIN-CONG SOIL?!
THIS IS AN ACT OF WAR!
WELL, WHAT DID YOU EXPECT...
...WHEN YOU COMMITTED GENOCIDE AGAINST A WARRIOR PEOPLE?

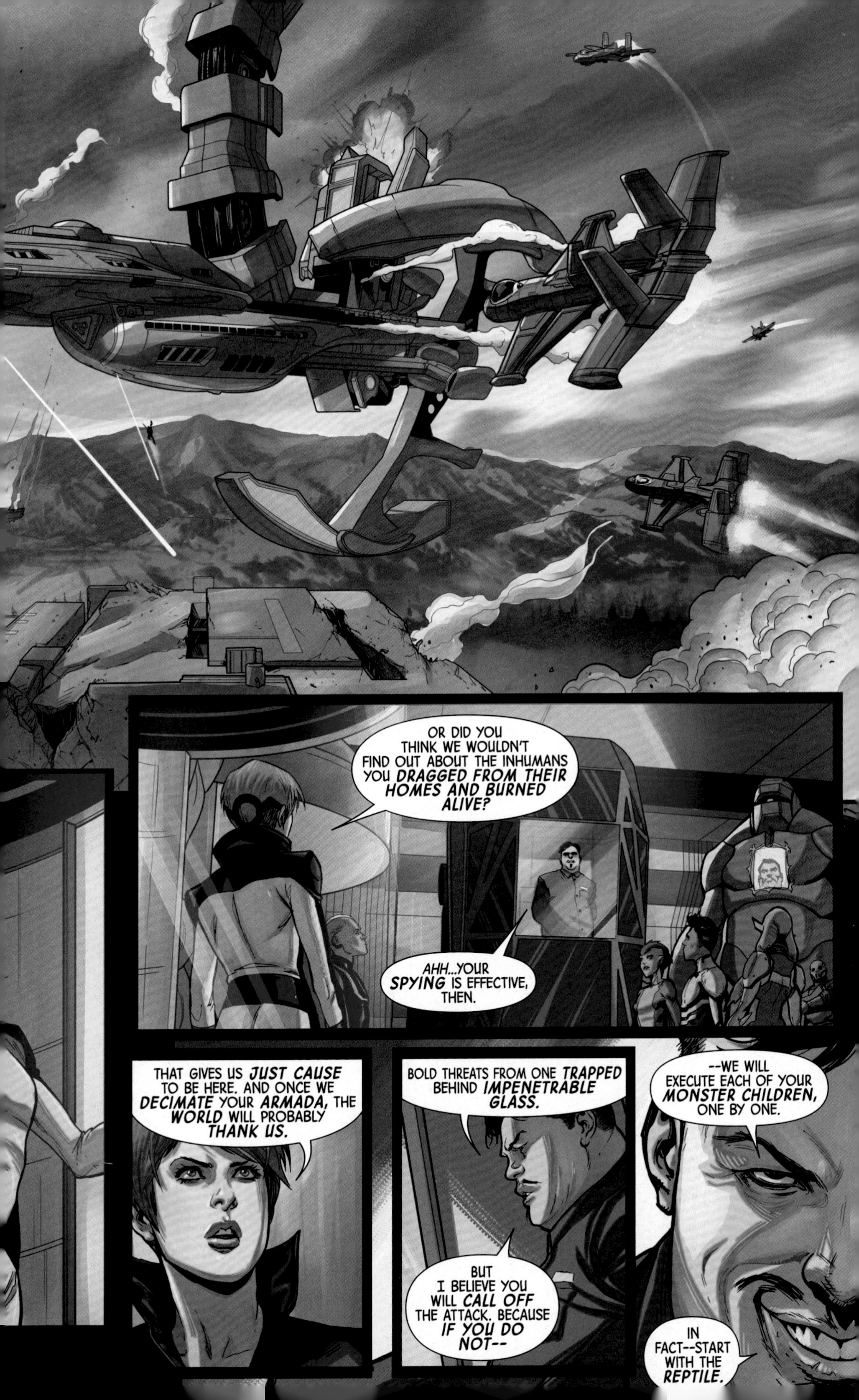
OR DID YOU THINK WE WOULDN'T FIND OUT ABOUT THE INHUMANS YOU DRAGGED FROM THEIR HOMES AND BURNED ALIVE?
AHH...YOUR SPYING IS EFFECTIVE, THEN.
THAT GIVES US JUST CAUSE TO BE HERE. AND ONCE WE DECIMATE YOUR ARMADA, THE WORLD WILL PROBABLY THANK US.
BOLD THREATS FROM ONE TRAPPED BEHIND IMPENETRABLE GLASS.
BUT I BELIEVE YOU WILL CALL OFF THE ATTACK. BECAUSE IF YOU DO NOT--
--WE WILL EXECUTE EACH OF YOUR MONSTER CHILDREN, ONE BY ONE.
IN FACT--START WITH THE REPTILE.

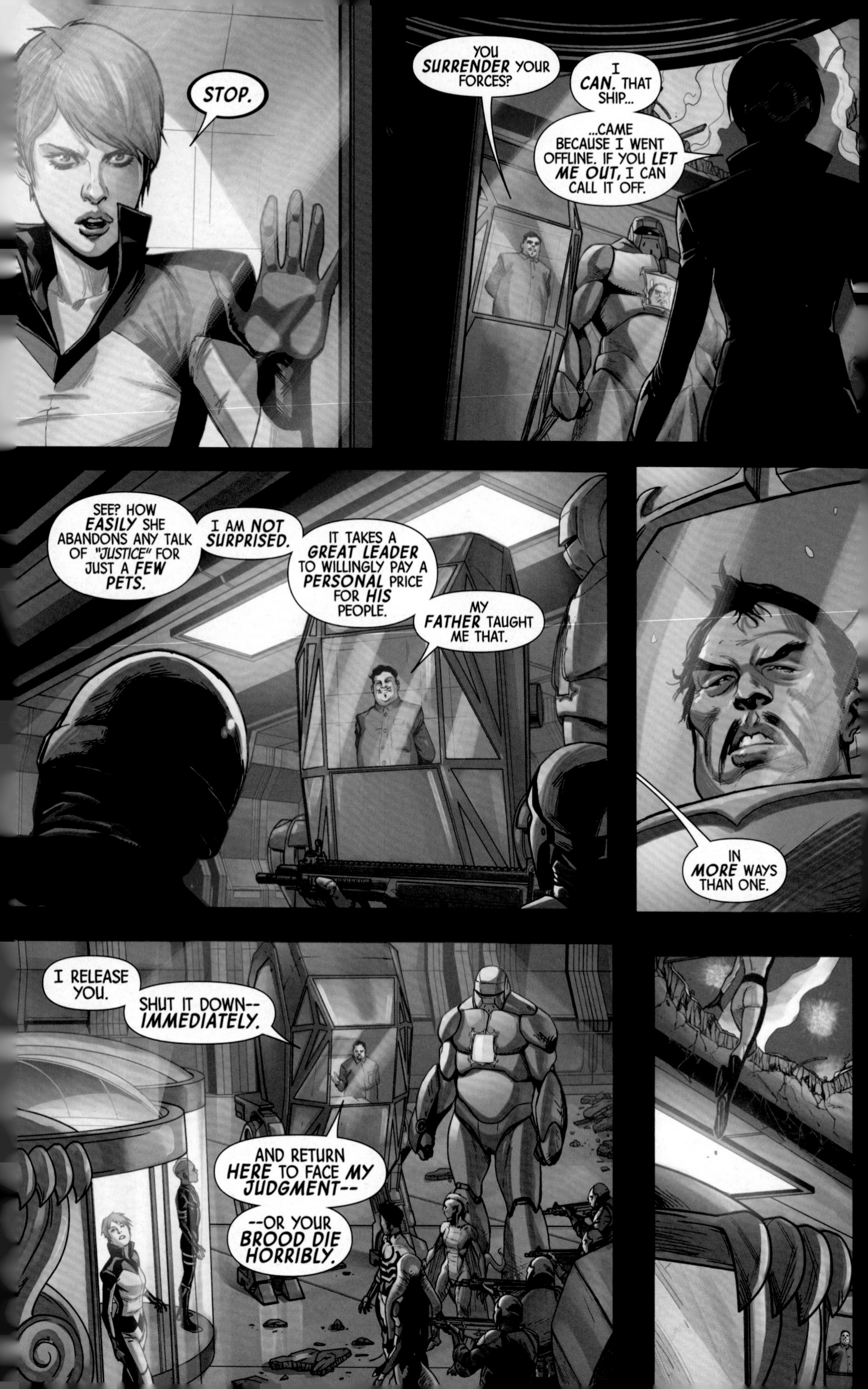
STOP.
YOU SURRENDER YOUR FORCES?
I CAN. THAT SHIP...
...CAME BECAUSE I WENT OFFLINE. IF YOU LET ME OUT, I CAN CALL IT OFF.
SEE? HOW EASILY SHE ABANDONS ANY TALK OF "JUSTICE" FOR JUST A FEW PETS.
I AM NOT SURPRISED.
IT TAKES A GREAT LEADER TO WILLINGLY PAY A PERSONAL PRICE FOR HIS PEOPLE.
MY FATHER TAUGHT ME THAT.
IN MORE WAYS THAN ONE.
I RELEASE YOU.
SHUT IT DOWN-- IMMEDIATELY.
AND RETURN HERE TO FACE MY JUDGMENT--
--OR YOUR BROOD DIE HORRIBLY.

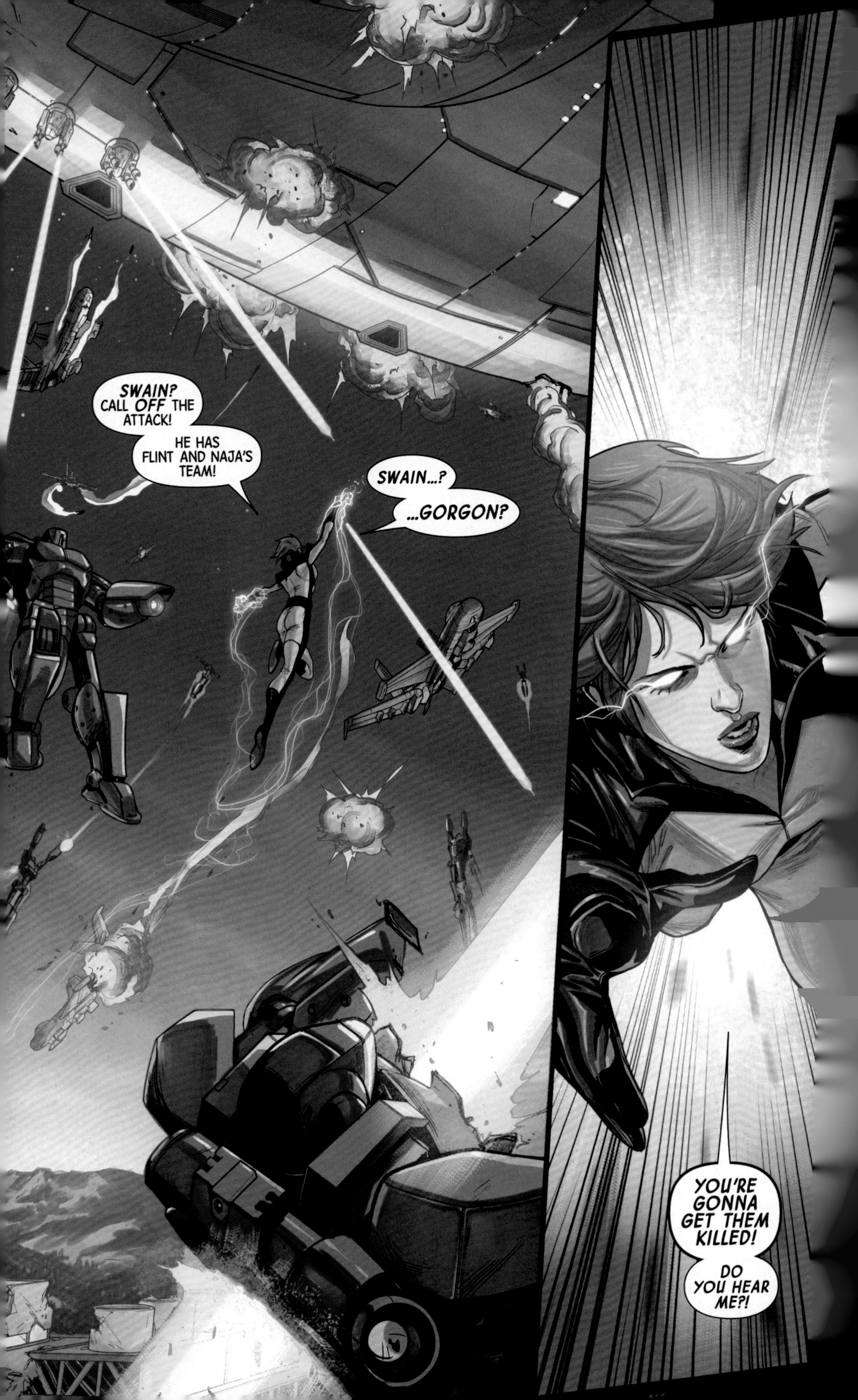
SWAIN? CALL OFF THE ATTACK!
HE HAS FLINT AND NAJA'S TEAM!
SWAIN...?
...GORGON?
YOU'RE GONNA GET THEM KILLED!
DO YOU HEAR ME?!

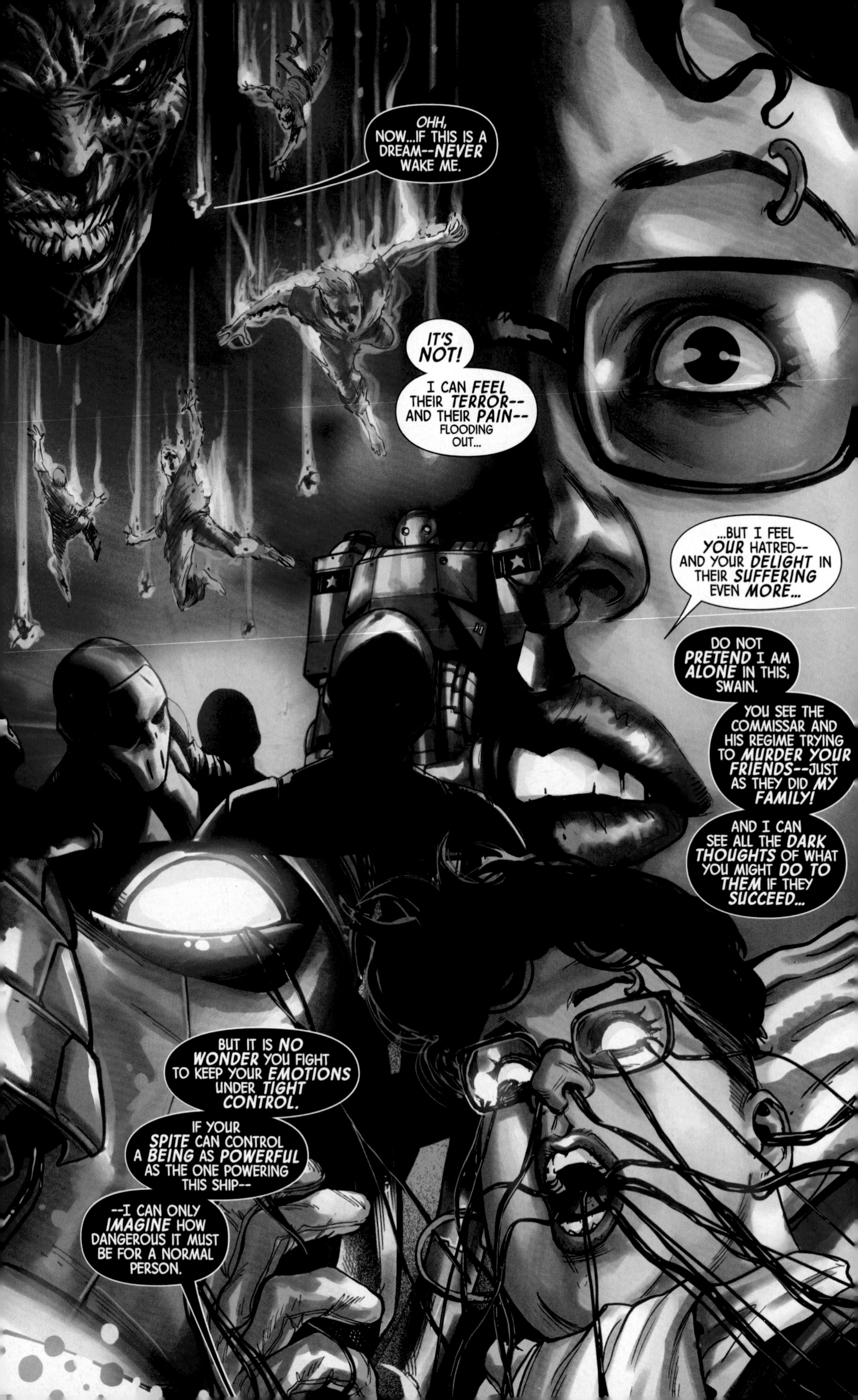
OHH, NOW...IF THIS IS A DREAM--NEVER WAKE ME.
IT'S NOT!
I CAN FEEL THEIR TERROR-- AND THEIR PAIN-- FLOODING OUT...
...BUT I FEEL YOUR HATRED-- AND YOUR DELIGHT IN THEIR SUFFERING EVEN MORE...
DO NOT PRETEND I AM ALONE IN THIS, SWAIN.
YOU SEE THE COMMISSAR AND HIS REGIME TRYING TO MURDER YOUR FRIENDS--JUST AS THEY DID MY FAMILY!
AND I CAN SEE ALL THE DARK THOUGHTS OF WHAT YOU MIGHT DO TO THEM IF THEY SUCCEED...
BUT IT IS NO WONDER YOU FIGHT TO KEEP YOUR EMOTIONS UNDER TIGHT CONTROL.
IF YOUR SPITE CAN CONTROL A BEING AS POWERFUL AS THE ONE POWERING THIS SHIP--
--I CAN ONLY IMAGINE HOW DANGEROUS IT MUST BE FOR A NORMAL PERSON.

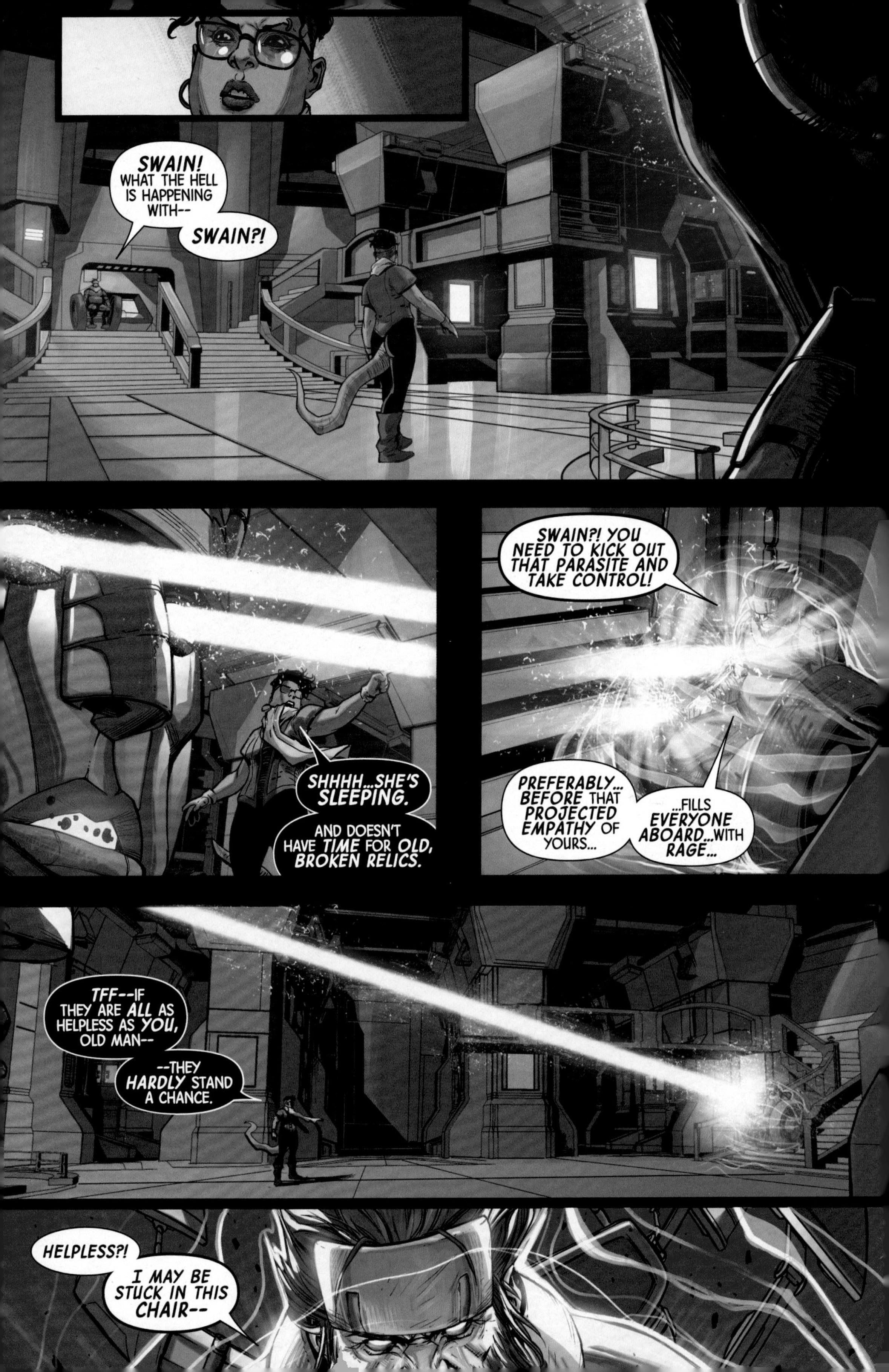
SWAIN! WHAT THE HELL IS HAPPENING WITH--
SWAIN?!
SHHHH...SHE'S SLEEPING.
AND DOESN'T HAVE TIME FOR OLD, BROKEN RELICS.
SWAIN?! YOU NEED TO KICK OUT THAT PARASITE AND TAKE CONTROL!
PREFERABLY... BEFORE THAT PROJECTED EMPATHY OF YOURS...
...FILLS EVERYONE ABOARD...WITH RAGE...
TFF--IF THEY ARE ALL AS HELPLESS AS YOU, OLD MAN--
--THEY HARDLY STAND A CHANCE.
HELPLESS?!
I MAY BE STUCK IN THIS CHAIR--

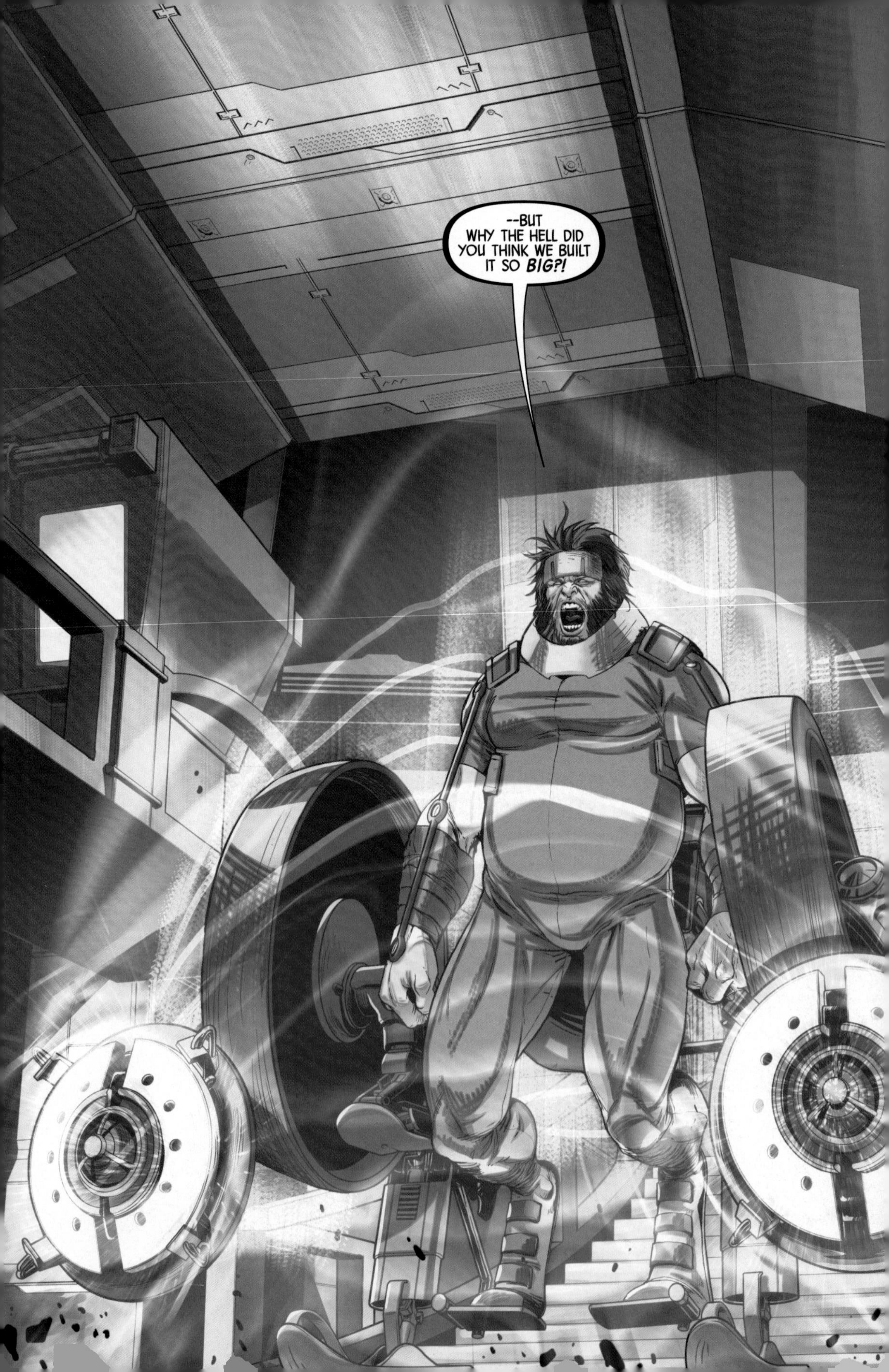
--BUT WHY THE HELL DID YOU THINK WE BUILT IT SO ***BIG?!***

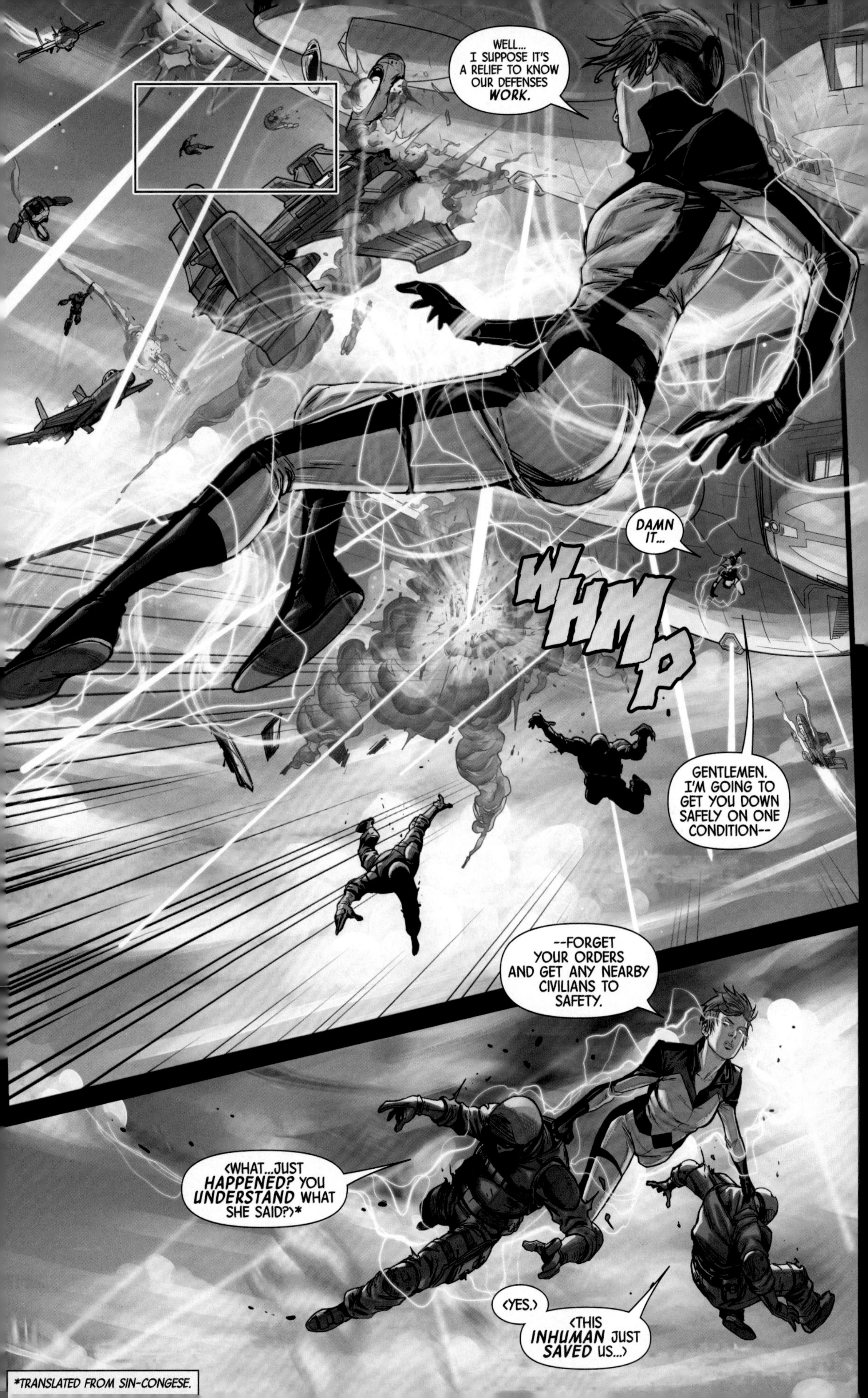
WELL... I SUPPOSE IT'S A RELIEF TO KNOW OUR DEFENSES WORK.
DAMN IT...
WHMP
GENTLEMEN. I'M GOING TO GET YOU DOWN SAFELY ON ONE CONDITION--
--FORGET YOUR ORDERS AND GET ANY NEARBY CIVILIANS TO SAFETY.
‹WHAT...JUST HAPPENED? YOU UNDERSTAND WHAT SHE SAID?›*
‹YES.›
‹THIS INHUMAN JUST SAVED US...›
*TRANSLATED FROM SIN-CONGESE.

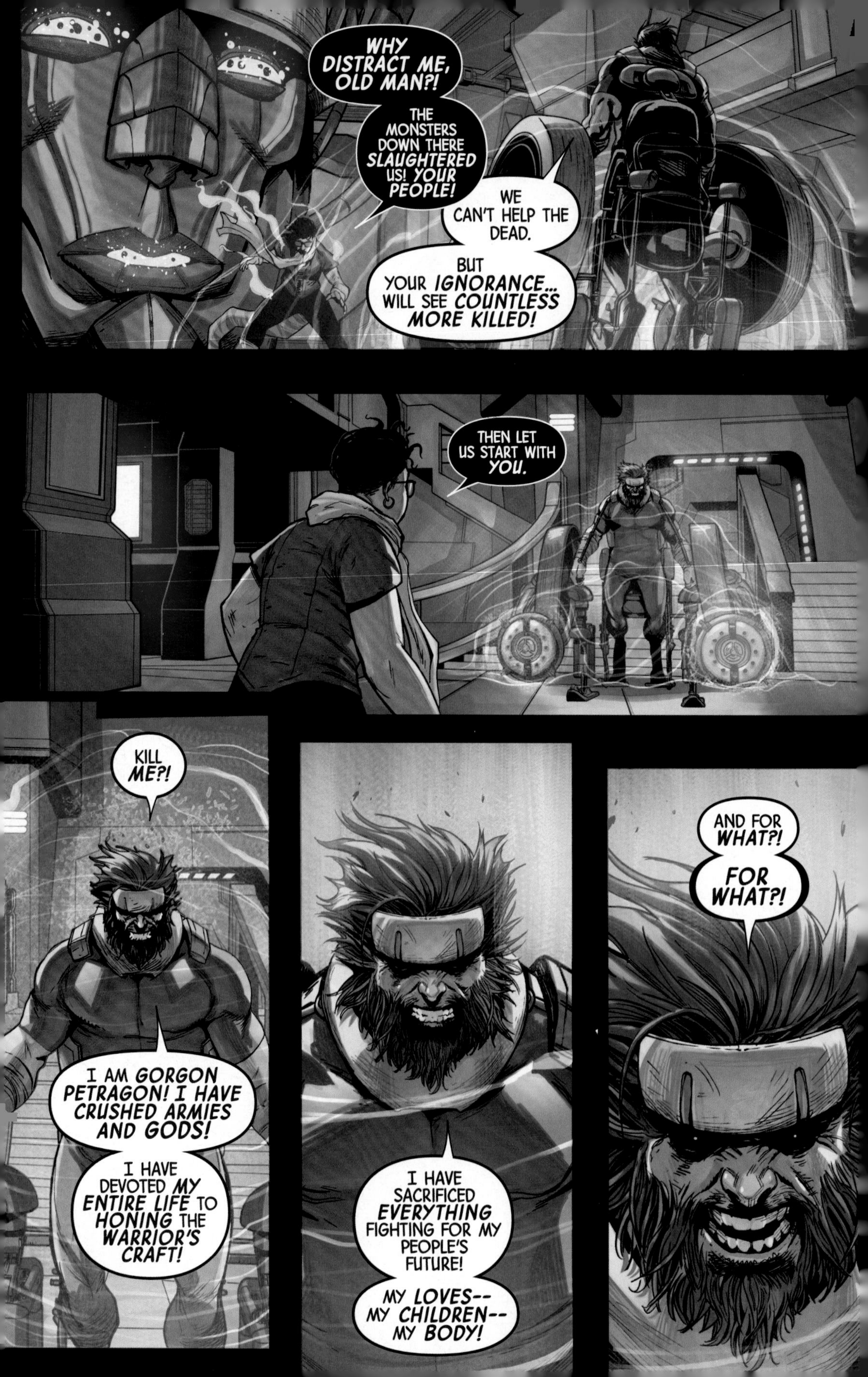
WHY DISTRACT ME, OLD MAN?!
THE MONSTERS DOWN THERE SLAUGHTERED US! YOUR PEOPLE!
WE CAN'T HELP THE DEAD.
BUT YOUR IGNORANCE... WILL SEE COUNTLESS MORE KILLED!
THEN LET US START WITH YOU.
KILL ME?!
I AM GORGON PETRAGON! I HAVE CRUSHED ARMIES AND GODS!
I HAVE DEVOTED MY ENTIRE LIFE TO HONING THE WARRIOR'S CRAFT!
I HAVE SACRIFICED EVERYTHING FIGHTING FOR MY PEOPLE'S FUTURE!
MY LOVES-- MY CHILDREN-- MY BODY!
AND FOR WHAT?!
FOR WHAT?!

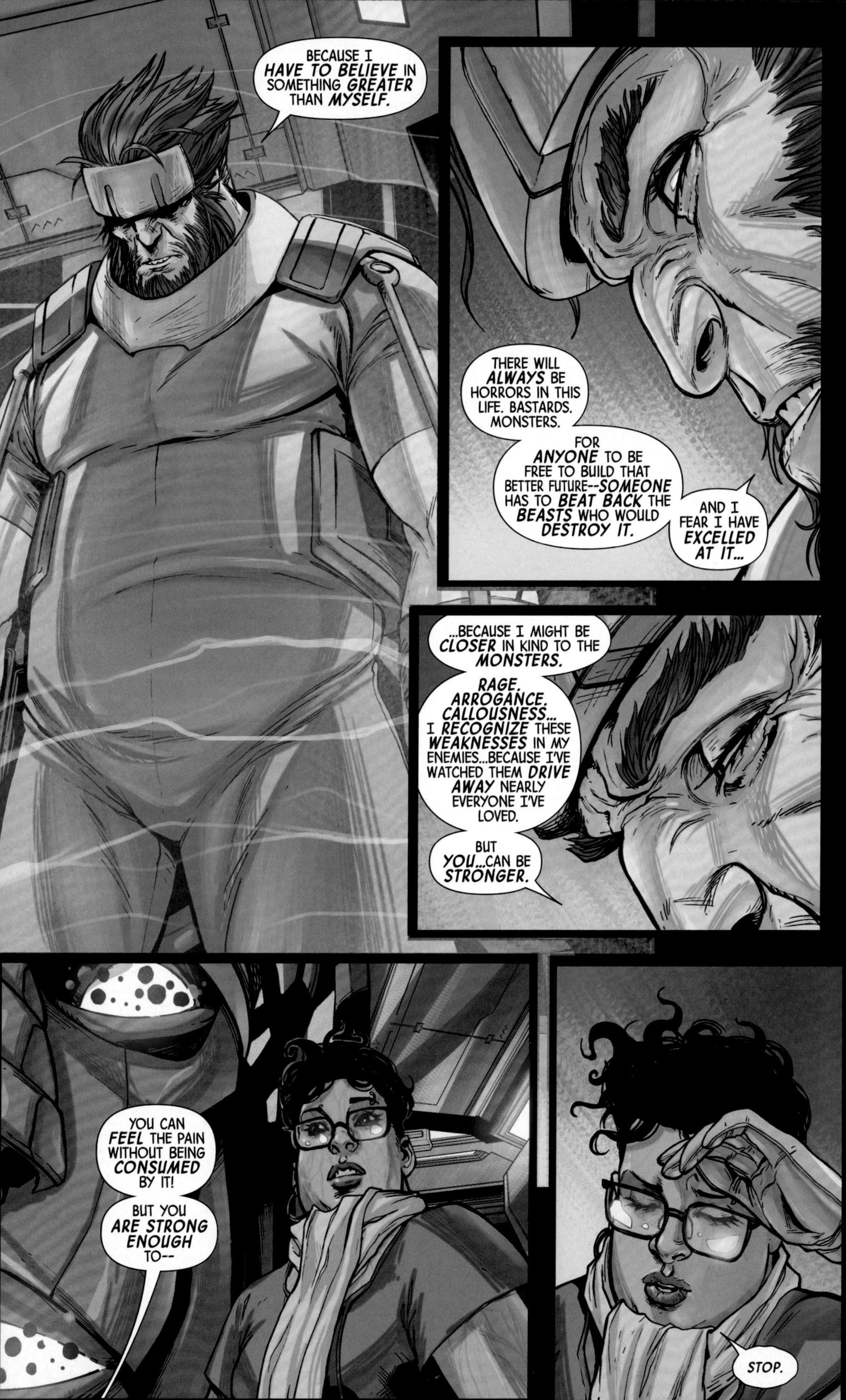

BECAUSE I HAVE TO BELIEVE IN SOMETHING GREATER THAN MYSELF.
THERE WILL ALWAYS BE HORRORS IN THIS LIFE. BASTARDS. MONSTERS.
FOR ANYONE TO BE FREE TO BUILD THAT BETTER FUTURE--SOMEONE HAS TO BEAT BACK THE BEASTS WHO WOULD DESTROY IT.
AND I FEAR I HAVE EXCELLED AT IT...
...BECAUSE I MIGHT BE CLOSER IN KIND TO THE MONSTERS.
RAGE. ARROGANCE. CALLOUSNESS... I RECOGNIZE THESE WEAKNESSES IN MY ENEMIES...BECAUSE I'VE WATCHED THEM DRIVE AWAY NEARLY EVERYONE I'VE LOVED.
BUT YOU...CAN BE STRONGER.
YOU CAN FEEL THE PAIN WITHOUT BEING CONSUMED BY IT!
BUT YOU ARE STRONG ENOUGH TO--
STOP.

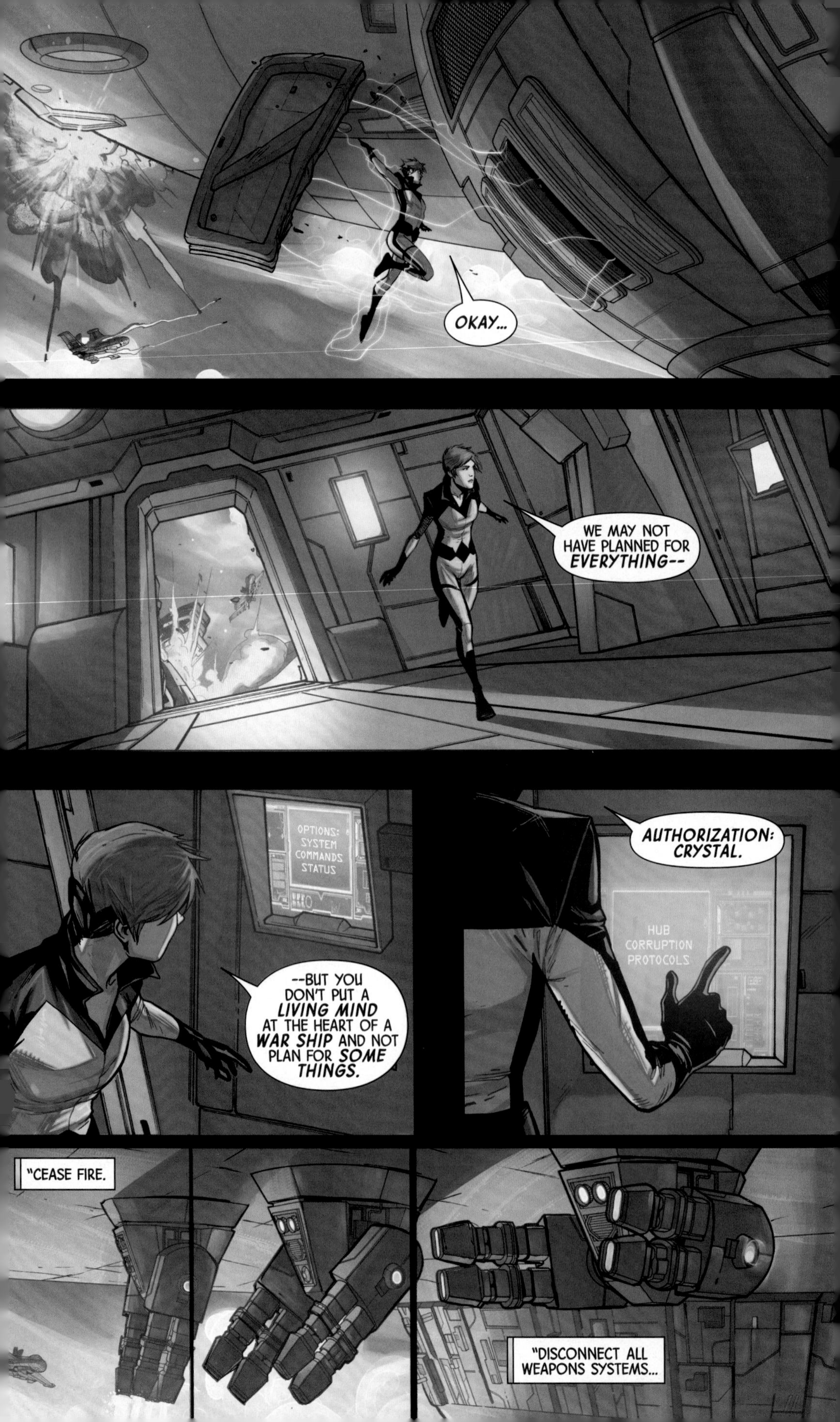
OKAY...
WE MAY NOT HAVE PLANNED FOR EVERYTHING--
OPTIONS: SYSTEM COMMANDS STATUS
--BUT YOU DON'T PUT A LIVING MIND AT THE HEART OF A WAR SHIP AND NOT PLAN FOR SOME THINGS.
AUTHORIZATION: CRYSTAL.
HUB CORRUPTION PROTOCOLS
"CEASE FIRE.
"DISCONNECT ALL WEAPONS SYSTEMS...

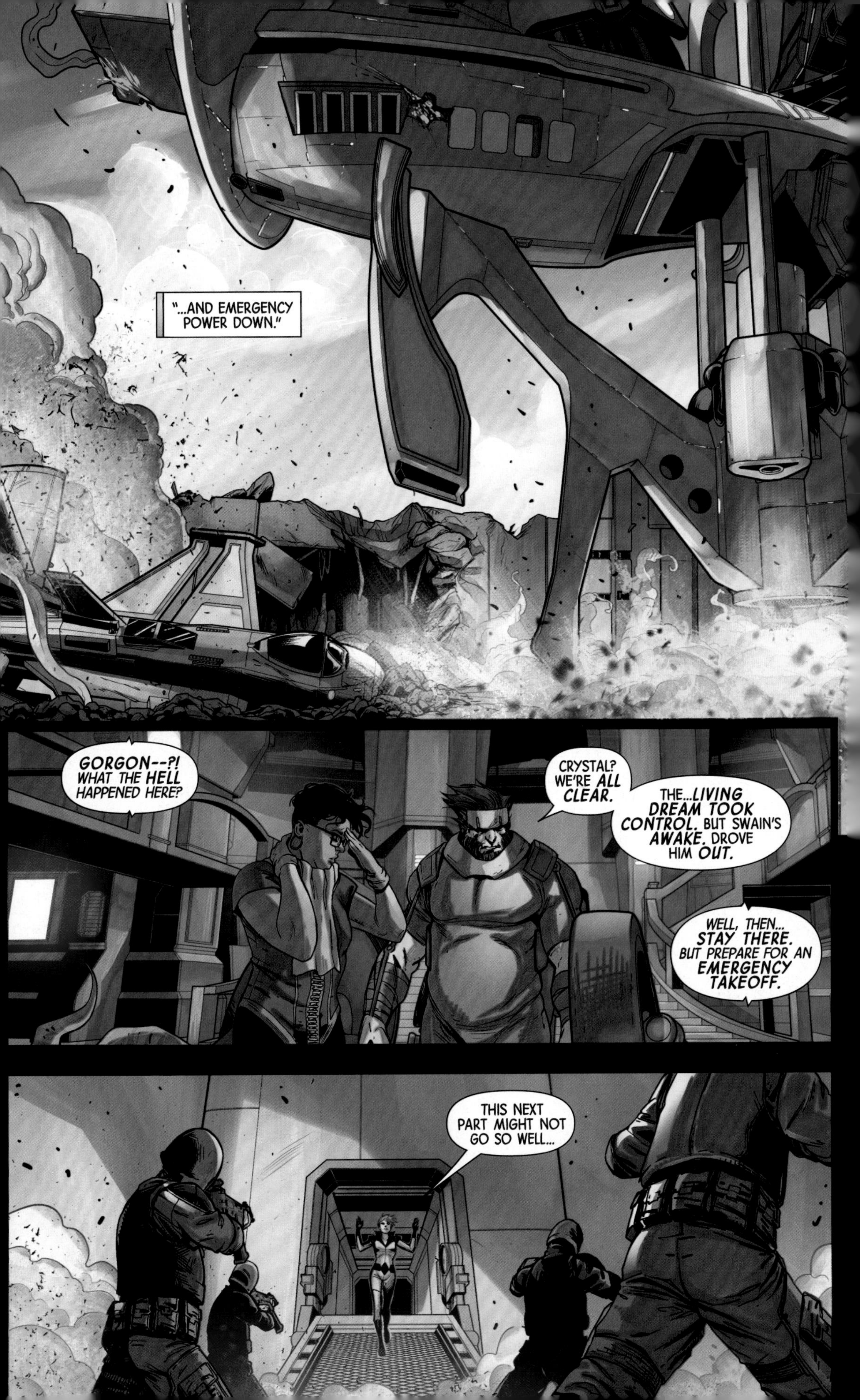
"...AND EMERGENCY POWER DOWN."
GORGON--?! WHAT THE HELL HAPPENED HERE?
CRYSTAL? WE'RE ALL CLEAR.
THE...LIVING DREAM TOOK CONTROL. BUT SWAIN'S AWAKE. DROVE HIM OUT.
WELL, THEN... STAY THERE. BUT PREPARE FOR AN EMERGENCY TAKEOFF.
THIS NEXT PART MIGHT NOT GO SO WELL...

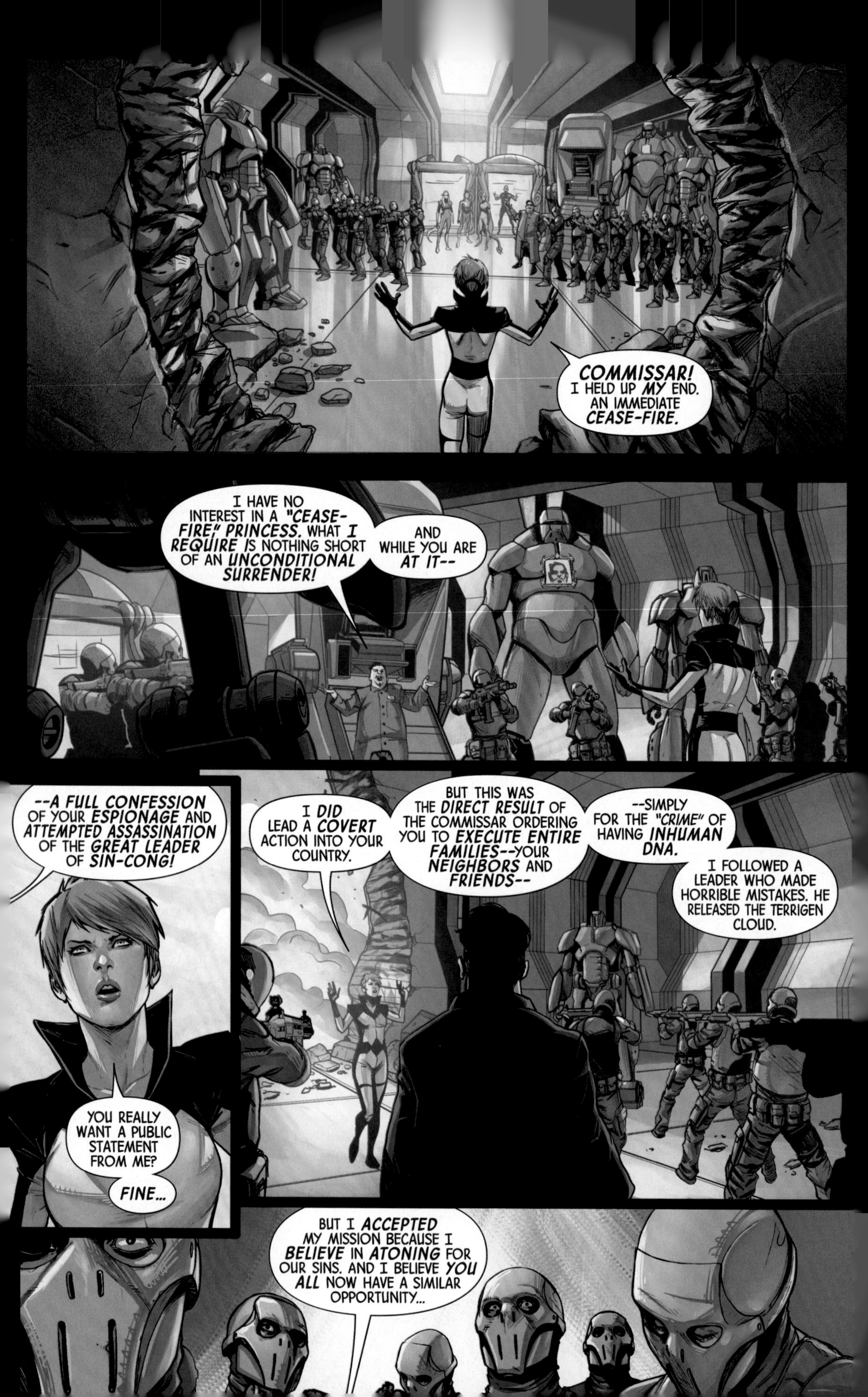
COMMISSAR! I HELD UP MY END. AN IMMEDIATE CEASE-FIRE.
I HAVE NO INTEREST IN A "CEASE-FIRE," PRINCESS. WHAT I REQUIRE IS NOTHING SHORT OF AN UNCONDITIONAL SURRENDER!
AND WHILE YOU ARE AT IT--
--A FULL CONFESSION OF YOUR ESPIONAGE AND ATTEMPTED ASSASSINATION OF THE GREAT LEADER OF SIN-CONG!
YOU REALLY WANT A PUBLIC STATEMENT FROM ME?
FINE...
I DID LEAD A COVERT ACTION INTO YOUR COUNTRY.
BUT THIS WAS THE DIRECT RESULT OF THE COMMISSAR ORDERING YOU TO EXECUTE ENTIRE FAMILIES--YOUR NEIGHBORS AND FRIENDS--
--SIMPLY FOR THE "CRIME" OF HAVING INHUMAN DNA.
I FOLLOWED A LEADER WHO MADE HORRIBLE MISTAKES. HE RELEASED THE TERRIGEN CLOUD.
BUT I ACCEPTED MY MISSION BECAUSE I BELIEVE IN ATONING FOR OUR SINS. AND I BELIEVE YOU ALL NOW HAVE A SIMILAR OPPORTUNITY...

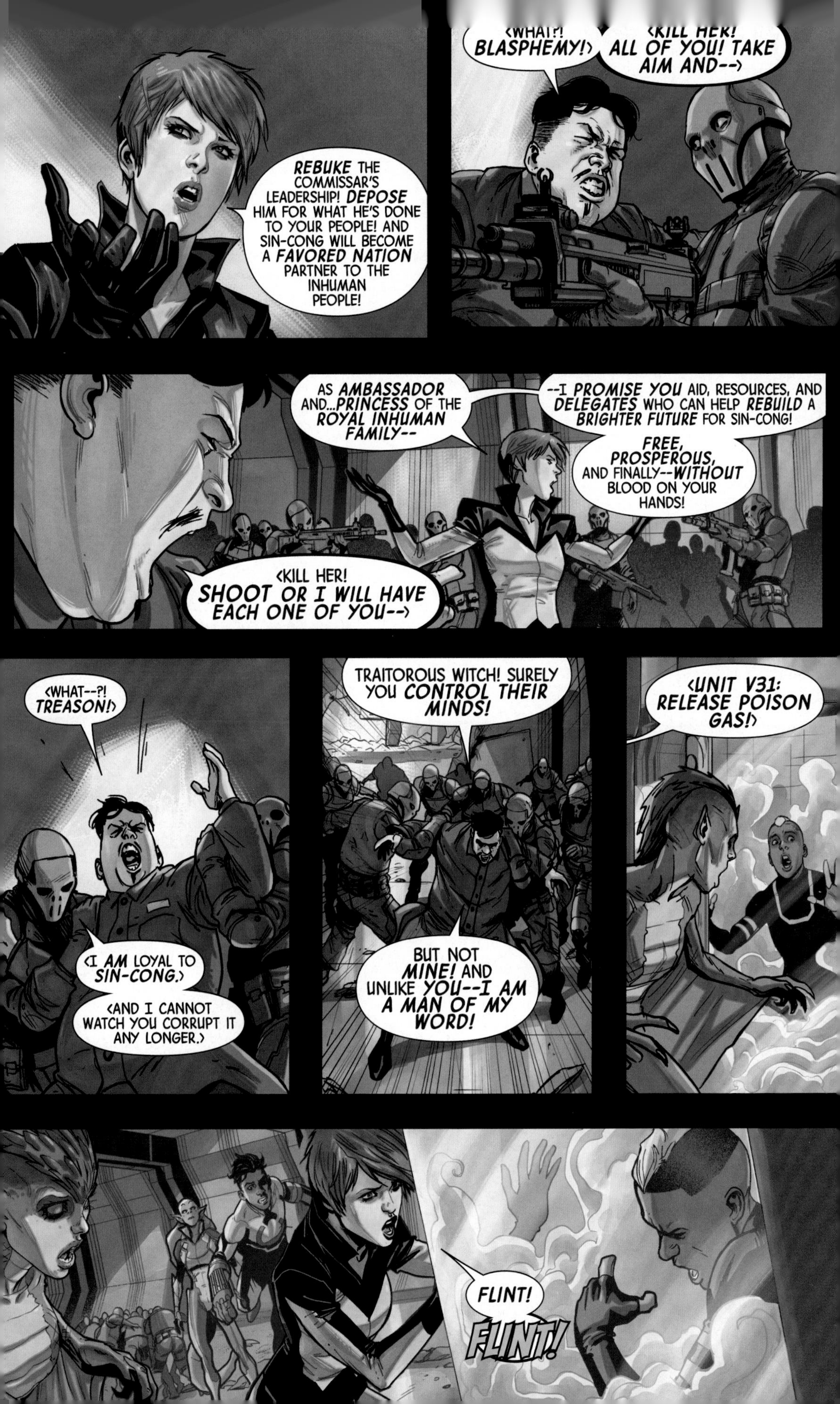
REBUKE THE COMMISSAR'S LEADERSHIP! DEPOSE HIM FOR WHAT HE'S DONE TO YOUR PEOPLE! AND SIN-CONG WILL BECOME A FAVORED NATION PARTNER TO THE INHUMAN PEOPLE!
‹WHAT?! BLASPHEMY!›
‹KILL HER! ALL OF YOU! TAKE AIM AND--›
AS AMBASSADOR AND...PRINCESS OF THE ROYAL INHUMAN FAMILY--
--I PROMISE YOU AID, RESOURCES, AND DELEGATES WHO CAN HELP REBUILD A BRIGHTER FUTURE FOR SIN-CONG!
FREE, PROSPEROUS, AND FINALLY--WITHOUT BLOOD ON YOUR HANDS!
‹KILL HER! SHOOT OR I WILL HAVE EACH ONE OF YOU--›
‹WHAT--?! TREASON!›
‹I AM LOYAL TO SIN-CONG.›
‹AND I CANNOT WATCH YOU CORRUPT IT ANY LONGER.›
TRAITOROUS WITCH! SURELY YOU CONTROL THEIR MINDS!
BUT NOT MINE! AND UNLIKE YOU--I AM A MAN OF MY WORD!
‹UNIT V31: RELEASE POISON GAS!›
FLINT!
FLINT!

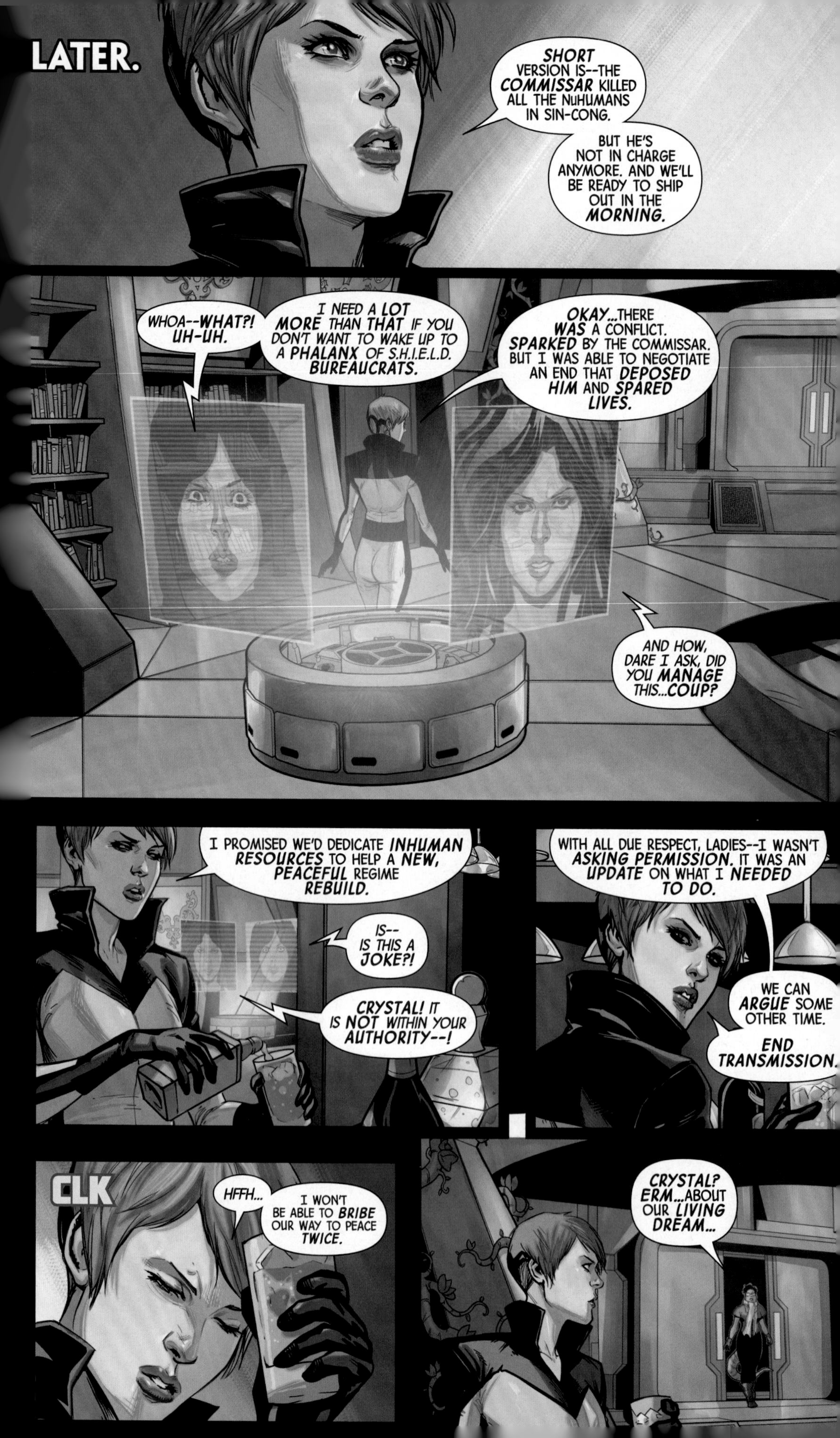
LATER.
SHORT VERSION IS--THE COMMISSAR KILLED ALL THE NuHUMANS IN SIN-CONG.
BUT HE'S NOT IN CHARGE ANYMORE. AND WE'LL BE READY TO SHIP OUT IN THE MORNING.
WHOA--WHAT?! UH-UH.
I NEED A LOT MORE THAN THAT IF YOU DON'T WANT TO WAKE UP TO A PHALANX OF S.H.I.E.L.D. BUREAUCRATS.
OKAY...THERE WAS A CONFLICT. SPARKED BY THE COMMISSAR. BUT I WAS ABLE TO NEGOTIATE AN END THAT DEPOSED HIM AND SPARED LIVES.
AND HOW, DARE I ASK, DID YOU MANAGE THIS...COUP?
I PROMISED WE'D DEDICATE INHUMAN RESOURCES TO HELP A NEW, PEACEFUL REGIME REBUILD.
IS-- IS THIS A JOKE?!
CRYSTAL! IT IS NOT WITHIN YOUR AUTHORITY--!
WITH ALL DUE RESPECT, LADIES--I WASN'T ASKING PERMISSION. IT WAS AN UPDATE ON WHAT I NEEDED TO DO.
WE CAN ARGUE SOME OTHER TIME.
END TRANSMISSION.
CLK
HFFH...
I WON'T BE ABLE TO BRIBE OUR WAY TO PEACE TWICE.
CRYSTAL? ERM...ABOUT OUR LIVING DREAM...

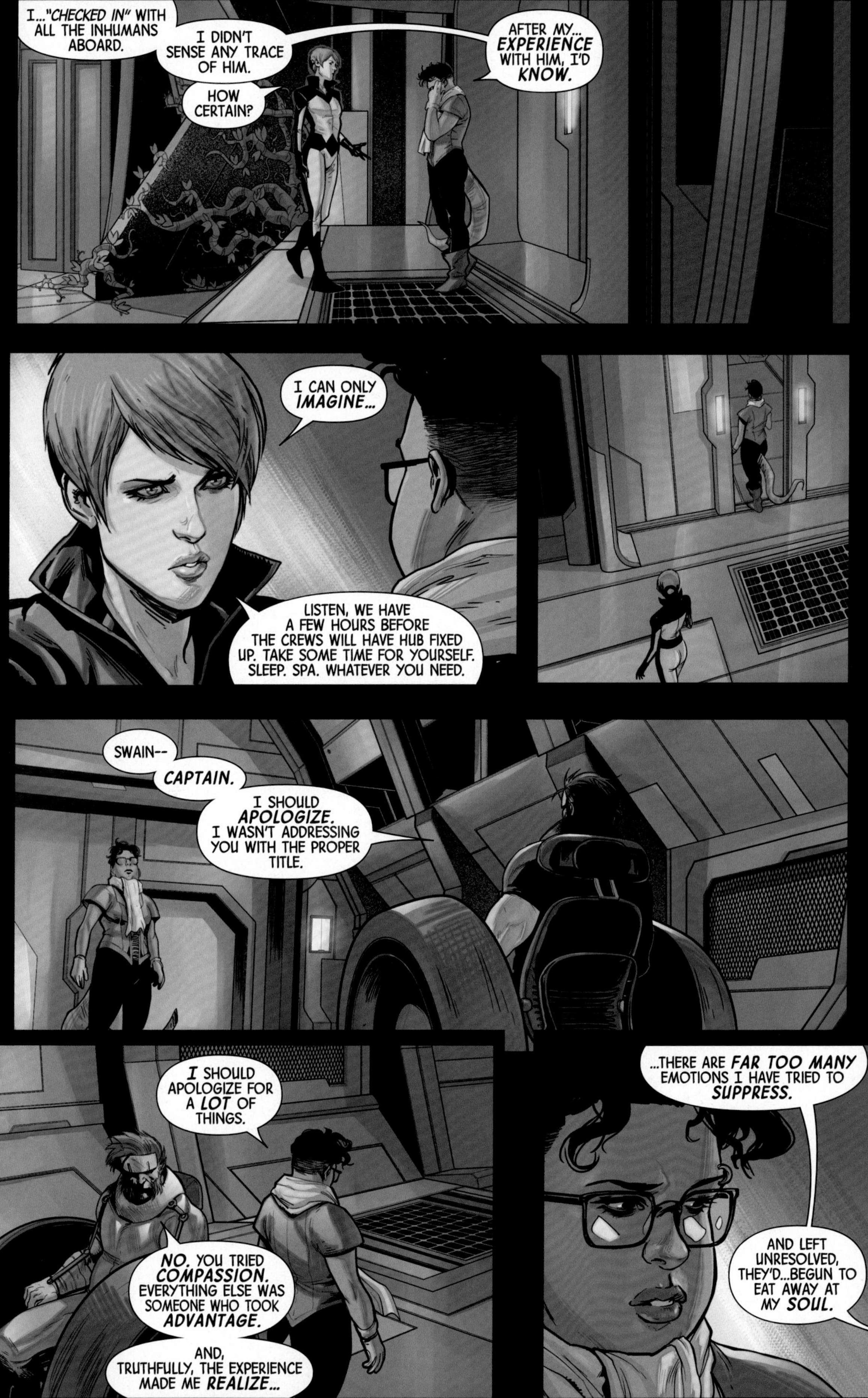

I..."CHECKED IN" WITH ALL THE INHUMANS ABOARD.
I DIDN'T SENSE ANY TRACE OF HIM.
HOW CERTAIN?
AFTER MY... EXPERIENCE WITH HIM, I'D KNOW.
I CAN ONLY IMAGINE...
LISTEN, WE HAVE A FEW HOURS BEFORE THE CREWS WILL HAVE HUB FIXED UP. TAKE SOME TIME FOR YOURSELF. SLEEP. SPA. WHATEVER YOU NEED.
SWAIN--
CAPTAIN.
I SHOULD APOLOGIZE. I WASN'T ADDRESSING YOU WITH THE PROPER TITLE.
I SHOULD APOLOGIZE FOR A LOT OF THINGS.
NO. YOU TRIED COMPASSION. EVERYTHING ELSE WAS SOMEONE WHO TOOK ADVANTAGE.
AND, TRUTHFULLY, THE EXPERIENCE MADE ME REALIZE...
...THERE ARE FAR TOO MANY EMOTIONS I HAVE TRIED TO SUPPRESS.
AND LEFT UNRESOLVED, THEY'D...BEGUN TO EAT AWAY AT MY SOUL.

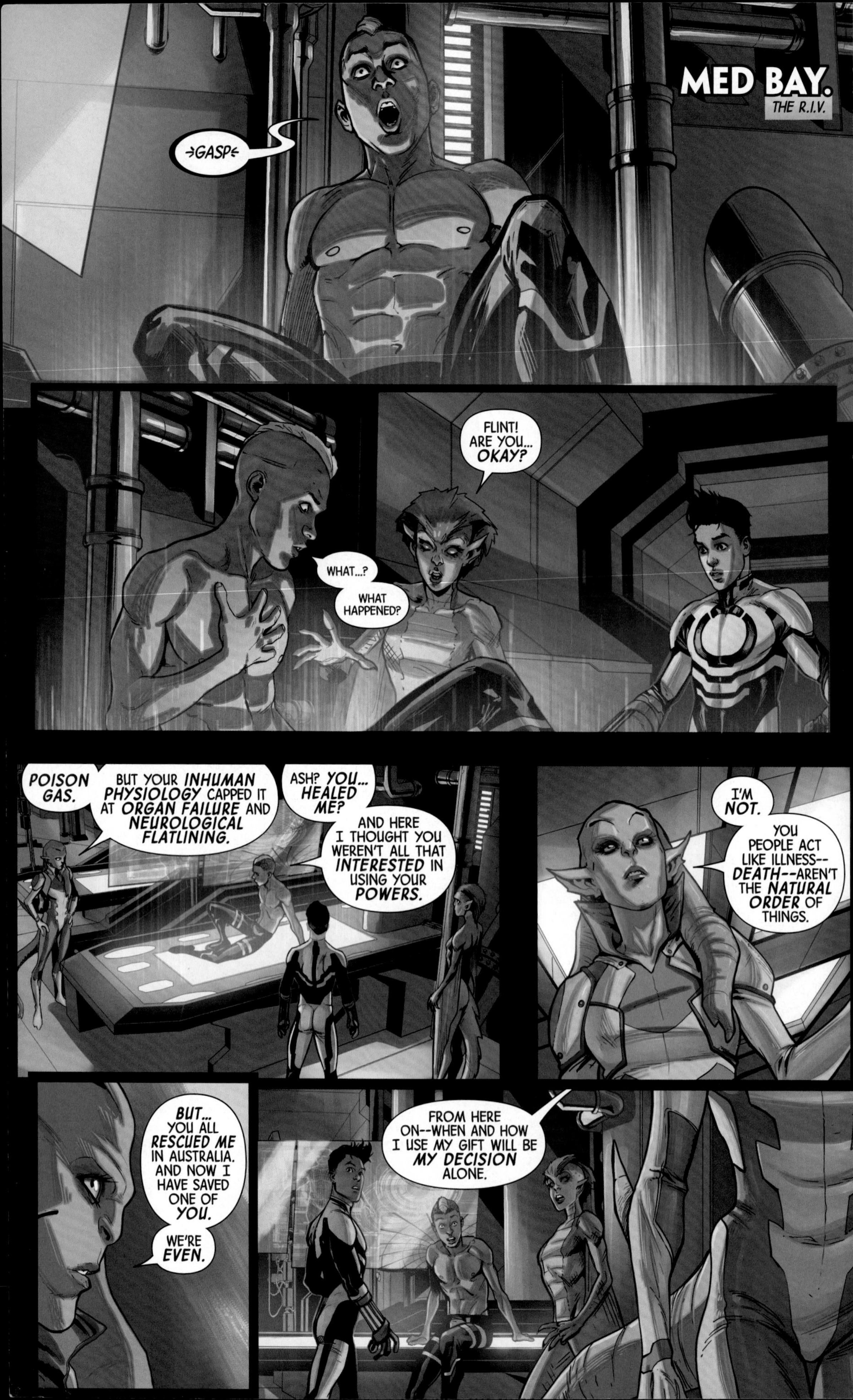
MED BAY.
THE R.I.V.
GASP
FLINT! ARE YOU... OKAY?
WHAT...?
WHAT HAPPENED?
POISON GAS.
BUT YOUR INHUMAN PHYSIOLOGY CAPPED IT AT ORGAN FAILURE AND NEUROLOGICAL FLATLINING.
ASH? YOU... HEALED ME?
AND HERE I THOUGHT YOU WEREN'T ALL THAT INTERESTED IN USING YOUR POWERS.
I'M NOT.
YOU PEOPLE ACT LIKE ILLNESS--DEATH--AREN'T THE NATURAL ORDER OF THINGS.
BUT... YOU ALL RESCUED ME IN AUSTRALIA. AND NOW I HAVE SAVED ONE OF YOU.
WE'RE EVEN.
FROM HERE ON--WHEN AND HOW I USE MY GIFT WILL BE MY DECISION ALONE.

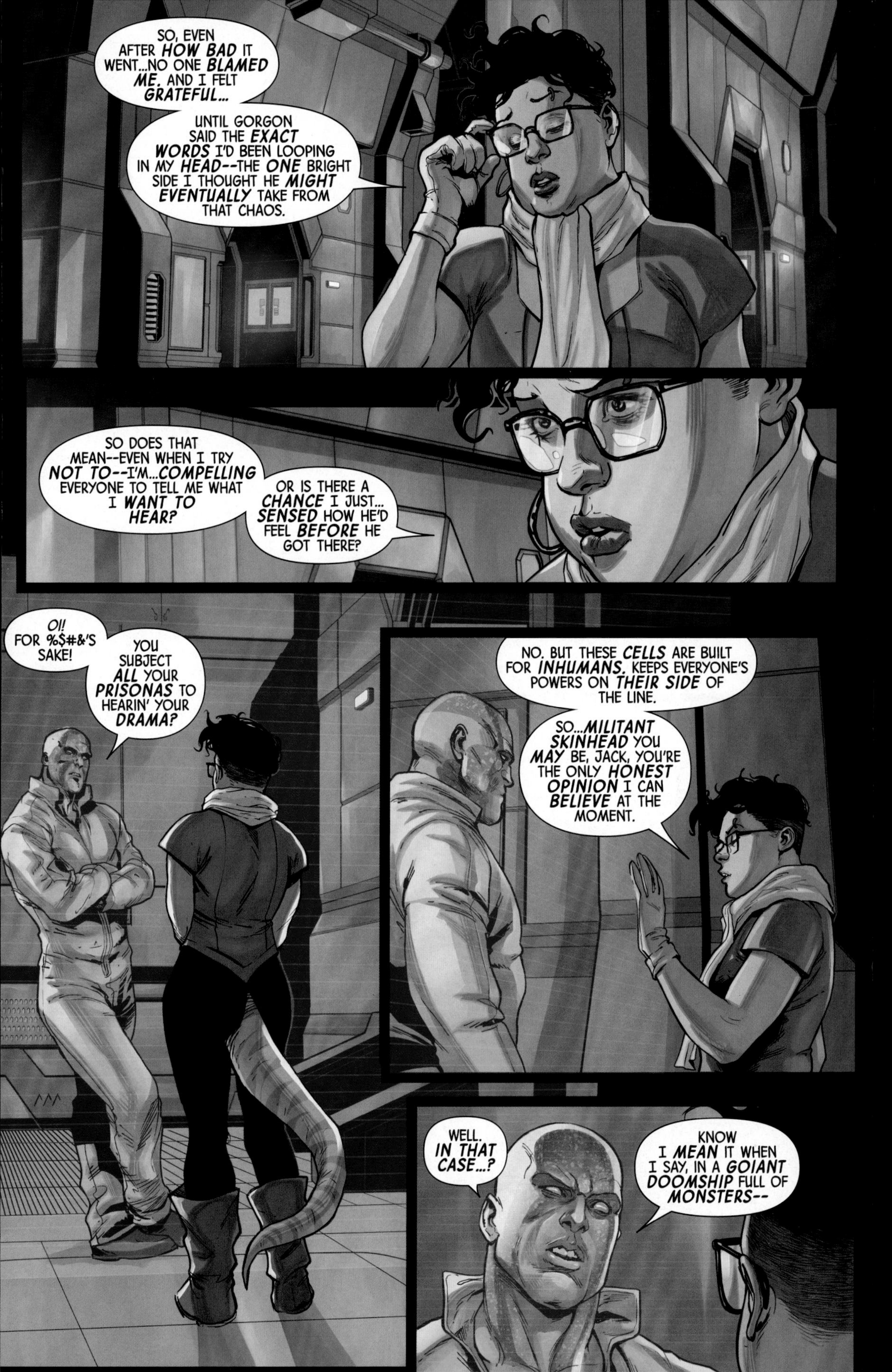
SO, EVEN AFTER HOW BAD IT WENT...NO ONE BLAMED ME. AND I FELT GRATEFUL...
UNTIL GORGON SAID THE EXACT WORDS I'D BEEN LOOPING IN MY HEAD--THE ONE BRIGHT SIDE I THOUGHT HE MIGHT EVENTUALLY TAKE FROM THAT CHAOS.
SO DOES THAT MEAN--EVEN WHEN I TRY NOT TO--I'M...COMPELLING EVERYONE TO TELL ME WHAT I WANT TO HEAR?
OR IS THERE A CHANCE I JUST... SENSED HOW HE'D FEEL BEFORE HE GOT THERE?
OI! FOR %$#&'S SAKE!
YOU SUBJECT ALL YOUR PRISONAS TO HEARIN' YOUR DRAMA?
NO. BUT THESE CELLS ARE BUILT FOR INHUMANS. KEEPS EVERYONE'S POWERS ON THEIR SIDE OF THE LINE.
SO...MILITANT SKINHEAD YOU MAY BE, JACK, YOU'RE THE ONLY HONEST OPINION I CAN BELIEVE AT THE MOMENT.
WELL. IN THAT CASE...?
KNOW I MEAN IT WHEN I SAY, IN A GOIANT DOOMSHIP FULL OF MONSTERS--

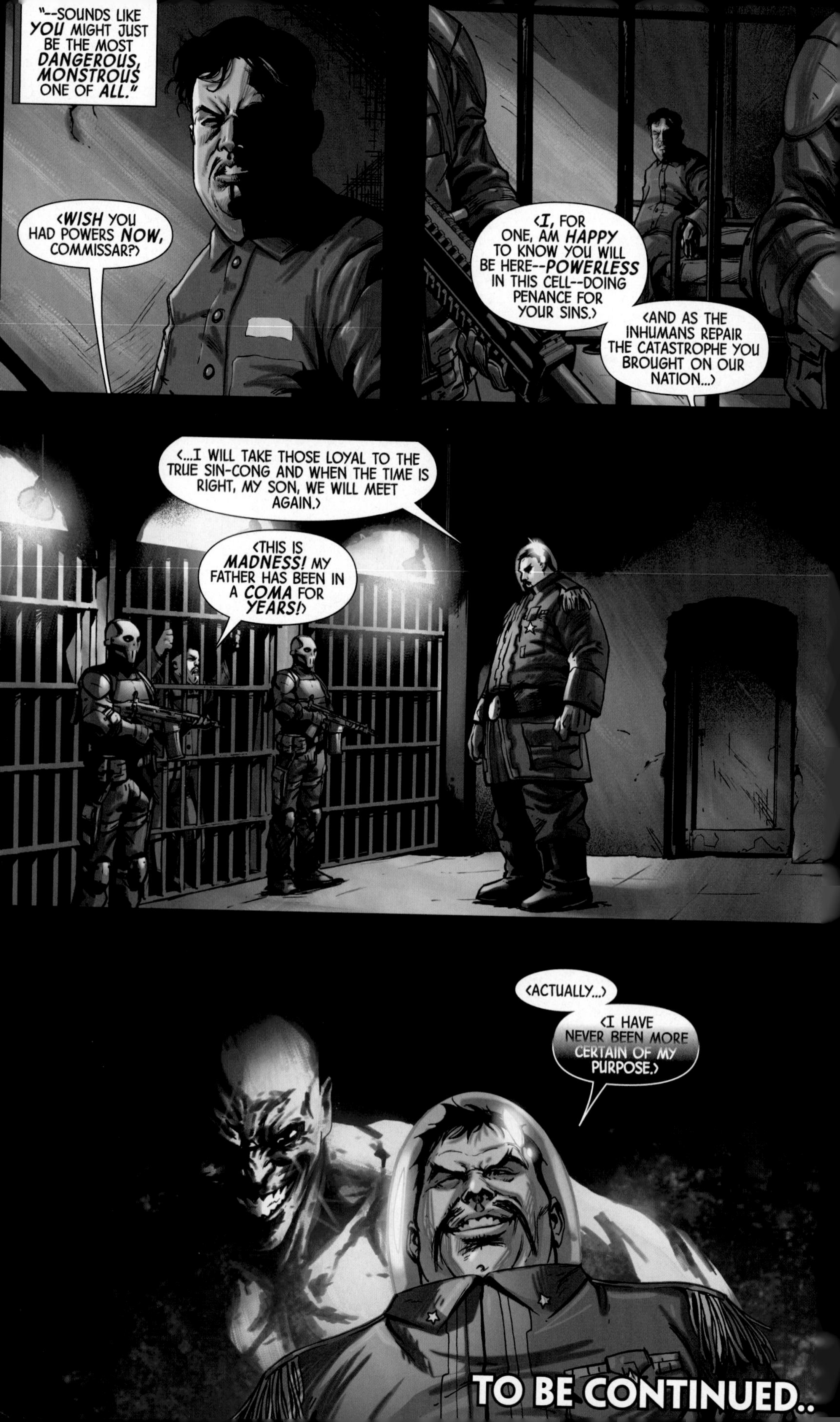
"--SOUNDS LIKE YOU MIGHT JUST BE THE MOST DANGEROUS, MONSTROUS ONE OF ALL."
‹WISH YOU HAD POWERS NOW, COMMISSAR?›
‹I, FOR ONE, AM HAPPY TO KNOW YOU WILL BE HERE--POWERLESS IN THIS CELL--DOING PENANCE FOR YOUR SINS.›
‹AND AS THE INHUMANS REPAIR THE CATASTROPHE YOU BROUGHT ON OUR NATION...›
‹...I WILL TAKE THOSE LOYAL TO THE TRUE SIN-CONG AND WHEN THE TIME IS RIGHT, MY SON, WE WILL MEET AGAIN.›
‹THIS IS MADNESS! MY FATHER HAS BEEN IN A COMA FOR YEARS!›
‹ACTUALLY...›
‹I HAVE NEVER BEEN MORE CERTAIN OF MY PURPOSE.›
TO BE CONTINUED..

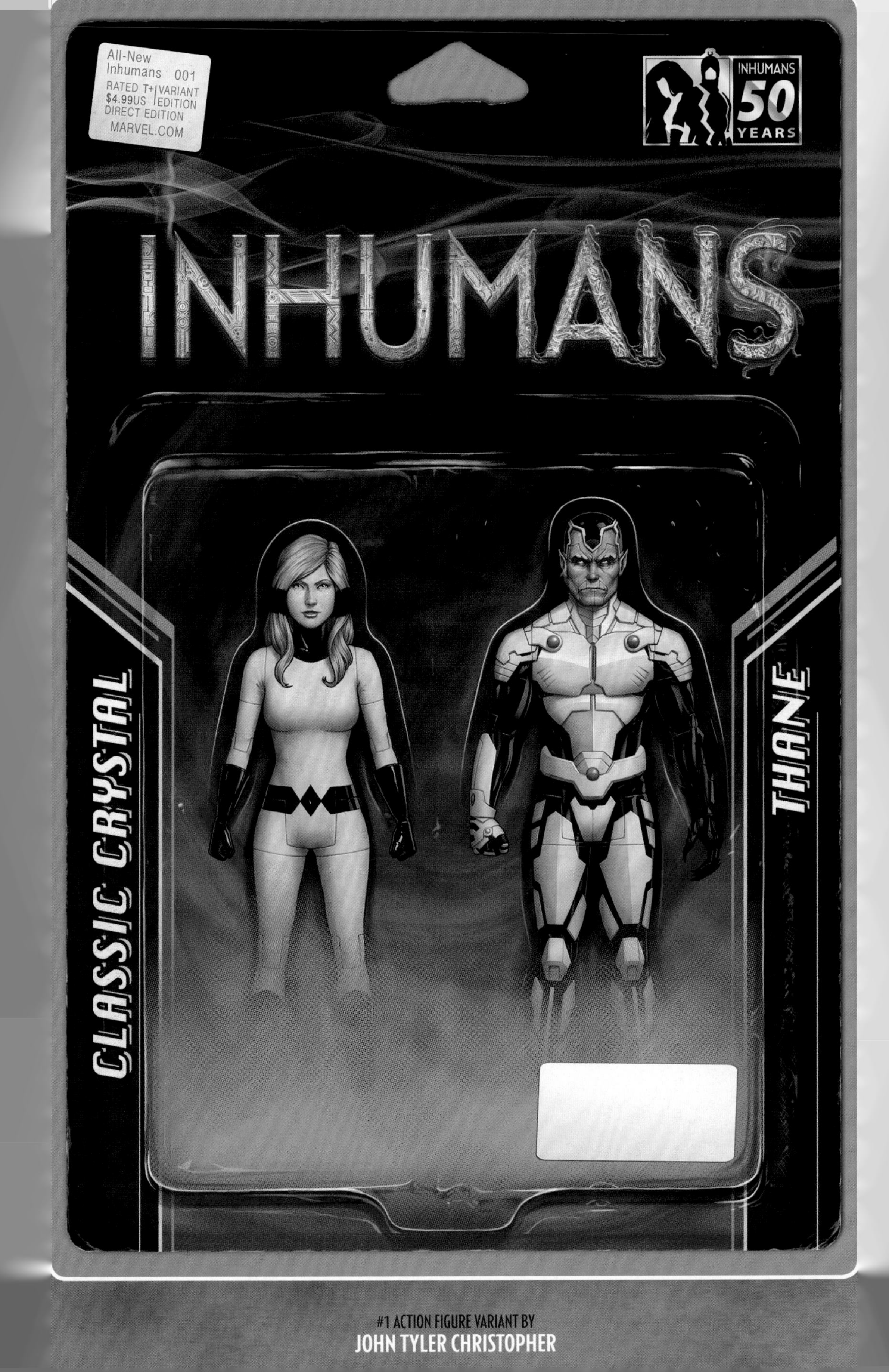
All-New
Inhumans 001
RATED T+ VARIANT EDITION
$4.99US
DIRECT EDITION
MARVEL.COM
INHUMANS 50 YEARS
INHUMANS
CLASSIC CRYSTAL
THANE

#1 ACTION FIGURE VARIANT BY
JOHN TYLER CHRISTOPHER

UNCANNY INHUMANS #0-2, ALL-NEW INHUMANS #1 & KARNAK #1 CONNECTING VARIANTS BY
JIM CHEUNG & **JUSTIN PONSOR**

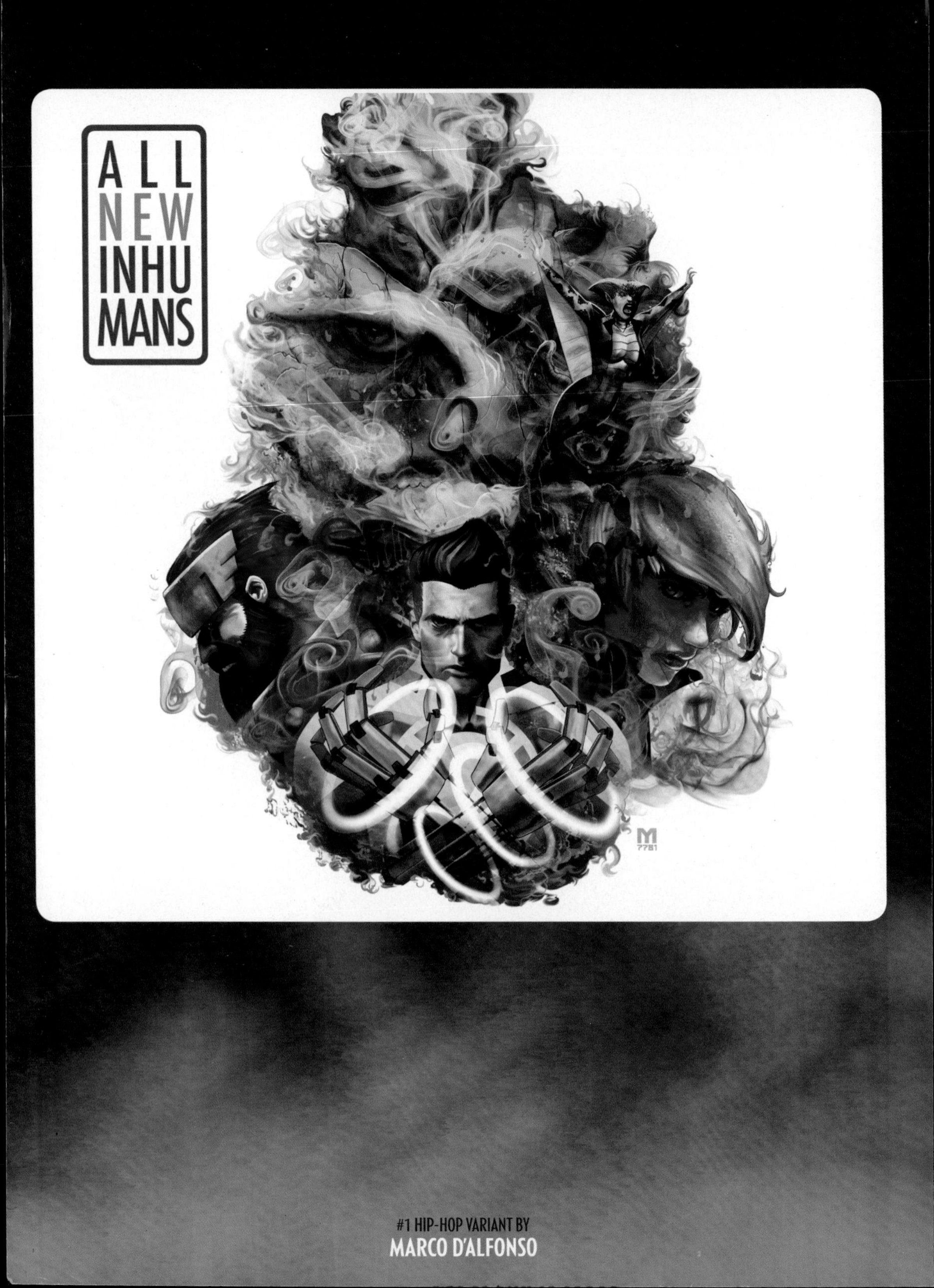
ALL
NEW
INHU
MANS

#1 HIP-HOP VARIANT BY
MARCO D'ALFONSO

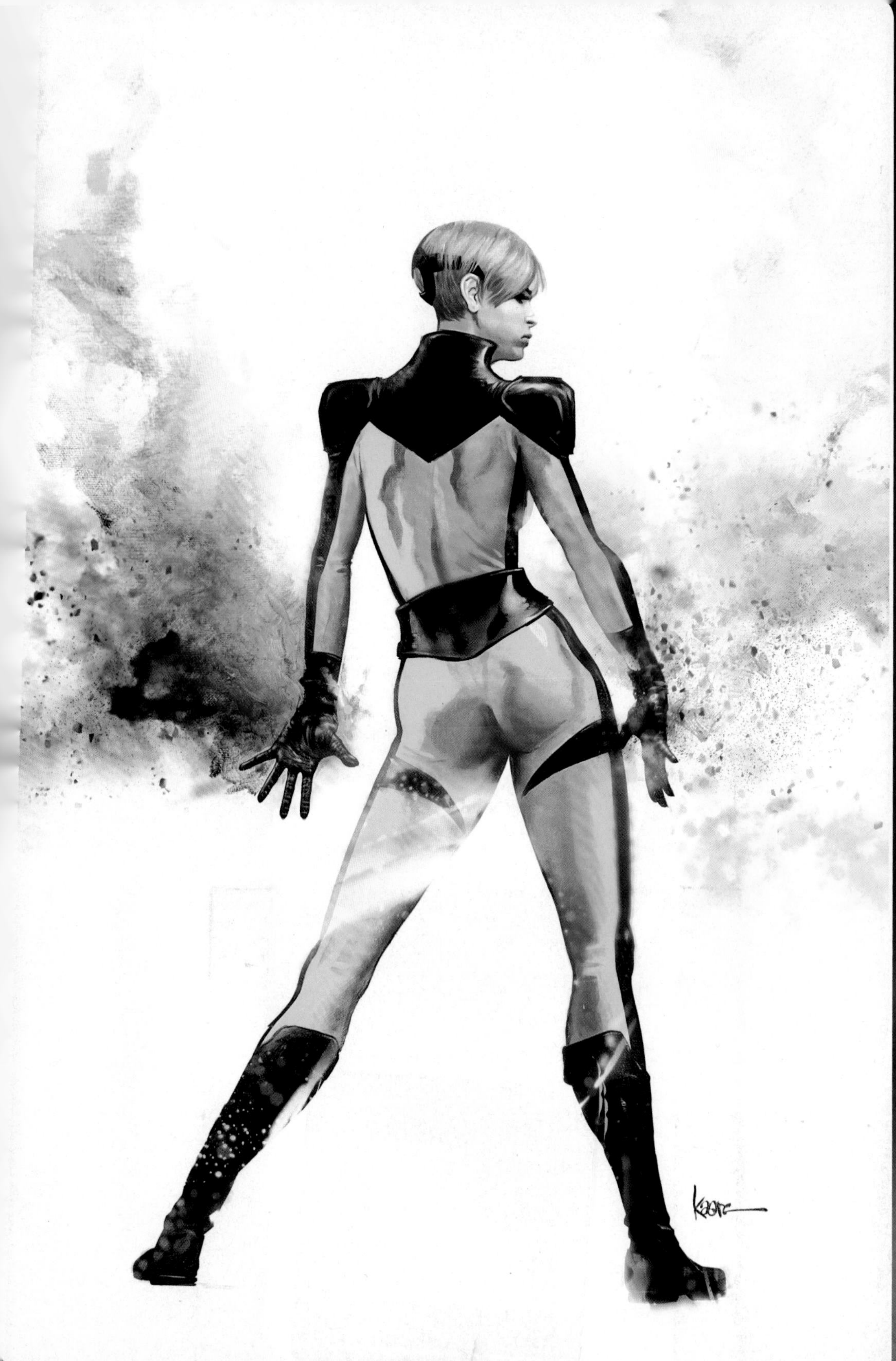

#2 VARIANT BY
KAARE ANDREWS

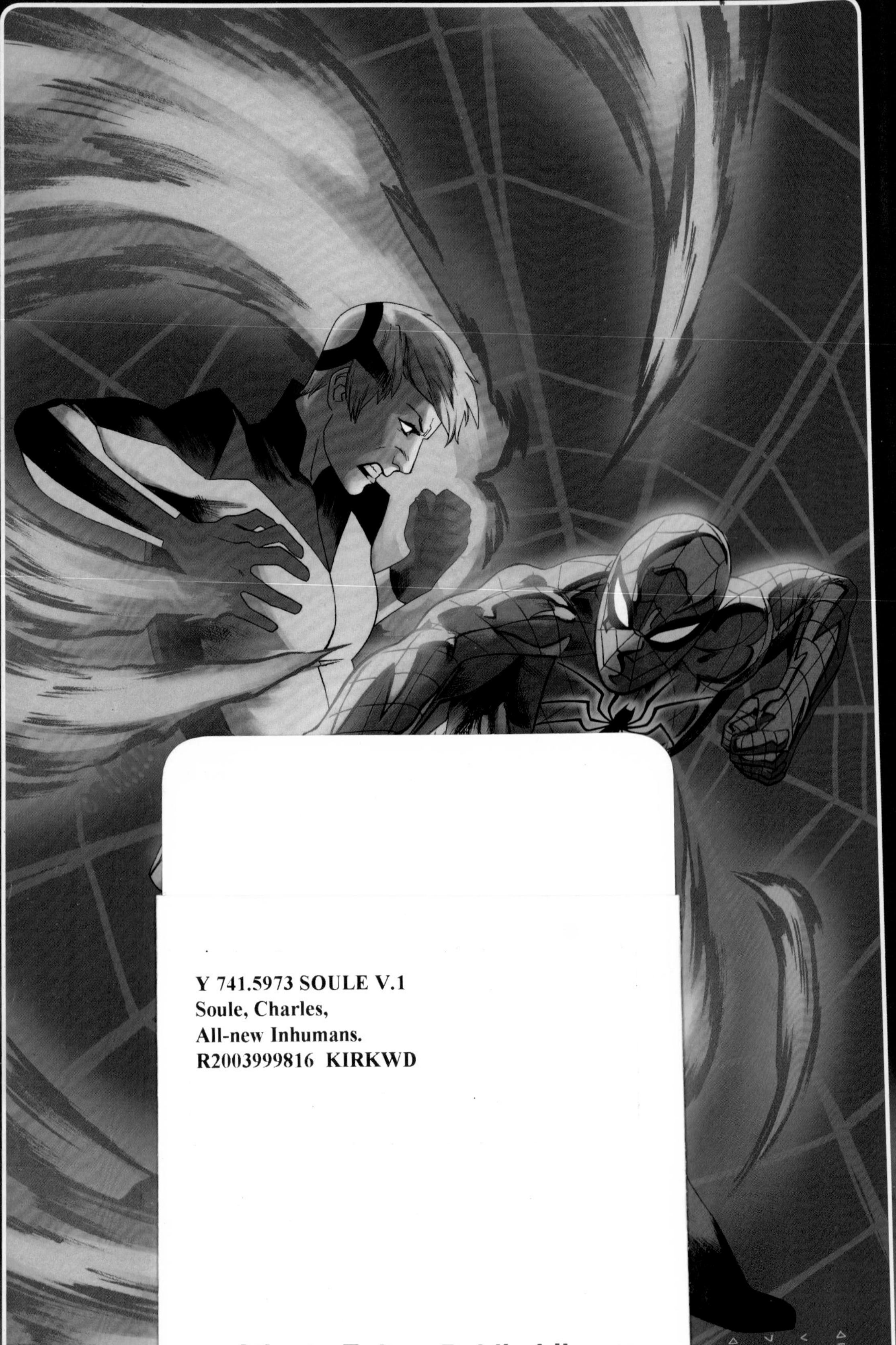